# LYNN FISCHER'S
## *Quick*
## *LOW CHOLESTEROL*
# *GOURMET*

## DELICIOUS AND HEALTHY MEALS YOU CAN PREPARE IN 20 MINUTES OR LESS

Lynn Fischer

**LIVING PLANET**

P R E S S

WASHINGTON, DC

**Warning:** The instructions and advice presented in this book are in no way
intended as a substitute for medical counseling. Always check with your
physician before beginning any change in diet or exercise. Ask if certain
foods or vitamins will interfere with any drugs you are taking.

The nutritional values given in this book cover total fat, saturated fat,
percent of fat, cholesterol, sodium and calories and are computed by a
registered nutritionist using USDA figures. Dietary saturated fat is the
primary culprit in elevating our cholesterol counts, causing atheroscle-
rosis and other heart and artery problems.

Although many brands are mentioned, no payment or favor was received
by the author for that mention. The recommendations are solely the opin-
ion of Lynn Fischer.

Discounts on bulk orders of this book are available from the
publisher. For information, call (202) 686-6262.

**Cover design:** Mary Challinor
**Cover photo:** Anthony Loew
**Interior design and page layout:** Karen Bowers

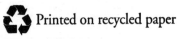 Printed on recycled paper

ISBN 1-879326-21-3

Manufactured in the United States of America

10 9 8 7 6 5 4 3 2 1

# CONTENTS

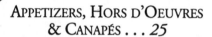

# Acknowledgments

First, I acknowledge and thank you, the reader—for buying the book, for being a fan of the "Low Cholesterol Gourmet" television show, for reading my column or writing me, or just for caring about your health or the health of others. I write cookbooks and cooking columns, do healthy cooking on television and give demonstrations to share my recipes, tips and hints. I do it for me just as much as for you. I want to give you good healthy cooking ideas in a book you will love, a book that pleases and helps you. That is my real satisfaction and really, my passion. My feelings about you are even on my license plate, which reads BE WELL.

Since this is my own very personal acknowledgment, I want to acknowledge my beloved daughter Lisa Bialac Jehle, her John, my curious grandchild Wolf whom I miss, and my talented, sweet and very smart son Cary Warren Bialac, of whom I am justifiably proud and who loves nature, horses, and all animals and birds just as I do, and who has wonderful Brit in his life.

I adore my brothers Tom, Bob and Jim, and their wives, especially Mary, Tom's wife, who because of a shorter distance, I see more often. I pay special tribute to my dad, attorney Addison Connor, who started us all off in Detroit being aware and careful of our health. He's 87 now, roller blades in Naples, Florida, plays tennis daily and golf weekly, and is always thinking of marrying again. Usually just thinking. So if you see an older guy roller blading (he's very good), just say "Hi Addie." And I thank my late mother, Mary Connor of Detroit, who at my age was a world-ranking athlete, the U.S. Open champion in badminton.

Professionally, I thank my agent and friend Gail Ross, who has watched out for me for seven years (with no itch on either side), the book's editor Kateri Alexander, who is a gem, never pedantic and nearly always right, Dianne Woo, my eagle-eyed final arbiter of style, nutritional analysts Diane Welland, a registered nutritionist, and Jeanne Voltz, who has more food experience in her little finger than most of us will ever have, and all the great television cooks whom I have learned from—Jacques (a great dancer and superb cook), Jeff (TV's best), Pierre (clever), Madeleine (really knows her stuff), Paul (so smart), Julia (my idol), Marcia (very nice), Arlen (knows what he's talking about), Martin (entertaining), Burt (durable), Graham (funny man), Justin (I *garannteee*), Merle (exceptionally nice), and Nathalie (my compadre). They are all eminently great cooks and chefs who, to my delight, OCCASIONALLY use their genius making low-fat recipes, and who really paved the way in television cooking. I am proud when they agree to be guests on my show.

My friends: I gratefully thank my mentor, speech coach and wonderful friend Ginnie von Fremd, who is beautiful, patient, and who advises me on everything and has a halo; and my buddies—Jennifer Douglas, with whom I work out every day (she writes the show too), professionals Nina Miller, Manuel Trujillo, man friends Stanford Adelstein, Robert Furman and Henry Cole (where are you?), Susie Hart Wydler (how many years?), Kathy McLain (six feet of gorgeousness), Jeanne Morressy (knew me in my Hollywood days), Joanie La Belle (knew me before that), Anthony Loew (a doll—took the cover photo too), Phil Beuth (ABC-TV's best), Terry Frantz McKenzie (saved me), and DC pals Beth Mendleson, Peggy Lampl, Susie Tomai, Jonathan Adelstein (Stan's son), Diana Winthrop, Andrea Fleischer and Joy Roller. And I thank my shiny, smart, hardworking, enthusiastic friend and assistant Mary Schaheen, whose efforts I greatly appreciate.

I also give a special thanks to Senator David Pryor, chairman of the Aging Committee (with Senator William Cohen of Maine), who asked me to prepare a nutritious breakfast for Hillary Rodham Clinton and 20 senators. The breakfast, which included traditional Arkansas dried blueberry-wheat-pecan multi-grain bread and an Arkansas dried blueberry sourdough wheat walnut bread, was served just prior to a hearing on the causes of preventable health problems. It is rewarding to know that our country's leaders are recognizing that a healthy diet is essential for a more fulfilling life.

— *Lynn Fischer*

# *Preface*

People often ask me if I really do eat this way. YES! ARE YOU KIDDING?! I couldn't do all that I do—write books and my television series, host the series, do radio interviews, research and write my column, give seminars, speeches, judge contests, teach cooking classes, search for great items for my catalog* and still spend time with family and friends, if I didn't.

If you're like me, you simply don't have time to fuss over food every day. That's the common refrain in the hundreds of letters I get each week from viewers of my "Low Cholesterol Gourmet" show.

My first book, *The Low Cholesterol Gourmet,* introduced you to delicious low-fat, low cholesterol cooking. In this book, I've devised over 200 quick ways to treat yourself, family and friends to sumptuous, lush food that also happens to be healthy and contains the lowest fat possible. What more could you ask for? Lunch or dinner prepared in 20 minutes or less, with simple, easy-to-follow directions.

Nearly all of these delicious and quick meals are from my show. I've also tucked in a few of my personal favorites for you. And they have all the nutritional data you need to maintain a heart-healthy diet: total fat, saturated fat, cholesterol, calories, sodium and percentage of fat. And most important, you'll save precious time without having to compromise on flavor or variety. Because low in fat and low in cholesterol never means low in taste or imagination.

These recipes provide a wide variety of low-fat foods. I believe you increase your energy when you cut out the fat, and that energy increases dramatically when you exercise daily, too. Another bonus of low-fat eating is weight loss. It's easy to strip off pounds

* Catalog number is 1-800-8-FLAVOR

when you've stripped off the fat in foods. Your plate can still be full but it will be full of lots of different low-fat foods. Seeing is believing. Mark White, the handsome director of my TV show, lost 100 pounds as he learned about low-fat eating from the show.

So, lose the fat in your food. There is no biological reason for any added fat in the diet, anyway. The experts say the fat that occurs naturally in vegetables (yes, even in radishes there are trace amounts), fruits, cereals, nuts, and grains is all the fat you need.

My philosophy for great healthy eating includes widening your variety of foods, eating lots of small servings of many kinds of foods, and using animal products sparingly as suggested by the United States Department of Agriculture (USDA) food pyramid.

I began learning about healthy eating when I worked as a medical newsletter writer and medical television reporter and anchor in Washington, DC. When I married a man whose diet needed to change because of heart disease, I translated that knowledge into creating delicious low-fat, low cholesterol meals that we and our two sets of children loved. With this new healthy diet, exercise and careful business lunch planning, his cholesterol dropped a dramatic 100 milligrams. When we divorced 15 years later, I wrote my first book and created my television show so you could actually see how easy healthy cooking is. Now I hope you're ready to see how quick it can be, too.

Join me on this wonderful journey of delicious foods. Explore all the creative ways to enjoy the great tastes of low-fat cooking. Food is one of life's most enjoyable experiences. When you eat well, you feel good. When you feel good, YOU CAN DO ANY-THING!

—*Lynn Fischer*
Washington, DC

# *Introduction*

W hy go to all this trouble to change the way we eat? Actually, there are excellent reasons. Current research has shown us how diet affects our bodies, our health and our lives. You may not live longer on a low-fat menu plan, but your quality of life has the potential to be so much greater when you feel good and look good. Also, many researchers think low-fat foods are what we were meant to eat anyway. We know we have fewer health problems such as excess weight and some kinds of cancers when our fuel isn't so rich. But the major reason to eat low-fat food is to keep our heart healthy. Eating is more enjoyable when you know your food is not only delicious, but good for you.

## Cholesterol and Heart Disease

As a medical reporter I learned heart disease still ends life prematurely for over 1,000,000 Americans each year. It is the number one medical problem for men and women alike—regardless of ethnicity. An astounding half of all American men and a third of all women over age 24 have a cholesterol number that indicates heart disease or the beginnings of heart disease. It doesn't need to be this way, and you can change it for yourself this very day.

Long-term studies have shown that lowering your blood cholesterol, especially if it is over 200 milligrams, is an important step in not just prolonging life, but improving the quality of life. A good diet, even with cholesterol lowering medication, is still the first line of defense.

The word *cholesterol* can be confusing. There are two ways we use the word. One is in the food we eat, called "dietary cholesterol," which is measured in milligrams. You'll see it at the end of each recipe as "mg." Most of us eat close to 600 milligrams of cholesterol a day, which is considered far too high.

The other way we use the word cholesterol is in your own cholesterol number, the one given when blood is drawn and analyzed. If you haven't fasted (taken only water for 12 hours), that number is given as a combination of high density, low density and very low density lipoproteins (HDL, LDL and VLDL). If you have fasted, you can get your individual HDL and LDL numbers so you know what steps to take to change one or the other, or both. As an example, if your HDL isn't high enough, exercise raises it, and that can lower your blood cholesterol. If your LDL is too high, diet or other means can lower it. If you have heard the terms *good cholesterol* and *bad cholesterol,* they refer to your HDL, which is considered good if the number is high because it helps your body get rid of saturated fats, and LDL, which is bad because if the number is high your body will make more cholesterol plaque.

The National Cholesterol Education Program guidelines in 1989 state that cholesterol can be higher than 200 and still be considered healthy. But as time goes on and we learn more, we may need to know what each value of those HDL, LDL and VLDL numbers is in order to assess heart and artery health.

How do we get a blood cholesterol that is too high? Perhaps it's from our own bodies. A few of us have an inherited proclivity to make too much—more than we can get rid of so it forms a plaque in our arteries. But most of us get too much cholesterol from the food we eat. However, it is primarily the saturated fat in our diet that raises our blood cholesterol and forms the plaque. Dietary cholesterol is also a culprit, but it isn't as significant as our total fat and especially saturated fat intake. That's why shellfish such as lobster, which has a lot of cholesterol but not much fat, isn't as consequential as some cuts of red meat which have a high sat fat content. Shellfish and some ocean fish also contain omega-3 fatty acids, thought to help lower blood cholesterol.

Since the fat on red meat has been identified as containing saturates, for some it is easier to forsake all red meat, but it isn't necessary. It is true that broiled or grilled fish consistently has less saturated fat than most red meat or poultry. But some meat such as very lean beef, ham, lamb and pork, and some poultry such as lean, skinless duck is as low in saturates as some fish. Conversely, some fish and especially chicken can be prepared so it is higher in saturated fats than some red meat. We can eat almost any lean meat or any chicken if we prepare it without the saturated fats and in amounts that are under 3-1/2 ounces, about the size of the palm of your hand, and we don't eat it every day.

Cholesterol is only in animal products: meat, especially organ meats such as brains, liver, sweetbreads and kidneys and it is especially high in egg yolks. Cholesterol is in the muscle as well as the fat. Our typical American diets, which have been historically healthier than many other countries and have made us a comparatively healthy nation (even with our fast-food obsession), are now thought to be too rich. Actually, we don't need to eat any cholesterol, as our bodies make enough naturally.

Saturated fatty acids (the correct term) are primarily in the fat of red meats, chicken, processed meat such as bologna and hot dogs, and surprisingly, sat fats are in some plants such as coconut, and in tropical oils such as palm kernel and palm oil. In this book, you'll see the saturated fat number at the end of each recipe, and it's in grams. They are easy to count and keep track of. I try and keep my intake of sat fats under 10 grams a day. Way under. Total fats are also important, but usually, if you keep the saturated very fats low, the total fats will be low too.

A word about avocados and nuts. Avocados are considered to be high in fat but they have little saturated fat, so I don't omit them. As for nuts, some, such as walnuts and pecans, contain few saturated fats too, so I use them also.

When buying foods, be wary of the words NO CHO-LESTEROL found on many products. If it's on cookies, for example, and they contain fat, it may be a high saturated fat product. Although there is no cholesterol, that doesn't pre-clude the more ominous sat fats. Select brands with labels that give you nutrient values, and pick the ones that have the comparatively lowest saturated fats and total fats (see "A Word About Labels" on page 295). Also be aware of the word *margarine* in commercial cakes and cookies. Margarine can legally contain beef tallow or tropical oils.

DON'T BE TRICKED. When comparing brands, notice serving size. One may list the cholesterol and fat content for a tablespoon serving size and another for ounces.

So, at first glance one brand may look more low-fat or low in cholesterol and not be!

## Nutritional Values

The nutritional values given in this book are total fat, saturated fat, percent of fat, cholesterol, sodium and calories. They are compiled by a registered nutritionist using USDA figures, which are the most reliable we have.

For my purposes (which is to eat a delicious, easy to prepare, but heart-healthy menu), the number to watch out for when buying food, eating in a restaurant, or preparing a recipe is the saturated fat number. Only then do I glance at the total fat number. If I keep my sat fat number low, under (way under) 10 grams a day, and total fat under 20 grams a day, which is easy when you eat large amounts of fruits, vegetables, bread, pasta, beans, potatoes, rice and the meat portions are kept very small or have little fat, then I can eat that occasional brownie with abandon.

It isn't what is in any one dish or meal that is important, but the cumulative amount of saturated fat and cholesterol. Form your own dietary plan with that in mind. Be careful about how much saturated fat and total fat you are actually consuming and want to consume.

## Total Fat

Keeping dietary fats low isn't always easy in this country. We want and are used to juicy hamburgers, fatty salad dressings, and rich ice cream. Figuring the fat in your diet isn't easy, especially if you eat out. Nevertheless, you may want to write down exactly what you eat for a week and make a realistic guess about the fat amounts. People are always surprised when they find out how much fat they actually ingest. They may not know one potato chip has more fat than ten potatoes until they analyze their intake.

But going back to the juicy hamburger, it is nice to know there are delicious, almost nonfat (and some non-meat), juicy burgers (loaded of course with tomatoes, lettuce and nonfat dressing) that contain little sat fat, maybe no cholesterol (page 201), and that there are many delicious nonfat salad dressings (pages 92–98). Don't forget there are also incredibly good and rich-tasting commercial varieties of nonfat ice cream, yogurt, sour cream and cottage cheese.

### *The American Heart Association's Ten Dietary Guidelines:*

1  Total fat intake should be less than 30% of calories.
2  Saturated fat intake should be less than 10% of calories.
3  Polyunsaturated fat intake should not exceed 10% of calories.
4  Cholesterol intake should not exceed 300 mg/day.
5  Carbohydrate intake should constitute 50% or more of calories, with emphasis on complex carbohydrates.
6  Protein intake should provide the remainder of the calories.
7  Sodium intake should not exceed 3 g/day.
8  Alcoholic consumption should not exceed 1–2 oz of ethanol per day. Two ounces of 100 proof whisky, 8 oz of wine, or 24 oz of beer each contain 1 oz of ethanol.
9  Total calories should be sufficient to maintain the individual's recommended body weight.
10 A wide variety of foods should be consumed.

For a free copy of the American Heart Association Diet call the American Heart Association at 1-800-242-8721.

Note: I and the medical experts I consult feel an intake of cholesterol and fat that is lower than the numbers listed above is more beneficial to health care.

## Margarine versus Butter

A major question I am often asked is, "Which fat is the best to eat on a low-fat menu plan: butter or margarine?" For lower saturated fat, margarine, no matter how you slice it, has about half. Diet, and sometimes liquid, margarine has even less. It doesn't taste like butter, however, and many people simply want butter, because they are used to it and like the taste. Both butter and margarine contain salt and coloring. Margarine does have trans fatty acids and some hydrogenated fats which make them saturated, but even with that, most margarine still has half the saturated fat as butter.

Select the brand that is made of vegetable products where only oils such as canola, safflower, sunflower, corn or soy are used. If the margarine is diet or whipped, it may have up to 30 percent water, which is fine for heating or flavoring cooked foods, and for recipes where the fat content won't significantly change the recipe. It can make toast and popcorn soggy. The way to get around that is to let the toast and popcorn cool. Read the labels on the margarine for the saturated fat grams as they differ, and select the brand with the lowest, which would be 1 or 2 grams of saturated fat per serving.

Other foods high in saturated fatty acids are most meat, cheeses, cream, butter and ice cream. As far as we know, like cholesterol, there is no biological reason to eat any saturated fat.

## Microwaving and Other Time-saving Gadgets*

If there is one appliance where it pays to purchase the largest and finest version, it is probably the microwave. Microwave cooking offers a fast heating method that needs no fat, perfect for those of us who want our meals delicious and on the table quickly. The microwave has been around for about 35 years and as far as I know, there has never been

* Catalog number is 1-800-8-FLAVOR

a case of radiation or any kind of contamination caused by a microwave.

Microwaves differ widely in quality and size, both outside and inside, and they differ in features and cooking speed. If you understand and utilize it well, you will use it more than any other appliance in your kitchen except your refrigerator.

It helps in the cooking process to microwave many foods such as nonfat chicken and vegetables in plastic bags or wraps marked "safe for microwaving," because they keep the moisture in.

Food on or in plates or bowls should be raised slightly on a trivet so they don't get soggy, and so the heat generated by the food can circulate around and under it. Most dishes need turning or stirring during heating, so buy a turntable if your microwave doesn't have one, or just turn the plate or vegetable a couple of times during the heating cycle. Microwaves cook notoriously unevenly, leaving some areas unheated, and the thinner edges tend to cook first, the thicker center last, so arrange the food accordingly.

Covered food cooks more quickly in the microwave and all foods stay more moist if covered, but a covered dish always needs ventilating so poke a few holes in plastic wrap, or tilt the glass lid. Some foods like eggs will explode if cooked in the shell, and some meats like ham or beef will pop if not rotated often.

Also, be aware that in most microwaves you usually can't use foil, metal cookware, china or ceramic plates that contain metal. I don't know of any that can handle dishes or bowls that have gold or silver edging.

Enjoy your microwave to the max. Use it to defrost and cook frozen foods, especially vegetables, right in the package (bang them on the counter first to loosen). Use it to make your air-popped popcorn and to cook just about everything quickly and deliciously (except bread and most cakes). It makes rich applesauce, bakes potatoes, cooks corn in the husk, and boils artichokes quickly. Vegetables keep their color and nutrients just as they do in stove-top steaming.

Incidentally, even if you bought your first microwave decades ago, you do not need to keep a glass of water in it. Just read your directions carefully, use it often, and enjoy a truly modern miracle that helps you speed up and simplify the food you want to eat.

Another appliance that helps speedy cooking is the updated pressure cooker. These new pressure cookers are beautiful in design, and speed up the cooking of some vegetables such as potatoes, beans (which I recommend not soaking), soups and stews.

Another great item is the tiny electric hot water dispenser you put under your sink. The hot water dispensers are handy for bringing water to boil for pasta, for steaming vegetables with water that is already very hot, for packaged soup mixes and for tea or coffee as the water is almost to the boiling point. Instead of taking 6 to 7 minutes to boil a full pot of water for pasta, when you put it on the burner, it takes about two.

There are other fast heating and preparation gadgets and methods, and new appliances are being developed continually. I buy and try them all—processors, mixers, blenders, mini-processors and mini-mixers, immersion blenders, toaster ovens, bread machines, rice makers, juicers, convection ovens, anything to speed up the cooking process when I am in a hurry.

I finally put a 6-foot-line of plugs along the edge of my counter so I can run them all at once. I never know when I might need to.

None of these speedy methods should ever diminish your love of good food. Yes, fix it fast when you're in a hurry, but try and serve your delicious food on fine china, buy or pick some flowers for your table, and slow down. Enjoy and savor your every meal with relish and gusto.

# Adaptations or Substitutions to Lower the Fat

W hy is it some people can eat twice as much food as others and still keep their cholesterol at a healthy level (some cholesterol problems can't be controlled by diet alone) and their weight exactly where they want it? It is because of fat. They know where fat is hiding, what to eat, how to substitute and how to adapt without changing the flavor of the food. They don't eat less food, often they eat more. They know fat, especially saturated fat, is what makes blood cholesterol levels rise and that fat has double the calories of either carbohydrates or protein.

They also know there are delicious new nonfat foods to enjoy, such as low-fat Danish pastry; that a beef stew for four with one pound of lean top round and lots of incredible fresh vegetables and herbs tastes just as good as a beef stew for with two fatty pounds of meat and a few vegetables.

They know that even most gourmands can't tell the difference between some brands of ice cream that have no fat and no cholesterol, and ice cream made with egg yolks and cream. They still enjoy their chocolate cake, banana splits and ice cream sodas, but they just select the nonfat varieties.

Here's another astounding fact. Did you know the largest percentage of calories per day for the average woman comes from her salad dressing? That statistic comes from the Center for Science in the Public Interest, and it's reliable. Yet, we think of salads as healthy and low in fat but if several fat grams and several hundred calories can be eliminated just in the choice of salad dressing, think what you can do by making educated substitutions for other foods like the cream in your coffee, cream cheese, cottage cheese, cookies, yogurt and many other foods. Most of us interested in reducing our fat intake don't use any oil in our dressing. Salad oil is often the first fat to go. We know instead how to make great flavorful vinegars, delicious Caesar salads without eggs and oil and other nonfat dressings.

You may already know that skim milk is 4 percent fat per cup and you may see such things as ground turkey advertised as 85 percent fat-free. Not much fat you say? Fifteen percent is enormous. One percent milk translates to 17 grams of saturated fat, so it pays to use skim. Skim milk too blue for you? Add a few spoonfuls of nonfat dry milk powder and shake it up. But watch the labels as skim milk can be legally 1 percent fat. As for the 85 percent fat-free ground turkey? Don't buy it. Instead have the meat cutter grind your own selection of turkey breast (or thigh if it is completely defatted), skinning it and removing the fat.

A recent study indicates there is only a little difference in people's metabolism. Less than one tenth of 1 percent of us have physical problems that would keep weight on us. However, almost 50 percent of all men and a third of all women have a cholesterol that is too high and some 60 percent of us are too heavy. The difference is in what we eat. People who want their fat intake low, their cholesterol intake low, their energy high and to eat as healthy a diet as possible (without eating just nuts and twigs) know which foods can be exchanged or easily substituted. This is why I made the substitution list on the following pages. So, you will know too.

Choosing what you put into your mouth may be the biggest and most important health decision you make, and you have an opportunity to do it in a delicious and healthy way several times a day.

# Low-fat Substitutions and Adaptations

| If Recipe/Meal Calls For: | Use Instead: |
|---|---|
| **Butter** | Butter sprinkles, margarine with the least amount of saturates, or part butter, part margarine. The more liquid the margarine, the less hydrogenation and the fewer saturated fats. |
| **Oil** | Water. When a recipe says "2 tablespoons of oil," omit it entirely. If sautéing or frying anything, use vegetable spray and/or defatted stock, wines, juices or flavored vinegar. If it is in salad dressing and you have to have the taste of olive oil, spray on a small amount. You can purchase your own container, fill it with the oil of your choice and spritz it on. |
| **Margarine** | Whipped, diet or liquid margarines. Diet margarine becomes soggy on hot toast or muffins, bread, scones, biscuits. |
| **Cheese** | Low-fat, including some nonfat varieties (most are fine when melting isn't required—then use a slightly higher fat variety) or use half nonfat and half regular. |

| | |
|---|---|
| **Cottage Cheese** | Nonfat cottage cheese, farmers cheese, hoop cheese and pot cheese. If these cheeses are too thick, thin with skim milk or a whisk. |
| **Sour Cream** | Nonfat or low-fat sour creams, or evaporated skim milk sediment (the inch at the bottom of a can that has set undisturbed for a month) mixed with 1/4 teaspoon of lemon juice, or nonfat yogurt or yogurt cheese. |
| **Whipped Cream** | Skim milk whipped with an immersion blender. |
| **Yogurt** | Nonfat yogurt. |
| **Thick Yogurt** | Yogurt cheese made by letting yogurt sit in a clean towel hung on the faucet over the sink to drain the whey, or thickened in a yogurt strainer made for that purpose (call 1-800-8-FLAVOR), until the yogurt becomes thick. |
| **Salad Dressing** | Nonfat or plain balsamic or other flavored vinegars such as raspberry, blueberry, tarragon, sherry or champagne flavors, for example, or lemon juice and a pinch of sugar. |
| **Cream Cheese** | Nonfat or low-fat. |
| **Cream Sauce** | Nonfat or low-fat (page 249). |
| **Gravy** | Nonfat or low-fat (page 244–247). |

| | |
|---|---|
| **Buttermilk** | Low-fat. Check the labeling. Skim milk is often called SKIM but labeled 1 percent, which is 17 percent higher in saturated fat than skim. Nonfat soy and nonfat rice milk. |
| **Cream** | Evaporated skim milk with a few teaspoons of nonfat dry milk. |
| **Ice Cream** | Nonfat ice cream, Nonfat frozen yogurt, or sorbet, frozen fruit frappé. |
| **Sherbet** | Sorbet or frappé. |
| **Cakes, Cupcakes** | Nonfat cookies or Fig Newtons (many are delicious) and other low-fat varieties like raisin crackers, graham crackers, and cookies made with little fat. |
| **Danishes** | Fat-free varieties of danishes and coffee cakes (many are delicious), toast and honey, nonfat danishes, nonfried donuts. |
| **Mayonnaise** | Nonfat or low-fat, low-cholesterol varieties, mustard made without eggs, yogurt cheese (page 256), or homemade tofu mayonnaise (page 94). |
| **Fat for Frying** | Water, wine, juice, defatted stock or spray-on olive or canola oil. Make your own spray using the type or brand of oil you like (page 91). |
| **Sandwich Spreads** | Nonfat mayonnaise or other low-fat spreads, bean dips, tofu dips. |

| | |
|---|---|
| **Dips** | Nonfat or light or make your own. All in this book are low- or nonfat. |
| **Eggs** | Substitute eggs (in addition to the no cholesterol and lowered fat benefits, they are better for you because they have been pasteurized, killing any salmonella bacteria). Some brands fluff up better than others in cooking such foods as omelets. All do well in baking, but try several kinds as they keep improving; or 2 egg whites for each whole egg. Powdered egg replacers also work well. |
| **Meat** | Buy naturally lean cuts, have smaller servings (3-1/2 ounces) and remove all visible fat, or use skinless defatted chicken, duck and especially turkey, which has less saturated fat; or fish or meat substitute made of soy products, wheat products, vegetables, or combinations of them. |
| **Steak** | Lean tenderloin, choice or select beef, all visible fat removed; a smaller portion, or omit and have a large vegetarian meal. |
| **Hamburger** | Grain burgers, or low-fat turkey or chicken burgers, veggie burgers, earth burgers, nut burgers (check packages for fat content, some are as low as 1 gram fat and others higher than 10) or Zero trim, lean top round ground by the meat cutter. If you are making hamburgers, add back a few teaspoons per pound of a less saturated fat such as canola oil so the burgers will stick together. |

| | |
|---|---|
| **Chicken** | Fish. Or turkey. Or defat and skin the chicken. |
| **Chicken or Meat Stock** | Water, vegetable stock or defatted stock using a defatting cup, or chilling and picking off the fat, or spooning off the fat. Vegetable juices, vegetable stock, bouillon cubes, veggie tea. |
| **Fish** | Lean fish such as halibut, or shellfish, which has almost no fat (although it has more cholesterol). |
| **Bacon** | Canadian bacon or very lean bacon, cooked in paper towels in the microwave and remove all the fat, even for your BLT sandwich and spinach salad. Tempeh (a soy product). Nonmeat bacon or sausage. |
| **Pork** | Lean such as tenderloin and a smaller portion. |
| **Ribs** | Lean ham or pork tenderloin. |
| **Sausage** | Soy, turkey, if it is low in saturated fat, lean ham, Canadian bacon or make your own with unsaturated fat. |
| **Hot Dogs** | Soy or those lowest in saturated fat (hot dogs range from 60 to 2 percent fat). Vegetarian hot dogs. |
| **Marinades** | Omit all oil. Marinade always enters any meat, fruit or vegetable faster without oil. Also, poultry without skin is infused with flavor more quickly. Use soups, water, wines, |

brandy, defatted stock, soy sauce or juice as the base.

**Sugar**            Less. All sugars, whether honey, fructose, sucrose, glucose, maple, Demerara, beet, brown, molasses, corn syrup, or others are sugar and contain the same number of calories, about 16 per teaspoon. Fructose is however sweeter than others, so you can use less.

**Salt**             Lemon juice, Lite Salt, herbs and spices or your own mixture of potassium and salt. Vegetable and herb based salt substitutes.

# Terms and Ingredients Used in Low-fat Cooking

### Lean Meat

Look at the meat before you buy it and purchase only lean versions. The fat on the edge can be removed. The fat in the middle, the marbling, can't. Buy leaner cuts like lean ham, pork tenderloin, top round. Lean, as in hamburger, often isn't lean enough for a heart-healthy diet.

### Defatting Poultry

The grocery store meat cutters can do most of the work for you. Often, they aren't as thorough as you might be. If *you* decide to do it, start by placing your whole hand under the breast skin from the open area at the legs, pull off all the skin, peeling it off over the legs. With a knife and scissors remove any fat that remains.

### Defatting Meat

With a sharp knife zero trim all fat, meaning there is no fat at all on the edges and interior fat is also removed. It helps if you purchase naturally lean cuts of meat. For hamburger, never buy it pre-ground. Select a lean top round, have the meat cutter remove all the fat and then grind.

### Sauté

Sauté is French for fry (in fat); however, in this book, license is taken and it can mean fry or steam in small amounts of liquid or combinations of stock and olive oil, wine or juice.

### Steam

Steaming means using the steam from boiling water (usually) or a mixture of juice or wine to cook food. It is a moist form of cooking, versus broiling, which is a dry form. It can be accomplished with an inexpensive basket steamer, a double boiler set where the top pan has a perforated bottom, with a wire colander, or just placing food in a saucepan or skillet where the liquid is only 1/4 to 1/2 inch deep. Although some of the food may be partially submerged, the boil is so rapid, the effect steams the food. Usually the pan is covered, but not always.

Steam is also used effectively to bake crustier exterior, softer interior bread by throwing ice cubes in a boiling pot of water in the bottom of the oven during the first part of baking, then removing the pot after 10 minutes.

### Broil

Broiling is a controlled version of outdoor roasting, and is usually done under a gas flame or electric oven burner.

### Bake

Ovens are found in standard cooking stoves and bake the food using radiant heat from above and below, either with gas flame or electric coils. Ovens take a longer time to cook food than boiling, broiling or microwaving, but offer a melding of flavors that only long cooking methods can impart.

## Chill

Chill means to cool or serve colder than room temperature. To quickly chill, spread the food on a metal tray and put it in the freezer for a few minutes, or if vegetables or bottled wine, plunge them into ice water. When you don't want the foods to become wet or soggy, chill by placing them in a waterproof plastic bag, and holding the top, dunk the bag in ice water and swish it around.

## Plunging in Ice Water

In the cooking context, ice water is used to quickly chill foods and wine, and has just enough water to move the ice around. Cooking can be halted immediately by plunging, say, par-boiled green beans in the water, and red potatoes can be chilled to make a cold potato salad. Be sure the foods are well drained after plunging them in water for a minute or two.

## Nonfat

All foods whether a radish or a rabbit have fat or traces of fat. If it has just trace amounts, amounts less than a gram, it is, for our purposes, considered nonfat.

## Low-fat

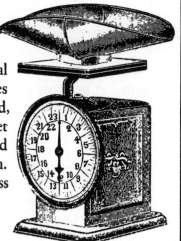

Low-fat means the food item has a lowered fat content compared to the usual or traditional amount. There are percentages that are supposed to be followed, but many manufacturers can get around this, so low-fat or lowered fat usually means a relative term. It is supposed to be 25 percent less in calories than similar products.

## Lite or Light

Lite is used for salt in this book, which means the salt contains half or part potassium chloride and half or part sodium chloride. Brands differ, so check the amount, or buy granulated potassium chloride and salt (with or without iodine) and make your own blend. Lite or light, as used in commercial products can indicate it has lower than the usual amount of fat, sugar, salt or calories and is in many products such as "light chips," "light cola," "light cheese," and even "light beer." In meat, it is supposed to mean it has 25 percent less fat than similar products. Low-fat does not necessarily mean nutritious or heart healthy.

## Calories

Calories are a measure of energy produced by the food we eat. The food with the highest number of calories is fat. Carbohydrates and protein have half as many calories as fat. Calories are burned at different levels by different people, and exercise helps burn calories.

## Carbohydrates

Sugar is a simple carbohydrate, potatoes are a complex one. They are produced only by living organisms, not water. The dominate ingredients are starch and cellulose.

## Proteins

Proteins can be made up of a wide variety of polymers and often contain as many as 22 amino acids. Proteins are in everything from jellyfish to gelatin, beans to Brazil nuts, sunflower seeds to salmon, tacos to toast. We need proteins and amino acids in the diet. One grain, quinoa (keen-wah), has all 8 necessary amino acids.

Proteins from animal sources are eggs, meat, fish and dairy products and are called complete proteins. Those from vegetables sources, whole grains, nuts, seeds and legumes and soy beans are incomplete proteins. This means that a diet of just corn, an incomplete protein, would be lacking and dangerous; as would a diet of just steak, even though meat is a complete protein. Adding rice to the beans makes it a complete protein. However, it isn't necessary to do that with every meal or with every food. The value of the protein in brown rice is nearly the same as in white rice.

Many experts feel that because of our long intestines and flattish teeth (more similar to herbivores rather than carnivores), animal protein may not be a necessary element in the human diet.

### Low-calorie

Low-calorie means it is supposed to have no more than 40 calories per serving, but check what they call a serving and what they call low.

### Reduced Calorie

Reduced calorie means it is supposed to be one third less in calories than similar products, but check the label for the serving size.

### Zero trim

Zero trim is how meat should be cut on a heart-healthy diet, and means there is no fat on the edge.

# APPETIZERS, HORS D'OEUVRES & CANAPÉS

*Mock Caviar • Hummus • Cream Cheese and Spicy
Bengal Chutney • Stuffed Celery (or Endive)
Black Bean Dip • Smoked Salmon Canapés • Antipasto
Baba Ghanoush • Prosciutto and Melon, Asparagus or
Pear • Cajun Chicken Wings • Guacamole
Tortilla or Taco Chips for Guacamole • Vegetarian Tacos*

*Clam Dip • Tofu-Yogurt Onion Dip
Vegetable Onion Dip
Dill Dip • Smoked Salmon Dip
Cottage Cheese Dip*

# Appetizers, Hors d'Oeuvres & Canapés

G reat appetizers host your party. They introduce your imagination and thoughtfulness as a party-giver. Their taste and aroma evoke oohs and ahs from your guests, making friends of strangers.

Delicious food livens any party. I have seen more dull gatherings gain energy when great food, whether old favorites or magnificently fashioned expensive fare, comes into the room.

To keep your party lively and lean offer steamy, hot stuffed mushrooms, or a cold, spicy mock caviar eggplant dip with crisp lavosh, carrots sliced into large, thin diagonals, lemony hummus with hot baked pita triangles, and fresh celery stuffed with nonfat cream cheese and huge green olive slices.

*Applause. Applause.* These heart-healthy appetizers will bring down the house with a roar of "great food," "great party."

# MOCK CAVIAR

SERVES 8 AS A DIP

This is the fast version of caponata, a Sicilian side dish. Serve it cold with crackers, corn chips or vegetables like celery or green beans. It makes a great filling for hard cooked egg whites. For the quickest preparation, use your processor for chopping, your microwave for cooking and your freezer for cooling.

1 large eggplant, unpeeled but pierced
1 large onion, unpeeled but pierced
1 medium onion, peeled
2 cloves garlic, minced
1 celery stalk
4 ripe olives
4 green olives
1/2 green pepper
1/2 red pepper
2 tablespoons cider vinegar
1 tablespoon cumin
2 tablespoons lemon juice
2 teaspoons drained capers
1/2 teaspoon sugar

In the microwave, cook the eggplant and unpeeled onion on high for 10 to 12 minutes. Slip the peel off the onion, and in the processor, lightly process the eggplant and cooked onion. Add the raw peeled onion, garlic, celery, olives, peppers, vinegar, cumin and juice and lightly process. Add the capers and sugar and mix well. Refrigerate until cold. If you want to serve it immediately, spread the mixture on a cookie sheet or other metal tray and place in freezer for five minutes. Serve cold.

◆ Per Serving:    Saturated fat: Trace   Total fat: 1gr    Cholesterol: 0
                  Sodium: 82mg    Calories: 36   Calories from fat: 14%

## WITH OLIVE OIL
Add 2 tablespoons of olive oil.

♦ Per Serving:    Saturated fat: 1gr    Total fat: 4gr    Cholesterol: 0
                  Sodium: 83mg    Calories: 66    Calories from fat: 50%

# HUMMUS

MAKES ABOUT 2 CUPS

Hummus (Humus) is a Middle Eastern specialty that has become so popular in America, it is even available ready-made in many food markets. The homemade variety has a fresher taste and you can control the salt, garlic, lemon and oil. Its most unusual ingredient, tahini, is a paste made from sesame seeds. Pour off the unnecessary oil which rises to the top.

Hummus can be served with the traditional bread, which is torn or cut into triangles; with crackers; or with cold vegetables such as celery and endive. It can even be stuffed into hard cooked egg whites and topped with a ripe or green olive half or a sun-dried tomato slice.

1 16-ounce can garbanzo beans (chick peas), drained
1/2 cup tahini, drained of sesame oil
2 cloves garlic, finely minced
1/4 cup fresh squeezed lemon juice
1/4 cup chopped black olives
1/4 teaspoon low-sodium salt (optional)

Garnish:
Chopped parsley
Cayenne
Chili paste
Chopped ripe olives
Chopped green olives
Slices of sun-dried tomatoes

In a food processor puree the beans, tahini, garlic, lemon juice, black olives and salt. Garnish and serve.

◆ **Per Tbsp:**   Saturated fat: Trace   Total fat: 1gr   Cholesterol: 0
                  Sodium: 26mg   Calories: 29   Calories from fat: 31%

WITH OLIVE OIL

After the hummus is put on a platter, pour a stream of 2 table-spoons of olive oil in a curly pattern or puddle across the top.

◆ **Per Tbsp:**   Saturated fat: .5gr   Total fat: 3gr   Cholesterol: 0
                  Sodium: 26mg   Calories: 51   Calories from fat: 57%

# CREAM CHEESE AND SPICY BENGAL CHUTNEY

SERVES 6

This is the lean update of a high cholesterol, high saturated fat piquant, spicy and mellow-tasting old favorite. I often keep the ingredients handy in case of unexpected company. Its color and interesting look always make it a hit.

It can be served in a mound on lettuce surrounded by melba toast, wheat or rye crackers, lavosh or you might prefer to use some 2- to 3-inch celery pieces or black olives.

**8 ounces substitute, nonfat or
    very low fat cream cheese
1 4-ounce jar Bengal Hot Chutney, chopped
    (or another sweet style, with 1/4 teaspoon hot sauce added)
1 avocado, diced and sprinkled with lemon
6 scallions cut into 1/2-inch pieces,
    white and light green part only**

Mound the cream cheese in a round half ball (on lettuce if desired) in the center of a round tray (or form it into a rectangle block for the rectangle tray). Pour the chutney over the top letting it slide off onto the sides. Place the avocado pieces firmly all over the top and poke in the scallions. Arrange the cracker and vegetables around the cheese.

◆ Per Serving:   Saturated fat: 5gr   Total fat: 17gr   Cholesterol: 0
                 Sodium: 217mg   Calories: 204   Calories from fat: 73%

## STUFFED CELERY (OR ENDIVE)

SERVES 4

Stuffed celery has been a favorite for decades. The new, very low saturated fat cream cheeses, the nonfat cream cheeses, and those made without dairy products, let us enjoy stuffed celery. Use a little less stuffing than usual and decorate each one. For variety, try stuffing the celery with a couple of tiny cooked, spiced shrimps, or larger shrimp halves (which take 3 minutes to steam), some strips of red, yellow and green peppers, parsley and other green herbs, or slivered kalamata olives.

For less formal gatherings, keep the celery whole, leaves and all. If you are stuffing endive, add more interesting toppings such as pickle slices, red pepper strips, a small, wafer-thin curl of lean ham or prosciutto, or even baby corn with a tiny sprig of parsley.

12 celery stalks, all one length, or different sizes,
   the leaves attached (picnic style), rinsed
8 ounces nonfat cream cheese, room temperature
2 to 4 tablespoons skim milk for thinning (optional)
12 large pimento-stuffed green olives, sliced into 1/4-inch slices
Paprika

Set the celery stalks out, hollow side up. In a small bowl mix the cream cheese, adding the skim milk when necessary to thin. With a knife, spread the mixture into the cavity of the celery, right up to the leaves. Push in several olive slices along the length of the celery, sprinkle with paprika, and serve.

◆ Per Serving:   Saturated fat: Trace   Total fat: 2gr   Cholesterol: 10mg
                 Sodium: 681mg   Calories: 93   Calories from fat: 21%

## WITH COTTAGE CHEESE
Substitute 4 ounces of pureed 1 percent fat cottage cheese for 4 ounces of the nondairy cream cheese.

- ◆ Per Serving:    Saturated fat: Trace   Total fat: 2gr    Cholesterol: 6mg
                    Sodium: 631mg   Calories: 83    Calories from fat: 23%

## WITH "LIGHT" CREAM CHEESE
Use dairy cream cheese with reduced fat.

- ◆ Per Serving:    Saturated fat: 6gr    Total fat: 12gr   Cholesterol: 20mg
                    Sodium: 671mg   Calories: 152   Calories from fat: 61%

## BLACK BEAN DIP

MAKES 1-1/2 CUPS

This is Southwestern in taste and style. Serve it with corn or tortilla chips, vegetables such as celery, carrots sliced thinly on the diagonal, or jalapeño flavored crackers, and sprinkle it with lime.

2 cups canned black beans, drained
1/2 to 1 cup nonfat sour cream drained, or thick,
    nonfat yogurt cheese, or pureed nonfat cottage cheese
1 onion, chopped
1/4 to 1/2 teaspoon cumin
1/2 cup chopped celery
2 tablespoons lime juice
2 tablespoons chopped cilantro
Several drops hot sauce

Garnish:
Chopped tomatoes
Chopped cilantro or parsley
Chopped scallions
Chopped red pepper
Lime wedges

In a small bowl, puree all the ingredients with an immersion blender or in a food processor. If you have neither, mash well with a fork. For more texture, puree only two thirds of the beans with the rest of the mixture, adding the whole beans to the pureed. Garnish. Serve cold.

◆ Per Tbsp:      Saturated fat: Trace   Total fat: Trace   Cholesterol: Trace
                 Sodium: 18mg     Calories: 25     Calories from fat: 3%

## SMOKED SALMON CANAPÉS

MAKES 16 CANAPÉS

These are small matzo or other cracker canapés that are tasty and attractive, yet have almost no saturated fat.

1 tablespoon canola margarine
2 teaspoons grated or shredded fresh horseradish
2 tablespoons minced fresh dill weed
Several matzos broken into 16 rectangles, or crackers
1/4 pound smoked salmon

Garnish:
16 tiny dill sprigs

Combine the margarine, horseradish and dill weed. Spread the mixture on each matzo rectangle. Cut the salmon slices into 2-inch squares. Cut each square in half, diagonally, to form two triangles. Form each triangle into a cone. Insert a dill sprig into each cone, and place each cone on the matzo rectangle.

◆ Per Canapé:    Saturated fat: Trace   Total fat: 1gr   Cholesterol: 2mg
                 Sodium: 63mg     Calories: 37     Calories from fat: 33%

## WITH IMITATION CREAM CHEESE

Place a small bit of imitation cream cheese (about 1/4 teaspoon) into each piece of salmon and fill with dill as directed.

◆ **Per Canapé:**   Saturated fat: Trace   Total fat: 2gr   Cholesterol: 2mg
Sodium: 70mg   Calories: 40   Calories from fat: 35%

## ANTIPASTO

SERVES 4

This colorful, flavorful dish is a selection of Italian-style foods, served on a large platter, usually before the first course of pasta. It can have many kinds of lean meats, vegetables and delicacies and with the selection of a wide range of foods, can easily be very low in saturated fat. Along with a good bread and perhaps soup, antipasto can be a meal in itself, or the first course of a larger dinner.

**Romaine or arugula to line a large platter**
**4 4 x 4-inch slices wafer thin lean ham or prosciutto, rolled and**
**secured with a toothpick**
**8 large slices ripe tomato**
**12 cucumber sticks**
**1 cup bottled ratatouille**
**8 sardines**
**4 hard cooked eggs, halved, yolks discarded, each half stuffed**
**with several tiny smoked canned oysters**
**20 marinated mushrooms**
**20 ripe olives**
**4 stuffed celery (page 30)**
**4 to 8 large dried figs**

Line a large tray or platter with lettuce. Arrange all of the food attractively, the ham together, the tomatoes and cucumbers together, the ratatouille in one mound, the sardines placed together, the hard cooked eggs side by side, and the mushrooms, olives, celery and figs placed around the edge of the rest of the food. Serve chilled.

◆ **Per Serving:**    Saturated fat: 1gr    Total fat: 9gr    Cholesterol: 62mg
                     Sodium: 932mg    Calories: 275    Calories from fat: 29%

## WITH MOZZARELLA
Add 2 ounces (4 slices) of fresh buffalo mozzarella to the platter.

◆ **Per Serving:**    Saturated fat: 3gr    Total fat: 11gr    Cholesterol: 70mg
                     Sodium: 998mg    Calories: 319    Calories from fat: 31%

# BABA GHANOUSH

SERVES 6–10

Every country has a favorite eggplant mixture. This flavorful one is Middle Eastern. Serve it as a dip with crackers, with pita bread, or vegetables or in hard cooked halved egg whites.

1 1 to 2-pound eggplant, unpeeled, pierced and microwaved
   whole for about 10 minutes
3 tablespoons tahini
2 teaspoons minced garlic
1/2 cup chopped Spanish onion
3 tablespoons lemon juice
1 tablespoon olive oil

Process all the ingredients and serve chilled.

◆ **Per Serving:**    Saturated fat: 1gr    Total fat: 5gr    Cholesterol: 0
                     Sodium: 6mg    Calories: 78    Calories from fat: 53%

# PROSCIUTTO AND MELON, ASPARAGUS OR PEAR

SERVES 20

This is a more formal or elegant hors d'oeuvre. Prosciutto ham is a special type of salty meat from Parma, Italy. It has an enticing aroma and a very distinctive flavor and it can vary widely in the amount of fat. Only purchase it if it is lean, remove all fat that is visible, and have the meat cutter slice it thinly. Luckily, hams are one of few meats where the fat is easy to see, so you can quickly decide whether or not to purchase a particular prosciutto.

**2 whole, different kinds of chilled melons, or 8 pears, or 2 pounds lightly steamed, chilled asparagus, flower heads only cut into 3 to 4-inch lengths, ends reserved for another use**
**1/4 pound (approximately) prosciutto, sliced wafer thin, all edge-fat removed, cut in 1 x 4-inch strips**
**Toothpicks**
**Coarsely ground black pepper**
**Parsley**
**Two lemons cut in wedges or thin slices**

Arrange the ham bundles on a large silver tray. Tuck in a few delicate greens like dill or small leaf parsley, place a few lemon or lime slices or wedges around the edge and you and your guests are in for a treat.

Prosciutto and melon does not keep for more than an hour or two so don't make it too far ahead of serving time. Cut the melons in half, scoop out the seeds, remove the rind and cut in long slender slices or in smaller chunks if the melons are large. If using sweet, plump pears, core them and slice lengthwise in 1/2 to 3/4-inch wide slices, trimming off the narrow end (which may break).

Wrap each piece of fruit or vegetable with a strip of prosciutto, hold it together with a toothpick and arrange on a large tray. Wrap the more slender asparagus with slightly smaller strips of prosciutto. Sprinkle lavishly with black pepper. Tuck in the parsley and lemon. Serve cold. As an hors d'oeuvre it makes about 80–100 pieces, serving 20–25, or 8 at a dinner party.

- **Per Serving:** Saturated fat: Trace   Total fat: Trace   Cholesterol: 3mg
  Sodium: 82mg   Calories: 13   Calories from fat: 21%

## CAJUN CHICKEN WINGS

SERVES 6 AS AN APPETIZER OR MEAT DISH (Four each)
SERVES 10 AS AN HORS D'OEUVRE (Two or so each)

Chicken wings are an inexpensive way to enjoy finger foods. They are usually high in fat, but if you use only the wing part closest to the bird and remove the skin you lower the fat. You can dip the wings in a sauce, or enjoy them without a dip.

If you want them crisp, bake them on a cookie sheet in a 400° oven for 20 minutes. You can also broil them (checking them often so they don't burn) for about 15 minutes. Or try a combination of first microwaving, then broiling to crisp. Chicken wings that have the skin removed marinate much more quickly, so adjust the flavor accordingly.

**24 chicken wings, all skin and fat removed**
**Cajun spice such as Zatarain's, Tony Chacherie's Creole**
**Seasoning, or a combination to taste of cayenne pepper,**
**paprika, black pepper, sugar, and garlic powder**

Shake the spices on the chicken and let it sit in an oven cooking bag, refrigerated, for one hour. In the same bag, bake the wings in the microwave on high for 8 minutes. Remove the bag and pour off all excess fat, and cook for 3 minutes more, or until done. To brown, remove the wings from the bag. Separate on a rack and broil for 3 to 5 minutes, checking often so they don't burn. Serve hot or cold.

- **Per Serving:** Saturated fat: 4gr   Total fat: 13gr   Cholesterol: 53mg
  Sodium: 56mg   Calories: 198   Calories from fat: 63%

# GUACAMOLE

SERVES 4

Our version of guacamole doesn't have the recent additions of sour cream, mayonnaise, or black olives but is wonderfully delicious and reminiscent of the original Mayan recipe which is thousands of years old.

Avocados have fat (if they're from California, it's at least 8 percent by law, and sometimes it's as much as 20 percent—Florida avocados have no law and less fat), but all avocados are primarily monounsaturated fat, a freebie for our concerns in a low saturated fat diet. So, unless you eat a lot of avocados, enjoy them because chances are you aren't even going to add that many calories. Three ounces have between 95 and 150 calories depending upon the time of year and where the avocados are from.

Serve with chips, celery, string beans, carrots, jicama or cucumber slices.

You can stuff guacamole in sugar-snap pods topped with a bright slice of red pepper, or place a few tablespoons on a ripe tomato slice as part of a salad or fill a whole tomato, hard cooked egg whites topped with some diced red peppers, or fill several cherry tomatoes, or fill half a small red, yellow, purple or green pepper. Then surround with chips for a colorful salad plate.

2 ripe avocados, peeled, one well mashed or pureed, the other diced in 1/4 -inch chunks
1 medium-small, fresh, very ripe tomato, diced (or dice a canned tomato)
1 small onion, chopped (about two full tablespoons)
1 tablespoon lemon juice
1 tablespoon lime juice
1/4–1/2 teaspoon finely cut fresh jalapeño or other hot peppers, or several squirts Tabasco sauce, or several shakes red pepper flakes
1/4–1 teaspoon chopped cilantro (optional)

Pinch of sugar (optional)
Dash of low-sodium salt (optional)

Garnish:
Salsa spooned in the center
Hot sauce squirted in the center
Diced fresh tomatoes in the center
Chopped Bermuda onions

Mix all ingredients well, blending the chunks with the well mashed avocado, but not mashing them completely. Authentic guacamole is lumpy and full of hearty texture. Taste. Adjust the seasonings. Serve immediately or chill covered with more lemon juice on top. Mix in the lemon juice before serving.

◆ Per Serving:  Saturated fat: 2gr  Total fat: 15gr  Cholesterol: 0
Sodium: 17mg  Calories: 170  Calories from fat: 73%

## WITH OLIVE OIL
Add 2 tablespoons of olive oil to the mixture.

◆ Per Serving:  Saturated fat: 3gr  Total fat: 22gr  Cholesterol: 0
Sodium: 17mg  Calories: 230  Calories from fat: 79%

## WITH NONFAT SOUR CREAM
Substitute 2 tablespoons of nonfat sour cream for the olive oil.

◆ Per Serving:  Saturated fat: 2gr  Total fat: 15gr  Cholesterol: 0
Sodium: 22mg  Calories: 175  Calories from fat: 71%

# TORTILLA OR TACO CHIPS FOR GUACAMOLE

Most corn chips are fried but there are several brands such as Bearitos Brand Tortilla Chips which aren't. You can make your own by toasting corn tortillas in the oven (350°, for 10–15 minutes) until crispy, and breaking them into smaller pieces.

For a different texture, you can make your own chips by frying them in an inch of canola/rapeseed or safflower oil, turning once or twice until the edges are quite crisp, leaving the center softer. Drain well and blot with paper towels and (optional) sprinkle lightly with low-sodium salt. Tear the chips into 1 by 2–3 inch pieces to serve.

A way to lessen the fat is to brush or spray the flat tortilla chips lightly with canola/rapeseed or safflower oil and bake.

◆ **Per Serving:** Saturated fat: Trace  Total fat: 4gr  Cholesterol: 0
Sodium: 80mg  Calories: 83  Calories from fat: 40%

## VEGETARIAN TACOS

SERVES 4–6

Most Mexican dishes adapt well to meatless versions. If served with refried beans, the taco shells and beans will combine to form a complete protein. To serve as appetizers put the mixture on small tacos. For dinner let guests assemble their own buffet-style.

Vegetable spray
1 clove garlic, minced
1 small onion, chopped
1 cup mashed canned beans
3 cups sliced mushrooms
1 carrot, shredded
2 tomatoes, cubed
1 8-ounce can tomato sauce
1 to 2 tablespoons chili powder
1/2 teaspoon ground cumin
dash of hot pepper sauce
8 regular size or 24 miniature taco shells, or uncooked corn tortillas
Taco hot sauce

Garnish:
**Salsa**
**1 head lettuce, shredded**
**Orange sections**
**Alfalfa sprouts**

In a large skillet, spray and add 1/4 inch water. Stir in the garlic, onion, beans, mushrooms, and carrot and heat over medium heat for about 4 minutes. Stir in 3/4 of the cubed tomatoes, tomato sauce, chili powder, cumin, and hot pepper sauce. Cover and simmer for about 5 minutes.

Meanwhile, if you are forming your own taco shells, preheat the oven to 350°. Place uncooked corn tortillas over the oven racks and bake for 10 minutes. To serve, spoon vegetable mixture into taco shells. Add salsa and lettuce. Top with a dash of hot sauce. Garnish plates with orange sections and alfalfa sprouts.

◆ **Per Serving:** **Saturated fat: 1gr    Total fat: 5gr    Cholesterol: 0**
**Sodium: 392mg    Calories: 208    Calories from fat: 20%**

# *Dips*

**O**ur old favorites become new favorites with the help of the new nonfat and low-fat mayonnaise, yogurt, sour cream, cream cheese and other cheeses. These creative new products are just as delicious as the fatty old ones. With a pinch of fresh herbs these dips are the "today" version of some heavier memories. Use the freshest ingredients you can find, for that just picked country flavor.

# CLAM DIP

MAKES ABOUT 1-1/2 CUPS

This is perfect for vegetables or crudites such as celery, green beans, carrot sticks, green, red, orange and yellow bell pepper sticks, endive, jicama, and carrots sliced diagonally so they make a big enough surface to hold this spicy dip that is full of clams. You can also use white melba rounds and other low-fat or nonfat crackers.

8 ounces nonfat cottage cheese
2 tablespoons Vermont's Fromage Blanc or very low fat cream cheese
1 or more tablespoons skim milk
2 teaspoons fresh lemon juice
Several drops Tabasco sauce
1 6-1/2 ounce container fresh (or canned) clams, drained and
    coarsely chopped
2 tablespoons chopped fresh parsley

In a blender or food processor, mix the cheeses, adding skim milk until it is smooth. Stir in the clams, lemon juice, Tabasco and parsley, mix well and refrigerate several hours. Serve chilled with crackers or dipping vegetables.

◆  **Per Tbsp:**      Saturated fat: Trace   Total fat: Trace   Cholesterol: 4mg
                                Sodium: 13mg     Calories: 20    Calories from fat: 17%

# TOFU-YOGURT ONION DIP

MAKES ABOUT 1-1/2 CUPS

This is a very smooth, flavorful dip for a vegetable platter or crackers. Don't be afraid to try tofu. You've probably had it before without even realizing it.

8 ounces tofu
1 tablespoon lemon juice

1/2 teaspoon sugar
1 tablespoon low-sodium soy sauce
1–2 tablespoons skim milk to thin if necessary
1/3 cup finely chopped onions
1/4 cup nonfat yogurt

Garnish:
Chopped parsley
Chopped chives
Chopped red pepper

In a blender or food processor combine all the ingredients except the parsley and chives and blend until very smooth. Refrigerate for several hours. Before serving, sprinkle with parsley and chives. Serve chilled.

◆ Per Tbsp:     Saturated fat: Trace   Total fat: 1gr     Cholesterol: Trace
                Sodium: 3mg     Calories: 12    Calories from fat: 38%

## VEGETABLE ONION DIP

MAKES 3 CUPS

Vegetable onion dip is a favorite to serve with crackers or vegetables, and the new, far less saturated fat versions of sour creams and cream cheeses make it possible to keep the saturated fats very low. You may wish to adjust the taste with a few drops of vinegar, low-sodium salt, a pinch of sugar, Tabasco or other flavorings as the imitation products vary in taste and sugar amounts. You want a piquant flavor that has a certain richness.

2 cups low saturated fat imitation sour cream
1/2 cup finely chopped onions
1/4 cup finely chopped scallions
1/4 cup finely chopped carrots

In a small bowl, mix the ingredients thoroughly. Serve chilled.

◆ Per Tbsp:    Saturated fat: 2gr    Total fat: 3gr    Cholesterol: 0
                Sodium: 15mg    Calories: 32    Calories from fat: 79%

## DILL DIP

MAKES 2 CUPS

Dill is one of those fresh, delightful herbs that is pleasant to almost everyone. This dill dip is further spiced with some of the new saltless dill pickles, available in large supermarkets. The cheese is Vermont's Fromage Blanc, also available in the same markets. It has virtually no fat.

1 cup nonfat cottage cheese
1/2 pint Vermont's Fromage Blanc
Skim milk if necessary to thin
4 tablespoons chopped fresh dill
4 teaspoons chopped salt-free dill pickles
1/4 cup chopped onion

In a food processor or blender, puree the cottage cheese and the Fromage Blanc using skim milk if necessary to thin. Fold in the other ingredients and serve chilled.

◆ Per Tbsp:    Saturated fat: Trace   Total fat: 1gr    Cholesterol: 3mg
                Sodium: 65mg    Calories: 28    Calories from fat: 40%

## SMOKED SALMON DIP

MAKES ABOUT 1-1/2 CUPS

This can be a vegetable or cracker dip, or served with jelly and toasted bagels for Sunday brunch. A teaspoonful or more of skim milk can always be used to thin the cheese, if necessary.

1 8-ounce package nonfat cream cheese
1/2 cup lowest fat part-skim ricotta cheese
2 tablespoons yogurt
Few drops hot sauce (optional)
4 ounces smoked salmon, finely chopped

Combine the cheeses, yogurt and hot sauce in a food processor and process until smooth. Fold in the smoked salmon.

◆ **Per Tbsp:**      Saturated fat: Trace    Total fat: 1gr     Cholesterol: 2mg
                        Sodium: 48mg     Calories: 18    Calories from fat: 36%

## COTTAGE CHEESE DIP

MAKES ABOUT 2 CUPS

Few people know cottage cheese can be processed to a satin smoothness if you just keep processing for 2 or 3 minutes. Then add just what you would like, date bits for a sweet dip, or spicy morsels for a more piquant taste. Use this as a dip for vegetables, and play with the flavors, getting it as spicy as you want. Use the skim milk sparingly, just enough to thin it to the desired consistency.

1 pint nonfat cottage cheese
Skim milk
1/4 cup dried parsley
2 teaspoons dried or fresh chives
1/2 teaspoon garlic powder
1/2 teaspoon low-sodium salt (optional)
1/ teaspoons celery seed
1/4 teaspoon black pepper

In the processor, blend the cottage cheese until very smooth. Add enough skim milk to thin the cheese, if necessary, then add all the other ingredients and process.

◆ **Per Tbsp:**      Saturated fat: Trace    Total fat: Trace    Cholesterol: 1mg
                        Sodium: 11mg     Calories: 8    Calories from fat: 5%

# SOUPS, STEWS & CHOWDERS

*Easiest Chicken Soup • Spring Pea Soup*
*Chicken and Corn Soup • Minestrone*
*Black Bean Soup • Vegetarian Bean and Rice Soup*
*Cream of Broccoli Soup • Cabbage Soup*
*Homemade Lentil Soup • Gazpacho*
*Tomato Soup • Oyster Stew • Two-Bean Corn Chili*
*Baked Bean Soup*

# Soups, Stews & Chowders

**T**ossing good food in just one pot is my idea of a great way to cook. Although some soups need a while to meld and blend, there are many fast and delicious ones, too. Almost every canned soup can be extended and freshened by separately steaming chopped vegetables, such as onions, leeks, scallions, garlic, mushrooms, carrots, parsley, celery or others, adding them to the soup, and heating them together for a few minutes. Sometimes just the addition of a juice such as tomato or carrot, perhaps some seasoning wines such as Pernod, Marsala, Madeira, Armagnac, sherry or vermouth helps. Or try incorporating a quick cooking rice or ramen noodles.

Canned corn chowder is better with fresh chopped steamed cibola or Spanish onions, plus some more frozen corn. Other soups such as mushroom might benefit from chopped steamed shallots, scallions and even chopped carrots.

Some soups such as tomato soup made from scratch are fast and easy with just a quick heating of few chopped fresh yellow or red tomatoes (even cherry tomatoes pureed), onions and basil. Quick soups such as defatted chicken can also be made from scratch in a relatively short time.

# EASIEST CHICKEN SOUP

SERVES 8

You can almost make this with your eyes closed, but you'll need a defatting cup or time to chill the soup to remove the fat that rises to the top. Use the giblets, including the neck, heart, and gizzard, the fat and skin but discard the liver. This soup can be flavored with sherry, fresh or dried sage, soy sauce, Worcestershire sauce and many other flavorings, herbs and spices, and of course you can add cooked noodles or rice once it is defatted.

1 whole chicken and parts except the liver, *or* the skin, neck, bones, fat and giblets
3 carrots, cut in fourths
1 very large onion, coarsely chopped
2 celery stalks including leaves, coarsely cut
2 leeks, sliced
5 cloves garlic
1/4 cup chopped parsley
Water to cover chicken and vegetables
Low-sodium salt (optional)
Pepper

Garnish:
Chopped parsley

In a large pot, cook everything but the salt, if using, and the pepper loosely covered for 15 minutes in the microwave (or 45 minutes on the stove over low heat). Remove the chicken and the vegetables and defat the stock. Remove the skin from the chicken if using a whole chicken, then all the meat from the bones and cut the meat into large pieces, removing all the visible fat. Add the chicken meat and giblets back into the stock after it has been defatted. If using only skin, fat, neck, bones and giblets, remove everything, discard the neck, fat, skin and bones, cut any fat off the giblets, defat the stock and add the defatted giblets back. Rinse the vegetables and cut into bite-size pieces and put them back into the soup. Season with salt and pepper and garnish. Serve hot.

- **Per Serving:**     Saturated fat: 1gr     Total fat: 3gr     Cholesterol: 57mg
  Sodium: 233mg     Calories: 125     Calories from fat: 19%

## STOCK WITHOUT MEAT

- **Per Serving:**     Saturated fat: Trace     Total fat: Trace     Cholesterol: 5mg
  Sodium: 175mg     Calories: 36     Calories from fat: 97%

## STOCK WITH MEAT

- **Per Serving:**     Saturated fat: 1gr     Total fat: 3gr     Cholesterol: 80mg
  Sodium: 236mg     Calories: 134     Calories from fat: 20%

## STOCK WITH NOODLES OR RICE

Add 1 cup of cooked noodles or rice just before serving. Unless you are going to use up all the soup at one time, don't add them directly to the soup while it cooks or is stored or they will get mushy. Instead, place heated pasta or rice in each individual bowl and pour the soup over it at the time of serving.

- **Per Serving:**     Saturated fat: Trace     Total fat: 1gr     Cholesterol: 11mg
  Sodium: 176mg     Calories: 63     Calories from fat: 9%

# SPRING PEA SOUP

SERVES 4–6

This is a thick, robust soup that is easy to prepare in a food processor and even easier if you have an immersion blender. It is nourishing enough to be a light meal when served with slices of crusty whole grain bread and fruit.

Vegetable spray
2 stalks celery, finely chopped
2 cloves garlic, minced

1 medium-size onion, chopped
Water to cover
2 cups vegetable or defatted chicken stock
1 16-ounce bag frozen peas, thawed
Dash of white pepper
1/2 cup nonfat milk
1/4 cup nonfat evaporated skim milk
Dash of nutmeg (preferably freshly ground)

Garnish:
Garlic Croutons

Spray a nonstick 3 1/2- to 5-quart saucepan, add the celery, garlic, onion and 1/4 inch water and cook until softened,
about 4 minutes. Add the stock, peas and white pepper. Over
medium heat, cover and simmer for 5 minutes.

Either transfer the mixture to the bowl of a food processor fitted with steel blade and puree, or use an immersion blender right
in the saucepan, and puree. Return mixture to the saucepan (if
using the processor) add the two milks and nutmeg and cook over
low heat for about 5 minutes, stirring constantly. Top each serving with your choice of garnish.

GARLIC CROUTONS
Rub sliced garlic on toast, spray lightly with olive oil spray and
bake on a tray in 350° oven for 10 minutes and cut into cubes.

◆ Per Serving:    Saturated fat: Trace    Total fat: 1gr    Cholesterol: 1mg
                  Sodium: 363mg    Calories: 118   Calories from fat: 5%

## CHICKEN AND CORN SOUP

SERVES 4–6

Chicken first marinated for 5 minutes in egg whites and sherry
becomes snowy white and velvety when cooked, and the egg
white separates into shreds for an interesting texture in the soup.

The method is borrowed from Asian cooking, but added vegetables and simple seasonings are all American.

**2 chicken breasts, skinned and defatted, partially defrosted**
**1 tablespoon dry sherry**
**1 egg white, beaten until foamy**
**2 cups defatted chicken stock**
**2 cups water**
**1-1/2 cups corn, cut off cobs or frozen whole kernel**
**4 tablespoons minced parsley**
**1/2 cup frozen green peas, partially defrosted**
**1/2 teaspoon low-sodium salt (optional)**
**Black pepper**

Cut the chicken in 1/8-inch strips. In a bowl, toss the chicken strips with the sherry and egg white. In a large saucepan, bring the stock and water to a boil. Add the chicken mixture, stir to separate the chicken and bring it to a boil again. Add the corn and 2 tablespoons of the parsley and return to a boil. Add the peas and return it to a boil and add the salt and pepper. Serve immediately in warm bowls, with the remaining parsley sprinkled over top.

◆ Per Serving:    Saturated fat: 1gr    Total fat: 3gr    Cholesterol: 58mg
                  Sodium: 387mg    Calories: 180    Calories from fat: 16%

WITH CHICKEN THIGHS
Substitute 10 ounces chicken thigh fillets (all fat and skin removed) for chicken breast.

◆ Per Serving:    Saturated fat: 1gr    Total fat: 3gr    Cholesterol: 47mg
                  Sodium: 388mg    Calories: 132    Calories from fat: 20%

# MINESTRONE

SERVES 10

This thick, hearty soup can be varied end-
lessly by using different vegetables, meat
and pasta. Use different brands for the
canned tomato paste, crushed tomatoes and
whole tomatoes, in case one brand is bitter,
too sweet or just off. Or use a canned paste
and fresh crushed and whole tomatoes. Fresh tomatoes can make a
more watery soup, so you may wish to cook it down or thicken it
with cornstarch first softened in a cool liquid, or flour sprinkled
on top and stirred in. Like many good soups this can be cooked
for 10 minutes or one hour. However, the pasta turns mushy
quickly so if it isn't all going to be eaten immediately, cook it separately and add it to the soup or each bowl just before serving.

3 cups canned white or navy beans
3 quarts water
1 15-ounce can or package crushed tomatoes
2 6-ounce cans tomato paste
2 pounds fresh tomatoes or 1 28-ounce can whole tomatoes,
    chopped
1 leek, finely chopped
2 onions, finely chopped
3 cloves garlic, minced
1/2 cup chopped parsley
3 carrots, finely chopped
1 potato, diced
2 cups finely chopped cabbage
1 cup thinly sliced zucchini
8 green beans, diced
1 teaspoon dried oregano flakes, or 1-1/2 teaspoons fresh
    chopped oregano
1 teaspoon dried sweet basil flakes, or 1-1/2 teaspoons fresh
    chopped basil

**3/4 cup small pasta noodles**
**Low-sodium salt (optional)**
**Pepper**

Garnish:
**Chopped or shredded fresh basil**

In a large pot, combine all the ingredients except the pasta, salt and pepper and cook for 15 minutes. Puree some of the soup right in the pot with an immersion blender or remove some of the beans and puree with a food processor and add them back to the soup. Meanwhile, cook the pasta for 8 to 10 minutes in boiling water. Drain it and add to the soup. Season to taste with salt, if using, and pepper. Sprinkle with basil and serve hot.

◆ **Per Serving:** Saturated fat: Trace  Total fat: 1gr  Cholesterol: 0
Sodium: 62mg  Calories: 215  Calories from fat: 6%

## WITH OLIVE OIL
Add 2 tablespoons olive oil to the soup.

◆ **Per Serving:** Saturated fat: 1gr  Total fat: 4gr  Cholesterol: 0
Sodium: 62mg  Calories: 239  Calories from fat: 15%

## WITH MEAT BROTH
Omit the tomatoes and use defatted beef stock instead of water.

◆ **Per Serving:** Saturated fat: Trace  Total fat: 1gr  Cholesterol: Trace
Sodium: 1420mg  Calories: 187  Calories from fat: 5%

## WITH PARMESAN CHEESE
Add 1 tablespoon Parmesan cheese to each serving.

◆ **Per Serving:** Saturated fat: 1gr  Total fat: 3gr  Cholesterol: 4mg
Sodium: 152mg  Calories: 229  Calories from fat: 11%

# BLACK BEAN SOUP

SERVES 8

This soup is a tradition in Latin America and the Caribbean. Often it is served with the soup bowl placed in the middle of each person's serving area, a bowl or mound of rice on one side, and chopped onions on the other. Add a bottle of hot sauce, a plate of some sweet limes and a cold, mild beer or soda pop to the table.

The garnish can be a very large hunk of avocado (Mexican style), wafer-thin slices of lemon or lime or a lemon-coated chunk of banana or papaya in the center (Florida style). If you aren't too brave about the avocado, banana or papaya in the soup, serve them in a salad next to the soup, add some crackers and you have a mighty fine lunch or dinner. This soup gets better each day, but only keeps for about 5 days in the refrigerator, and it can be frozen.

3 cups defatted beef or chicken stock
2 cups canned black beans, drained
1 large Spanish onion, finely chopped
1 large carrot, finely shredded
1 celery stalk with tops, finely shredded
1 leek, chopped
1 large tomato, finely chopped
2 cloves garlic, minced
1/4 teaspoon dried, flaked thyme
1/4 teaspoon turmeric
1 teaspoon ground cumin
1/2 bay leaf finely crumbled
1/4 teaspoon finely chopped jalapeño pepper
Low-sodium salt (optional)
Pepper
1/4 cup sherry

Garnish:
1 cup cooked rice for each serving
1 cup chopped onion for each serving
Chopped hard-cooked egg whites
Sliced banana
Sliced avocado
Lime or lemon slices or wedges

In a large pot, combine the stock, beans, onion, carrot, celery, leek, tomato, garlic, herbs and spices and jalapeño to the stock and simmer for 10 to 15 minutes. With an immersion blender, mash most of the beans and vegetables and serve hot with the garnishes.

◆ Per Serving: Saturated fat: Trace   Total fat: Trace   Cholesterol: Trace
Sodium: 512mg   Calories: 84   Calories from fat: 5%

WITH HAM
Dice the lean meat and add it to the soup.

◆ Per Serving: Saturated fat: Trace   Total fat: Trace   Cholesterol: Trace
Sodium: 924mg   Calories: 82   Calories from fat: 4%

## VEGETARIAN BEAN AND RICE SOUP

SERVES 8

This soup is a simpler, easier but just as delicious version of other black bean soups. It is served the traditional Caribbean way, with lemon and lime wedges for sprinkling and a bowl or mound of cooked white rice on one side, and chopped raw onions on the other. The garnish can be chopped tomatoes.

3 cups water
1 cup canned, drained black or other beans
1 Spanish onion, finely chopped
1 large carrot, cut into four pieces
5 cloves garlic, minced

1/2 teaspoon Cajun or New Orleans spice mix
1 teaspoon dried or fresh chopped parsley
2 teaspoons orange zest or three or four slices of orange peel
1 cup cooked rice for each serving
1 cup chopped onion for each serving
Chopped tomatoes

Garnish:
Lime or lemon slices or wedges
Sliced jalapeño rings

In a large pot, combine the water, beans, onion, carrot, garlic, Cajun spice, parsley and orange peel and simmer for 10 minutes, covered, adding more water if necessary. Partially puree with an immersion blender, add the rice and onions, sprinkle the top with tomatoes, lime wedges and a few rings of jalapeño peppers. Serve hot with the garnishes.

◆ Per Serving:   Saturated fat: Trace  Total fat: 1gr   Cholesterol: 0
                   Sodium: 16mg    Calories: 366  Calories from fat: 2%

# CREAM OF BROCCOLI SOUP

SERVES 4–6

Cream of broccoli soup is on nearly every restaurant menu. It is easy to make at home and makes good use of the stems of broccoli. Garnish it with wafer-thin slices of lemon or orange, nutmeg, chopped black olives, even a couple of mandarin oranges. The soup can be left all chunky, all pureed, or the stalks pureed with the extra small florets left whole. To make the soup extra thick, stir in 2 tablespoons of flour when you stir in the florets.

2 cups defatted chicken stock or water
2 cups skim milk
1 onion, finely chopped
1 cup chopped or pureed broccoli stems, peeled if needed
2 cups tiny broccoli florets
Low-sodium salt (optional)
1 8-ounce can evaporated skim milk
3 tablespoons flour

Garnish:
Grated orange peel
Sliced scallions

In a large pot, combine the stock, milk, onion and the chopped or pureed broccoli stems and heat covered for 15 minutes. Add the florets and heat for another 3 to 4 minutes until they get very green, stirring occasionally. In a small bowl, mix the salt, skim milk and the flour and stir in the soup, cooking 3 minutes more, until it thickens. Serve hot.

◆ Per Serving:    Saturated fat: Trace   Total fat: 1gr    Cholesterol: 3mg
                  Sodium: 444mg   Calories: 126   Calories from fat: 5%

# CABBAGE SOUP

SERVES 4

Cabbage soup is hearty and robust and the flavor improves overnight. A food processor for shredding the cabbage is helpful. This soup is a main dish and can be served with lots of good country-style or peasant bread and a dark green salad.

4 cups defatted chicken stock or water
1 onion, finely chopped
1 carrot, finely chopped
1 celery stalks, finely chopped
2 tablespoons chopped parsley
1/2 pound solid green or white head cabbage, finely shredded
1 small potato, diced or shredded
3 tablespoons flour
Low-sodium salt (optional)

Garnish:
Chopped fresh dill

In a large pot, combine the defatted chicken stock, onion, carrot, celery, parsley, cabbage and potato and boil covered for 10 minutes. With an immersion blender, puree the soup. Sift or shake the flour over the top, turn the heat to medium high, and stir until very thick, about 3 minutes. Serve hot.

◆ **Per Serving:**   Saturated fat: Trace   Total fat: Trace   Cholesterol: 0
Sodium: 656mg   Calories: 74   Calories from fat: 5%

WITH HOT DOGS
This version requires finding hot dogs with a very low fat content (usual fat in hot dogs is 60 percent) and kosher hot dogs have occasionally proved to be low, but Healthy Choice is 98% fat-free. Read the label and pass up any that don't supply the saturated fat content or have color added. Use 2 ounces of hot dogs.

In a separate saucepan, boil the hot dogs or franks for 7 minutes, then discard the water. Slice them and add them to the soup when the grated potato is added. The nutrient values given are for Healthy Choice hot dogs.

◆ **Per Serving:**   Saturated fat: Trace   Total fat: 1gr      Cholesterol: 6mg
Sodium: 755mg   Calories: 122   Calories from fat: 11%

## WITH HAM

Simmer a ham bone and completely defat the broth. Use the broth in place of all or part of the water in the recipe. Remove any visible fat from the meat. Dice it and add it to the soup.

◆ **Per Serving:**   Saturated fat: Trace   Total fat: 1gr      Cholesterol: 7mg
Sodium: 765mg   Calories: 118   Calories from fat: 10%

# HOMEMADE LENTIL SOUP

## SERVES 4

Dried beans, a few flavoring vegetables, and a little wine, make a great lentil soup. Even the dried lentils take just a few minutes to cook—just right for a quick, no fuss meal.

This is a hearty, dark soup, good with a salad, a crusty rye or walnut loaf and fruit for dessert. The brown lentils are more firm then the red, which almost disintegrate making a thick broth. Other wines such as Marsala or Madeira can be substituted for the Armagnac.

3/4 cup red lentils
4 cups water or defatted meat stock
1 turnip, thinly sliced
1 stalk celery, sliced (including tops)
1 small onion, chopped
1/2 teaspoon Cajun seasoning
2 tablespoons Armagnac

In a large saucepan with a lid, add all the ingredients except the Armagnac and cook covered over medium heat for 17 minutes. Stir in the wine just before serving. Serve hot.

◆ Per Serving:   Saturated fat: Trace  Total fat: Trace  Cholesterol: 0
                    Sodium: 35mg     Calories: 156  Calories from fat: 2%

## GAZPACHO

SERVES 6–8

Originally from Spain, this cold summertime soup takes advantage of delicious summer, vine ripened tomatoes. Interesting and varied garnishes are half the fun. Serve it with corn bread, tortillas, or a whole grain bread. For dessert serve something with chocolate which is a special treat in both Mexico and Spain.

1 large cucumber (peeled if waxed)
1 green pepper, pith and stem removed, seeds reserved
1/2 red pepper, seeds reserved
2 large stalk celery (use leaves)
1 large Spanish onion
3 large, very ripe tomatoes
2 cloves garlic, minced
1/4 cup cider or tarragon vinegar
2 tablespoon fresh lemon or lime juice
3 cups tomato juice, fresh if possible, or canned
Cayenne or Tabasco
Chopped cilantro (optional)
Low-sodium salt (optional)

Garnish:
Lime slices
Cucumber slices
Hot sauce
Slivered, hard cooked egg whites
Croutons
Chopped black olives
Chopped cilantro (if not used in recipe)
Chopped parsley
Chopped scallions

Process or with an immersion blender, puree half the vegetables until nearly smooth, reserving the other half which should be coarsely chopped. Combine all the vegetables with the vinegar, lemon and tomato juice, add the pepper seeds and seasoning, and if you have time, let the flavors blend in a covered bowl for several hours in the refrigerator. Serve chilled with lime slices, cucumber strips or other garnishes.

◆ **Per Serving:** Saturated fat: Trace   Total fat: Trace   Cholesterol: 0
Sodium: 395mg   Calories: 50   Calories from fat: 6%

## TOMATO SOUP

SERVES 6–8

Tomato soup and peanut butter sandwiches are nearly as traditional as displaying the American flag on July 4th. This soup can be hearty or smooth, creamed or spicy or used as a foundation red liquid for adding rice, wild rice, lentils, pasta and other good foods. If you make it with canned tomatoes, use the juice too. Garnish with lemon slices or chopped parsley, chopped cooked pepperoni (if lean and low in saturated fat) or chopped Greek olive or many other garnishes.

2-1/2 cups diced fresh or canned tomatoes
1 small onion, finely chopped
1/2 cup finely chopped celery including tops
1/2 teaspoon brown sugar
1/2 teaspoon chopped dried or fresh basil
Several shakes paprika
Low-sodium salt (optional)
2 cups defatted chicken stock or water
2 tablespoons flour
Pepper or Tabasco to taste

Garnish:
Nonfat sour cream
Chopped olives
Chopped parsley
Diced pepperoni

In a large pot combine the tomatoes, onion, celery, sugar, basil, paprika, and salt in the stock or water and simmer for 15 minutes, covered over low heat. Whisk in the flour and heat until thickened, about 3 to 5 minutes. Serve hot.

◆ Per Serving:  Saturated fat: Trace  Total fat: Trace  Cholesterol: 0
Sodium: 240mg  Calories: 33  Calories from fat: 9%

## OYSTER STEW

SERVES 4

This is the quickest and best oyster stew. It only takes 3 to 4 minutes to make. Serve it with the traditional oyster crackers or a good multi-grain bread and a cucumber or fruit salad.

To enrich the soup, steam in water or defatted stock in a separate nonstick skillet or saucepan, several tablespoons each of chopped onions, celery, carrots and a half dozen sliced mushroom for a couple of minutes, and add them to the heating skim milk along with the oysters.

1 pint shucked oysters with the liquor
2-1/2 cups evaporated skim milk
1/2 cup cream sherry
Oyster crackers

Garnish:
Parsley
Cayenne

Heat the oysters, liquor, milk and sherry until very hot, but not boiling and turn down the heat, just under a boil and heat for 1 or 2 minutes until the oysters are cooked. The oysters cook quickly, in about 2 minutes, so test the small ones so they don't get overcooked or they will be tough. Oysters become firm, opaque and shrink slightly when they are cooked. Serve hot.

◆ Per Serving:    Saturated fat: 1gr    Total fat: 3gr    Cholesterol: 74mg
                  Sodium: 324mg    Calories: 246    Calories from fat: 16%

## TWO-BEAN CORN CHILI

SERVES 6

This is a spicy hot Tex/Mex chili that is filling and colorful. Serve with corn chips and a salad.

1 cup cooked or canned black-eyed peas, drained
1 cup cooked or canned navy beans, drained
1 onion, coarsely chopped
1/2 cup tomato paste
2 teaspoons chili powder
1/2 teaspoon ground cumin
1 teaspoon prepared mustard
1/2 to 1 teaspoon dried oregano
1 cup fresh, frozen or canned corn kernels

1/2 cup chopped scallions
1/4 cup diced, pickled jalapeño peppers or 1/2 teaspoon
   chopped fresh
1 cup diced fresh tomatoes
Low-sodium salt (optional)


In a large nonstick skillet combine the black-eyed peas and beans with the onion, tomato paste and 1 cup water, the chili powder, cumin, mustard and oregano. Cook for 12 minutes, or until the onion is done (or cook, covered, in the microwave for 8 minutes). Add more water when necessary. Add the corn. Cook until everything is thoroughly heated. Add the scallions, jalapeño peppers and tomatoes, heating and stirring for another 2 minutes. Serve hot.

◆ **Per Serving:**   Saturated fat: Trace   Total fat: 1gr   Cholesterol: 0
                    Sodium: 126mg   Calories: 137   Calories from fat: 7%

## BAKED BEAN SOUP

SERVES 4

If you like the flavor of baked beans, you will like this rich, quick-fixing baked bean soup, perfect on a cold day. You can add corn to this too, but bacon really makes it better.

1 16-ounce can whole tomatoes, juice drained and reserved
1/2 onion, chopped coarsely
1/2 green pepper, chopped very coarsely
1/2 red pepper, chopped very coarsely
1/2 teaspoon brown sugar or maple syrup
1/2 teaspoon prepared mustard
1/2 teaspoon dried mustard
1/4 teaspoon Cajun seasoning or cayenne pepper
1 16-ounce can or jar vegetarian style beans

In a nonstick saucepan, heat the tomato juice. Add the onion to the juice and cook for 3 to 4 minutes. Very coarsely chop the tomatoes and add half of them to the pan, bring to a low boil and cook for 4 minutes. Add the peppers, sugar, mustard and seasoning and cook for 4 minutes. Add the rest of the tomatoes and beans and heat for 2 to 4 minutes. Serve hot.

- Per Serving:    Saturated fat: Trace   Total fat: 1gr    Cholesterol: 0
                 Sodium: 45mg    Calories: 102   Calories from fat: 4%

### WITH BACON
Add 1/4 cup crumbled cooked lean bacon, completely defatted with all the fat stripped away and discarded before measuring.

- Per Serving:    Saturated fat: Trace   Total fat: 1gr    Cholesterol: Trace
                 Sodium: 38mg    Calories: 200   Calories from fat: 6%

# SALADS &
# SALAD DRESSINGS

Tuna Salad Plate • Potato, Bacon and Green Bean Salad with
Sherry Vinaigrette • Chicken Salad • Three Bean Salad
Corn Salad • Arugula Salad • Black Bean Salad with
Mozzarella Cheese • Crunchy Rice Salad
Fennel, Beet and Carrot Salad • Jar Salad • Caesar Salad
Cobb Salad • Green Bean or Asparagus Bundle Salad
Greek Salad • Waldorf Salad • Classic Fresh Fruit Salad
(continued)

*Fresh Tomatoes, Basil and Buffalo Mozzarella*
*Classic Dinner Salad • Coleslaw*
*Carrot, Pineapple and Raisin Salad • Pineapple and*
*Cottage Cheese Salad • Oriental Cucumber Salad*
*Persian Cucumber Salad with Yogurt and Mint*
*Quick Pasta Salad • Pineapple Fruit Salad*

*Blue Cheese or Roquefort Dressing • French Dressing*
*Fruit Salad Dressing • Greek Dressing • Mayonnaise with Tofu*
*and Vinegar or Lemon • Seafood Dressing • Vinaigrette Classic*
*Caesar Salad Dressing • Thousand Island Dressing*
*Chutney Curry Dressing*

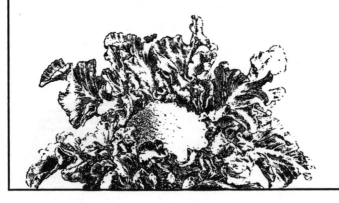

# Whole Meal Salads

**S**alads have been enjoyed for hundreds of years. There are records of "sallets" of lightly cooked asparagus topped with olive oil and vinegar as far back as the 12th century in England. Today, a huge salad on an oversized plate (it looks like enough for 4), along with a really good crusty bread, is a great quick dinner. The trick to making huge dinner salads successful is to keep them bountiful, beautiful and palatable.

Filling, wholesome, with the carbohydrates and protein you want, whole meal salads make use of the tiny bits of leftover lobster you have, an avocado half, the can of green beans in your cupboard, a few beets, or some Asian baby corn cobs. Out of tomatoes? There are some canned tomato wedges that actually work quite well.

For a beautiful presentation, first place some kind of green, usually a type of lettuce such as curly endive, or spinach covering the bottom of the plate. If you want the plate to have primarily greens, add another layer of cut or torn lettuce or spinach (or place a wedge of iceberg off to one side). When adding the vegetables, make separate mounds or bundles of all the different kinds. For instance, place three radishes in one spot, a bundle of asparagus with a stripe of red pepper in another, a dollop of corn relish off to one side, some tuna chunks with sweet pickle relish in the center somewhere else, and so on. You can place some items such as black olives around the edge. This untossed look is very alluring.

Since I have this kind of salad so often, my refrigerator and cupboards overflow with several kinds of capers, sun-dried tomatoes and zucchini, pickled peppercorns, canned plain and pickled red-roasted peppers, probably 10 varieties of olives and evenmore kinds of pickles. I am awash in items to make for interesting salads. This has helped to create exciting new salads for me and my guests.

The dressings are primarily old favorites; delicious classic Caesar without the raw egg, French—with flavor and little fat, Chutney Curry—bursting with tartness, even updated versions of Thousand Island and Green Goddess.

## TUNA SALAD PLATE

SERVES 8

You buy all the ingredients ready-made, just place them on lettuce on the plate.

Lettuce to line 8 plates
1 16-ounce can tuna packed in water, drained, divided for 8
    servings
12 sweet pickles
1 pint prepared potato salad, divided for 8 servings
1 pint prepared slaw, drained or squeezed to remove much of
    the dressing
4 stalks celery, each cut into serving slices
12 ripe olives
4 lemons cut in half

Line 8 plates with lettuce. Place a mound of tuna, three pickles, a mound of potato salad, a mound of slaw, the celery and olives on each plate. Serve with a half lemon.

♦ Per Serving:    Saturated fat: 2gr    Total fat: 11gr    Cholesterol: 53mg
                  Sodium: 1895mg   Calories: 475  Calories from fat: 20%

## POTATO, BACON AND GREEN BEAN SALAD WITH SHERRY VINAIGRETTE

SERVES 4

This can be served warm or chilled. The bacon is cooked by separating and heating in a microwave on paper towels, then picking off all the fat. The dressing and potatoes can be quickly chilled on a flat metal cookie tray in the freezer if you prefer the salad cold.

10 small new potatoes cut into quarters
1/4 cup white wine vinegar
2 tablespoons canola oil
Low-sodium salt (optional), and pepper
Vegetable spray
1/2 pound bacon slices, cooked in microwave
4 large shallots, thinly sliced
6 tablespoons (or more) imported Spanish sherry wine vinegar
1 teaspoon sugar
1 small head escarole, outer leaves discarded
1/2 pound green beans, cut into 2-inch-long pieces, steamed
    until crisp-tender

In a large saucepan in 1-inch water, steam potatoes until just tender, about 10 minutes. Peel if desired and transfer to a large bowl. Add vinegar, oil, salt, if using, and pepper.

Cook the bacon in a microwave, wrapped in paper towels. When done, pick off all the fat, leaving the meat chards. Spray a nonstick skillet with vegetable oil, add the bacon chards, the shallots and a few tablespoons of water and cook until softened, stirring frequently, about 3 minutes. Add the sherry vinegar and sugar and boil 1 minute. Taste and adjust the vinegar-sugar balance.

Cut the greens into bite-size pieces and divide among 4 large plates. Tuck potatoes and beans into greens. Spoon the dressing and bacon over the salad, toss and serve immediately.

◆ Per Serving:  Saturated fat: 2gr    Total fat: 10gr    Cholesterol: 21mg
                Sodium: 724mg    Calories: 294    Calories from fat: 30%

# CHICKEN SALAD

SERVES 4

A simple salad with a delicious dressing that makes leftover chicken, duck or turkey a treat.

2 cups diced cooked, skinless poultry
1 cup green grapes
1/2 cup walnuts
1 head lettuce, cut or torn
1 large bunch watercress, cut or torn
1/2 cup nonfat sour cream
1/2 to 2/3 cup orange juice
1/2 teaspoon low-sodium soy sauce
1/2 teaspoon jelly
Several shakes hot sauce

In a large bowl, mix the poultry, grapes, walnuts and lettuce and watercress. In a small bowl, mix well all the dressing ingredients, pour on the salad and toss well.

◆ Per Serving:  Saturated fat: 2gr  Total fat: 14gr  Cholesterol: 58mg
Sodium: 125mg  Calories: 315  Calories from fat: 41%

# THREE BEAN SALAD

SERVES 4–6

This is extra fast because you use the commercial three bean salad in a jar as a base. Adding to it makes this crunchy and fresher tasting. Other vegetables such as chopped red pepper, some cooked, drained corn, or scallions can also be added. It is colorful and attractive served on lettuce.

Several leaves of lettuce
1 16-ounce jar commercial three bean salad, liquid reserved
1 16-ounce can dark kidney beans, drained
1 8-ounce can garbanzo beans, drained
1/2 cup chopped celery
1/2 cup chopped onion
2 tablespoons cider vinegar
1/2 teaspoon sugar
1/2 teaspoon dried or chopped fresh rosemary

Arrange the lettuce on plates, mix all the other ingredients including the reserved bean liquid together and serve on the lettuce.

◆ Per Serving:   Saturated fat: Trace  Total fat: 2gr   Cholesterol: 0
                  Sodium: 1015mg  Calories: 261  Calories from fat: 6%

## CORN SALAD

SERVES 4

A soft salad that is high on taste and a corn lover's delight. The ripe tomatoes can be substituted with canned, drained tomato wedges.

2 tablespoons olive oil
1 16-ounce can corn, drained
2 red ripe tomatoes, diced
3 tablespoons white wine vinegar
1 teaspoon Dijon-style mustard
2 tablespoons chopped parsley
2 tablespoons chopped fresh basil
1-1/2 teaspoons chopped summer savory
Few squirts liquid hot pepper sauce, or to taste
Low-sodium salt and freshly ground black pepper, to taste

In a large bowl, add the olive oil and corn, and stir in the tomatoes. Add the vinegar, mustard, parsley, basil, savory and hot pepper sauce, then blend into the corn and tomatoes. Season with salt and pepper to taste.

◆ **Per Serving:**   Saturated fat: 2gr   Total fat: 14gr   Cholesterol: 0
Sodium: 234mg   Calories: 185   Calories from fat: 65%

## ARUGULA SALAD

SERVES 4

A refreshing, very green salad dotted with colorful yellow tomatoes and tossed with a tangy, lemony dressing.

1 substitute egg
1 large clove garlic, crushed
1 tablespoon fresh lemon juice
1 tablespoon balsamic vinegar
1-1/2 teaspoon Dijon mustard
Low-sodium salt (optional), freshly ground pepper
1/4 cup olive oil
12 ounces snow peas, stringed
4 ounces spinach leaves
1 bunches arugula, trimmed, torn into pieces
1 large red onion, cut into rings
1 cup fresh mint leaves with tender stems
2 cups yellow cherry tomatoes

In a small bowl, whisk substitute egg, garlic, lemon juice, vinegar, mustard, salt, and pepper together. Add oil and whisk until blended. Combine peas and remaining ingredients in salad bowl. Toss with dressing and serve at once.

◆ **Per Serving:**   Saturated fat: 2gr   Total fat: 16gr   Cholesterol: Trace
Sodium: 157mg   Calories: 207   Calories from fat: 66%

## BLACK BEAN SALAD WITH MOZZARELLA CHEESE

SERVES 4

This is a flavorful bean salad with a lot of texture. If this salad sits for any length of time, the black beans will discolor the cheese.

2 cups canned black beans, drained
1/2 cup chopped red onion
3/4 cup diced celery
1 tablespoon olive oil
3 to 4 tablespoons lemon or lime juice
1 tablespoon white wine vinegar
1/4 cup chopped parsley
Low-sodium salt (optional)
Pepper
1/4 cup diced low-fat mozzarella cheese

In a large mixing bowl, place all the ingredients, mixing carefully, and serve immediately.

◆ Per Serving:  Saturated fat: 1gr  Total fat: 4gr  Cholesterol: 2mg
Sodium: 166mg  Calories: 172  Calories from fat: 22%

## CRUNCHY RICE SALAD

SERVES 4

If cooked rice isn't on hand, it takes about 10 minutes total to make the instant in a bag, which is how it comes in some brands. To chill it, plunge the bag into ice water for a few seconds, drain, blot, open the bag and use as directed. Some foods gain flavor by sitting for several minutes. This does not, as the rice can absorb too much of the dressing, so use it immediately.

2 cups cooked rice

1 cup green beans, sliced into 1-inch pieces, or 1 cup sugar snap
  peas blanched and plunged into ice water

1/4 cup sliced radishes

1/4 cup chopped scallions

1/4 cup chopped green bell pepper

2 tablespoons chopped pared cucumber

2 tablespoons chopped tomato

1/2 tablespoon olive oil

1-1/2 teaspoons fresh lemon juice

1-1/2 teaspoons Dijon mustard

Low-sodium salt (optional)

Freshly ground pepper

In a large mixing bowl, toss all ingredients until thoroughly combined. Serve immediately or refrigerate covered, tossing again
before serving.

◆ **Per Serving:**   Saturated fat: Trace   Total fat: 2gr   Cholesterol: 0
                     Sodium: 100mg   Calories: 168   Calories from fat: 12%


## FENNEL, BEET AND CARROT SALAD

SERVES 4–6
OR MAKES 2 WHOLE MEALS

An Italian classic, this is a colorful and refreshing salad. Other
vegetables such as avocados and marinated mushrooms can be
added to make it a large dinner salad.

The salad needs to have the vegetables arranged in mounds
because if all the ingredients are tossed, the visual appeal is gone
and the delicate tastes of the different foods are lost. Place the lettuce on the plate, then arrange the vegetables in separate mounds;
one third of the plate space containing the slices of fennel, one
third a mound of the julienne carrots and the last third the beets.
In the center place the mushrooms, and tuck a few avocado slices
under each of the vegetable mounds, with the avocado ends stick-

ing out a little beyond the lettuce. This dinner or lunch salad can be served with soup and a good bread for a complete meal.

1 large bunch arugula, spinach or lettuce, cut or torn
2 cups thinly sliced raw fennel root
1-1/2 cups julienne carrots, steamed for 2 minutes if desired, then spread on a metal or aluminum sheet and chilled in the freezer for 2 minutes
1 16-ounce can sliced beets, drained
1 cup marinated cocktail mushrooms in a jar, drained
2 avocados, peeled and sliced lengthwise
Italian dressing or olive oil spray and several tablespoons balsamic, wine, or cider vinegar
Coarsely ground black pepper

Garnish:
Slivers of onions, chopped scallions or leeks, olives

Make a bed of greens on each plate and place the vegetables in separate mounds. Place the mushrooms in the center and the avocados around the edge. Sprinkle on the onions or scallions, and tuck in olives or other garnishes such as black or kalamata olives.

Pour on small amounts of Italian dressing or spray lightly with the olive oil, sprinkle with balsamic, wine, or cider vinegar and black pepper. Serve cold.

◆ Per Serving:    Saturated fat: 2gr    Total fat: 13gr    Cholesterol: Trace
                     Sodium: 383mg    Calories: 185    Calories from fat: 59%

## JAR SALAD

SERVES 4

Begin a quick, easy meal with apple or apricot juice and a lime slice, and end with anise toast or an amaretto cookie. Bread sticks add a crisp note to this salad. Other vegetables from a jar like beets, carrots, lima bean, etc., can also be used.

Iceberg lettuce, 4 to 8 outer leaves removed,
    center head cut into four wedges
1 4 to 6-ounce jar marinated artichoke hearts
1 4 to 6-ounce jar marinated mushrooms
Cucumbers
1 can (6-1/4 ounce) low-sodium tuna
    packed in water, drained
1 cup green pepper strips
1 cup diagonally sliced carrots
1 cup cauliflowerets
1 cup black pitted olives
1/2 cup green olives
12 slices red pepper
Cider vinegar

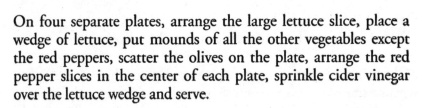

On four separate plates, arrange the large lettuce slice, place a
wedge of lettuce, put mounds of all the other vegetables except
the red peppers, scatter the olives on the plate, arrange the red
pepper slices in the center of each plate, sprinkle cider vinegar
over the lettuce wedge and serve.

◆ Per Serving:    Saturated fat: 2gr    Total fat: 12gr    Cholesterol: 26mg
                  Sodium: 218mg . Calories: 232   Calories from fat: 43%


## CAESAR SALAD

SERVES 4
OR MAKES 1 WHOLE MEAL

Made with dark green romaine (one of the most nutritious of all
the leafy green vegetables), anchovies, garlic, fresh lemon juice,
and freshly grated Parmesan cheese, this salad is special and
incredibly delicious even without the egg and the copious
amounts of oil. Guests are always surprised at the richness and
fresh taste even though the ingredients are slightly changed.

    Incidentally, you can prepare this with more authentic taste
by adding a quarter cup of substitute eggs to the dressing. Since

they've been pasteurized, these eggs are safe and they don't contain any yolk.

This salad is best served very cold. I will often make this for one (me). I add some avocado and onion slices and make it a whole meal.

Concerning instructions to "cut" the romaine (instead of tearing), tearing takes too much time, so just cut it, dress it and enjoy.

1 large head chilled dark romaine lettuce
Olive oil spray
2 large garlic cloves, minced
1 teaspoon Worcestershire sauce
1/2 teaspoon anchovy paste or 4 anchovies, patted dry
4 to 6 tablespoons lemon juice
1/4 cup freshly grated Parmesan cheese
Freshly ground coarse black pepper
Garlic croutons (page 49)

Wash and shake dry the romaine. Spray the leaves lightly with the olive oil. Gather the leaves together and cut them with a sharp knife into large pieces. In a separate dish, mix the garlic, Worcestershire sauce, anchovy paste, and lemon juice. If you are using substitute egg products, add 1/4 cup to the dressing and whisk in. Pour on the salad and toss. Sprinkle with cheese, pepper, and croutons.

♦ Per Serving:  Saturated fat: 1gr    Total fat: 2gr    Cholesterol: 7mg
Sodium: 280mg    Calories: 59    Calories from fat: 32%

## COBB SALAD

SERVES 4
OR MAKES 2 WHOLE MEALS

A Cobb salad is always different, depending upon which part of the country you live. In Los Angeles, it used to be a large plate of several different foods such as chicken, avocado, apples and lettuce, each taking up a quarter to an eighth of the plate, according to the number of foods. In the East, a Cobb salad is tossed and contains cheese and bacon.

In both versions there can be tuna, perhaps potatoes, and usually an olive oil dressing. My version is primarily lettuce, with other foods added in.

1 head iceberg lettuce, diced
2 tablespoons olive oil
2 tablespoons balsamic vinegar
1 tablespoon water
Low-sodium salt (optional) and pepper
1/2 cup diced avocado
1/2 cup diced red pepper
1/2 cup defatted, skinned chicken or tuna, diced

Cut the iceberg lettuce into 1/4-inch pieces making crosswise rows. Mix the remaining ingredients and toss with the dressing.

◆ Per Serving:  Saturated fat: 2gr    Total fat: 13gr    Cholesterol: 16mg
                Sodium: 32mg    Calories: 167   Calories from fat: 66%


## GREEN BEAN OR ASPARAGUS BUNDLE SALAD

SERVES 4

This is a crisp, bright green salad, with slivers of onions, sundried tomatoes and black olives. It is luxurious, countrylike, simple, and it is also quite elegant. It makes the most of the green bean or asparagus season. You can use half green beans and half yellow (wax) beans if you choose. Slightly undercook the beans or asparagus for the best results so they will be bright green. Arrange them all in the same direction whether serving on a platter or individual plates.

1 pound green beans, tipped and tailed or asparagus
1 cup sliced sun-dried tomatoes in olive oil, oil reserved
2 tablespoons olive oil from the sun-dried tomatoes
1 medium onion, quartered and sliced thin
1/2 to 3/4 cup very small pitted black olives
1 teaspoon lemon juice
4 tablespoons balsamic vinegar
Few strips pimento slices, or red pepper slices
Several lettuce leaves
Coarse ground black pepper

In a saucepan with 1 inch of water, steam the beans or asparagus for several minutes, remove from the stove, pour off the hot water and plunge the beans or asparagus immediately into cold water with ice cubes to stop the cooking. Drain them and add to a salad bowl with the sun-dried tomatoes, the sun-dried tomato flavored olive oil, the onion, olives, lemon juice, and vinegar, and mix well. Place the lettuce on a plate and gather the beans or asparagus and arrange them in an orderly bundle on the lettuce. Crisscross the green vegetables in the middle with a few 2 or 3-inch long but narrow strips of bright red pimento or red pepper. Just before serving, sprinkle coarse ground black pepper over the beans and serve cold.

♦ **Per Serving:**  Saturated fat: 1gr   Total fat: 9gr   Cholesterol: 0
Sodium: 333mg   Calories: 150   Calories from fat: 52%


## GREEK SALAD

SERVES 4

One of the cheeses lowest in saturated fats is the Greek feta cheese, a goat milk cheese. Feta varies in quality, and fresh feta, rather than packaged feta is usually better. If you can't find feta, use another goat cheese and call this a Mediterranean Salad. We don't use a lot of cheese, but more than enough to have the salad live up to its tangy reputation. For added interest, put in some sardines or a small amount of tuna. Pepperoncinis aren't usual in a Greek salad, but they add flavor and color. To pit the olives, invest in a small cherry pitter, which can be found in kitchen supply stores.

1 head lettuce or a mixture of lettuce and spinach (about 8
    cups)
20 Greek olives, pitted
2 ounces feta cheese, crumbled
1 ripe tomato, cut into 12 pieces
1 red onion, slivered
1 tablespoon sugar
2 tablespoons finely chopped parsley
1 teaspoon fresh chopped basil or 1/2 teaspoon dried basil
1 teaspoon fresh chopped oregano leaves or 1/2 teaspoon dried
    oregano
1/2 cup whole pepperoncinis (optional)
1/3 cup red wine vinegar
2 teaspoons fresh lemon juice
Freshly ground black pepper

Divide the lettuce among 4 salad plates. Arrange 5 olives around the edge of the lettuce, and 3 pieces of tomato in the center. Spread the red onion over the top and sprinkle a quarter of the feta cheese on each salad. Mix the sugar, parsley, basil, oregano, pepperoncinis (of using), vinegar and lemon juice, and pour over the salad. Grind black pepper on top and serve, or toss the salad with the dressing.

♦ **Per Serving:**    Saturated fat: 2gr    Total fat: 6gr    Cholesterol: 12mg
                       Sodium: 536mg   Calories: 100  Calories from fat: 47%

## WITH OLIVE OIL
Add 2 tablespoons olive oil to the dressing.

♦ **Per Serving:**    Saturated fat: 3gr    Total fat: 12gr    Cholesterol: 12mg
                       Sodium: 536mg   Calories: 160  Calories from fat: 66%

# WALDORF SALAD

SERVES 4

Waldorf salads work well on a low-cholesterol, low-saturated fat diet because of the new low-saturated fat mayonnaises available. This is almost too simple to be so good. Don't use the tasteless red Delicious apple but look for a Pippin or Nitney for a green Waldorf salad; for a red, try Winesap, Stayman, Jonathan or McIntosh. The apples are washed with soap and rubbed to remove the wax coating.

You can substitute pears for apples, and you can add raisins, chopped dried dates or figs, or pineapple for variations. Try topping the salad with one or several bright mandarin orange slices for color.

1 tablespoon lemon juice
1/4 teaspoon sugar
2 tablespoons skim milk
1/4 cup nonfat mayonnaise
4 large romaine or lettuce leaves
2 large apples, cored and coarsely chopped
2 celery stalks, including leaves, coarsely chopped
1/4 cup coarsely chopped walnuts
4 small sprigs parsley

In a small bowl, mix the lemon juice and sugar with the skim milk and mayonnaise. Place a lettuce leaf on each of 4 salad plates. Toss all the apples, celery and walnuts with the dressing and spoon onto the lettuce. Top each with a sprig of parsley.

◆ Per Serving:  Saturated fat: Trace  Total fat: 5gr  Cholesterol: Trace
  Sodium: 149mg  Calories: 106  Calories from fat: 36%

# CLASSIC FRESH FRUIT SALAD

SERVES 4

For zest, serve fresh fruit with honey mustard sauce (page 258), and a slice or two of lean prosciutto ham. If the ham is not available, substitute cooked chicken, pork or another ham such as Smithfield. The meat adds interest but can be left out.

Lettuce, mache, or spinach
1 cup fresh pineapple chunks
1 cup fresh peach or pear slices
4 bananas sprinkled with lime juice
1 cup fresh raspberries or blueberries
1 cup or 4 ounces sliced lean and defatted prosciutto, diced
   ham, chicken or pork

Arrange on each plate the greens, a mound of pineapple, the slices of peach or pear, surround the edge with the banana cut in two lengthwise, sprinkle with berries, place the meat on top or in a mound to one side. Serve chilled with dressing.

◆ **Per Serving:**   Saturated fat: 1gr   Total fat: 2gr   Cholesterol: 13mg
   Sodium: 405mg   Calories: 196   Calories from fat: 10%

# *Accompaniment Salads*

T hese are the piquant small salads to the left of your fork before you are served your main dish. To be most effective, they should be simple and refreshing but not filling or substantial.

With themes in mind, the cucumber salad is especially good with Asian food, and changing it slightly, adding mint and yogurt, it is perfect with Middle Eastern fare. There are also some simple carrot salads and coleslaw that are just right with casual country and picnic cooking. These small accompaniment salads are almost always tossed, contain just three or four ingredients, and are served with a light dressing that leaves you wanting more. Smaller versions of some of the whole-dinner salads can also be used effectively. You might enjoy trying a salad after the main course, as the Europeans do, for a refreshing change. One of the dietary benefits is that you don't feel like much dessert after the tangy lettuce.

## FRESH TOMATOES, BASIL AND BUFFALO MOZZARELLA

SERVES 4–6

Celebrate summer with a salad of fresh, vine ripened garden tomatoes, fresh basil leaves and fresh buffalo mozzarella. This salad can be served buffet-style in a large flat dish, with slices of tomato and rounds of mozzarella alternating, topped with chopped fresh basil and a basil leaf in the center, or on individual salad plates.

The mozzarella should be fresh buffalo. Choose a variety with the least amount of fat. Just use a thin slice for every three or four slices of tomato. Don't use store bought tomatoes, they just aren't the same at all.

8 to 12 large dark lettuce leaves, like romaine
2 to 3 large very ripe home grown tomatoes, thick sliced
1/2 pound fresh buffalo mozzarella, very thinly sliced
3 tablespoons chopped fresh basil leaves
1 teaspoon chopped fresh oregano leaves (optional)
1/4 cup red-wine or cider vinegar
1 tablespoon olive oil
Black pepper
Several basil leaves

Arrange the lettuce on individual plates or on a platter, place the two or three slices of tomato for each slice of mozzarella on the plate and tuck the mozzarella between every two tomatoes, with more of the mozzarella slice showing. Mix the basil and oregano with the vinegar and olive oil, and pour on the salad. Sprinkle with black pepper, garnish with several basil leaves and serve.

◆ Per Serving:    Saturated fat: 6gr    Total fat: 12gr    Cholesterol: 16mg
                  Sodium: 290mg    Calories: 219    Calories from fat: 50%

## CLASSIC DINNER SALAD

SERVES 4

This is an easy, piquant salad perfect for any meal. Use it with a nonfat vinaigrette dressing or the dressing here. Small amounts of sliced carrots, radishes and leftover vegetables can also be used.

1 pound mixed lettuces
12 ripe olives
1/2 cup slivered onion, scallions or shallots
1/2 cup cider vinegar

3/4 teaspoon sugar
1/4 teaspoon dry mustard
Black pepper
Several slices avocado (optional)

Garnish:
Pieces of leftover tuna or nonfat chicken
Ripe olives

In a salad bowl, toss the lettuce with the olives and onion. In a small bowl, mix the vinegar, sugar, mustard and black pepper. Toss on the lettuce mixture and serve chilled.

- **Per Serving:** Saturated fat: Trace   Total fat: 2gr   Cholesterol: 0
  Sodium: 125mg   Calories: 186   Calories from fat: 8%

## WITH OLIVE OIL
Add 1/4 cup olive oil to the dressing.

- **Per Serving:** Saturated fat: 2gr   Total fat: 15gr   Cholesterol: 0
  Sodium: 125mg   Calories: 305   Calories from fat: 43%

## COLESLAW

SERVES 6–8

Coleslaw can be very fast if you have a food processor, but you don't need one. Hand chopping doesn't cut the cabbage as finely, but it tastes just as good. You can use either or both white or red cabbage or a combination.

1 small cabbage, shredded
1 small onion, chopped
1/2 cup low-saturated fat or nonfat mayonnaise
1/2 teaspoon dry mustard (optional)

1 to 3 tablespoons cider vinegar
1/2 to 1 teaspoon sugar

In a large bowl, mix all the ingredients, and serve.

◆ Per Serving:   Saturated fat: Trace  Total fat: 1gr   Cholesterol: 0
                  Sodium: 9mg     Calories: 31   Calories from fat: 38%

## CARROT, PINEAPPLE AND RAISIN SALAD

SERVES 4–6

This is an old fashioned salad that can always be enjoyed on a low-cholesterol, low-saturated fat diet.

2 cups processor shredded carrots (about 3 large carrots)
1 medium celery stalk, cut into 1/4-inch pieces
3/4 cup crushed pineapple, drained
1/2 cup raisins
1/3 cup nonfat mayonnaise

Mix all the ingredients and serve chilled.

◆ Per Serving:   Saturated fat: Trace  Total fat: Trace  Cholesterol: 0
                  Sodium: 225mg   Calories: 99   Calories from fat: 2%

VARIATION
Substitute 1/4 cup cider vinegar with 1/4 teaspoon sugar for the nonfat mayonnaise. Taste and adjust seasonings.

◆ Per Serving:   Saturated fat: Trace  Total fat: Trace  Cholesterol: 0
                  Sodium: 24mg    Calories: 89   Calories from fat: 2%

# PINEAPPLE AND COTTAGE CHEESE SALAD

SERVES 4

Anyone over 50 knows this salad well as it was daily lunchtime fare in homes and restaurants. It was always made with canned pineapple, high fat cottage cheese, and occasionally it was placed on lettuce, with a bright red maraschino cherry on top. Without the lettuce and cherry, it was a school lunchroom staple. This old standby can be updated and made more delicious by switching to fresh, sweet pineapple, and one of the creamy nonfat cottage cheeses.

Several iceberg lettuce leaves
4 thick slices fresh pineapple or 12 thin slices canned pineapple
1-1/3 cups nonfat cottage cheese
4 large pitted prunes or maraschino cherries

Place the lettuce on each of 4 salad plates and arrange the pineapple on top. Add a mound of cottage cheese in the center. Top each with a prune and serve.

◆ Per Serving: Saturated fat: Trace   Total fat: Trace   Cholesterol: 3mg
Sodium: 12mg   Calories: 193   Calories from fat: 2%

# ORIENTAL CUCUMBER SALAD

SERVES 4

I first had this cucumber salad when I was 16 years old at the home of one of Detroit's finest photographers, George Kawamoto. I worked as a model for George and his wife Louise and I've never forgotten how sweet they were to me.

The salad is refreshing and has almost no fat at all. Since so many cucumbers are waxed, you may wish to either search out some that have no wax, or remove the skin, or you may want burpless cucumbers which have a more tender skin.

1 very large cucumber, unwaxed, or if waxed, peeled
2 tablespoons sugar
1/2 cup white rice wine vinegar
1 teaspoon sesame seeds, lightly toasted

Strip the cucumber skin with a fork, or use a lemon stripper and make 1/4-inch stripes about 1/4 inch apart. Slice it into 1/4-inch rounds. Mix the sugar and vinegar and add to the cucumbers. The mixture can be marinated in the refrigerator for up to half an hour. Spoon the cucumber rounds into small individual bowls, add a little dressing, and sprinkle with the sesame seeds.

◆ Per Serving:    Saturated fat: Trace    Total fat: Trace    Cholesterol: 0
                   Sodium: 2mg     Calories: 43    Calories from fat: 9%

## PERSIAN CUCUMBER SALAD WITH YOGURT AND MINT

SERVES 4

I have had versions of this salad in many homes and restaurants where the culture and food is Middle Eastern. The mixture of fresh mint, garlic and yogurt is refreshing.

1 very large cucumber, unwaxed preferably
1/2 Spanish, Vidalia or Bermuda onion quartered and slivered
    (optional)
2 tablespoons chopped fresh mint leaves or 1-1/2 tablespoon
    chopped dried mint
1 to 1-1/2 large cloves garlic, minced
1/2 to 3/4 cup nonfat plain yogurt
Low-sodium salt (optional)

Garnish:
**Several slices red pepper**

Slice the cucumber into long, narrow pieces, about 1/2-inch by 2 inches long. The onions, if used, should be wafer thin. In a bowl, mix the other ingredients, and toss with the cucumber and onions. Let the mixture marinate for 10 to 15 minutes, toss again to redistribute any settled liquid, garnish, and serve cold.

◆ **Per Serving:** Saturated fat: Trace  Total fat: Trace  Cholesterol: Trace
Sodium: 24mg    Calories: 27    Calories from fat: 5%

## QUICK PASTA SALAD

SERVES 4

When making macaroni for another dish, make extra. Store in the refrigerator in a plastic bag. It keeps for several days and you'll be able to make this delicious salad in a few minutes.

**2 cups cooked pasta, such as small shells or small elbow maca-**
    **roni**
**1/4 cup nonfat mayonnaise, or nonfat yogurt cheese**
**2 tablespoons cider vinegar**
**1/2 teaspoon lemon or lime juice**
**1/4 to 1/2 teaspoon sugar (optional)**
**1/2 cup chopped onion or scallion**
**1/2 cup diced celery**
**1/2 chopped black olives**
**Red pepper flakes**

In a large bowl, mix the mayonnaise, vinegar, lemon juice, and sugar, if using, together. Add all the other ingredients and toss. If the mixture seems to thick or heavy, thin with skim milk. Serve chilled.

◆ **Per Serving:** Saturated fat: Trace  Total fat: 2gr    Cholesterol: 0
Sodium: 262mg    Calories: 103   Calories from fat: 15%

# PINEAPPLE FRUIT SALAD

SERVES 4

A fresh fruit salad with a sprinkle of kirsch, champagne or other type of alcohol is refreshing and beautiful. Use fruit in season for the freshest taste.

1 cup fresh chunks of pineapple
1 cup blueberries
1 cup strawberries
2 bananas, sliced
Juice of 1 lemon (for the bananas)
4 plums, each pitted and sliced
12 ripe, dark cherries
8 1-inch wedges of melon
Lettuce

Arrange the lettuce on the plate, the melon around the edges and fill the center with any combination.

◆ **Per Serving:**  Saturated fat: Trace   Total fat: 1gr     Cholesterol: 0
                   Sodium: 9mg      Calories:148   Calories from fat: 5%

# Salad Dressings

**A**ccording to the Center for Science in the Public Interest, women get the highest percentage of daily calories from the fat in salad dressings.

Happily most Low Cholesterol Gourmet salad dressings are made without fatty oils. If you must have oil on your salad you can add it by the teaspoonful, or if you really want to watch those fat grams, just spray it on the greens and vegetables. Even olive oil spray is available in most grocery stores as is canola and corn oil. You can even make your own spray pump for oil, if you wish.

Oil, unless used within a week, should be kept refrigerated after opening. It starts to get rancid within 7 to 10 days. So, it is best to buy oil in small quantities. An additional benefit to using low-saturated fat oils is that they are the most liquid when cold.

All oils have the same number of fat grams and calories, but they differ in saturated fat content. The oil with the least amount of saturated fat is canola/rapeseed (rapeseed is the same as canola), then safflower, which is pretty close, then walnut and grapeseed, with slightly higher amounts, corn oil and olive oil are about double that of canola, and peanut oil is nearly triple with the highest amount of saturated fat of the regularly used household oils. Incidentally, canola and olive oil are nearly the same in monounsaturated fats.

All fats should be used sparingly. Most experts agree there is no biological reason to add fat to your diet. There is enough fat occurring naturally in healthy foods so trimming the fat in salad dressings makes good sense.

# BLUE CHEESE OR ROQUEFORT DRESSING

This dressing is fantastic, and although it contains cheese and a small amount of oil, they are both in amounts acceptable for a cholesterol lowering diet if used sparingly.

1 cup wine vinegar
3 tablespoons lemon juice
2 tablespoons olive oil
1 clove garlic, minced
1/2 teaspoon sugar
1/2 teaspoon dry mustard
 1/4 teaspoon dried rosemary
1/2 teaspoon paprika
1 teaspoon finely chopped parsley
1/4 pound blue or Roquefort cheese, crumbled

Mix together the vinegar, lemon juice and oil. Add the garlic, sugar, mustard, rosemary, paprika and parsley. Add the cheese. Use immediately if you want the parsley to remain a fresh green color.

◆ Per Tbsp:    Saturated fat: 1gr    Total fat: 2gr    Cholesterol: 3mg
               Sodium: 66mg    Calories: 29    Calories from fat: 73%


# FRENCH DRESSING

MAKES ABOUT 1 CUP

Authentic French dressing is just salt, fine olive oil and wine vinegar. American versions are sweeter and sometimes ketchup-red in color. This is an adaptation of the American version.

1/2 cup wine vinegar
1/4 cup water
2 tablespoons lemon or lime juice
1 clove garlic, minced
1/4 teaspoon sugar (optional)
1/2 teaspoon paprika
3 tablespoons olive oil

In a small bowl, mix all the ingredients except the oil. Whisk in the oil last.

◆ **Per Tbsp:**     Saturated fat: Trace   Total fat: 2gr     Cholesterol: 0
                    Sodium: Trace      Calories: 36    Calories from fat: 60%

## FRUIT SALAD DRESSING

MAKES ABOUT 1-1/4 CUPS

An excellent dressing for oranges, mixed fruits like bananas, apples and peaches, or for more exotic varieties such as mangoes and star fruit.

1/2 cup honey
1/4 cup lemon juice
1/4 cup water
1 tablespoon walnut oil
1/2 teaspoon lemon zest
1/4 cup frozen raspberries

Mix all the ingredients in a blender or food processor. Makes about 1-1/4 cups.

◆ **Per Tbsp:**     Saturated fat: Trace   Total fat: 1gr     Cholesterol: 0
                    Sodium: 1mg      Calories: 45    Calories from fat: 16%

# GREEK DRESSING

MAKES ABOUT 3/4 CUP

The feta cheese is added last, as are the Greek olives. The olives can be easily pitted with a cherry pitter.

1 small red onion, finely chopped
2 tablespoons finely chopped parsley
1 teaspoon fresh basil or 1/2 teaspoon dried basil
1 teaspoon fresh oregano or 1/2 teaspoon dried oregano
1/3 cup red wine vinegar
2 teaspoons fresh lemon juice
2 teaspoons sugar
1/4 cup pitted and sliced kalamata olives
Black pepper

Mix all the ingredients together.

◆ **Per Tbsp:** Saturated fat: Trace  Total fat: Trace  Cholesterol: 0
Sodium: 28mg  Calories: 18  Calories from fat: 16%

WITH FETA CHEESE
Add 2 ounces of feta cheese, crumbled or diced.

◆ **Per Tbsp:** Saturated fat: 1gr  Total fat: 1gr  Cholesterol: 4mg
Sodium: 76mg  Calories: 27  Calories from fat: 40%

# MAYONNAISE WITH TOFU AND VINEGAR OR LEMON

MAKES ABOUT 1 CUP

This is an exceptionally smooth mayonnaise. An immersion blender can also be used to make this.

1 cup soft tofu
2 tablespoons cider vinegar or lemon
1 teaspoon sugar
1 teaspoon dry mustard
Dash white pepper

In a small bowl, mix well, using electric mixer on low.

◆ Per Tbsp:      Saturated fat: Trace  Total fat: 1gr    Cholesterol: 0
                  Sodium: 1mg     Calories: 13   Calories from fat: 47%

## SEAFOOD DRESSING

MAKES ABOUT 3/4 CUP

This dressing is excellent on any seafood mixture such as shrimp, celery and avocado, or a cold cooked fish and vegetables. For a slightly different taste, substitute nonfat yogurt for the mayonnaise.

1/2 cup nonfat mayonnaise
2 tablespoons skim milk
3 tablespoons lemon juice
Tabasco sauce to taste
1/2 teaspoon dry mustard
1 teaspoon chopped dill pickles
3 teaspoons chopped chives
Paprika to taste

Mix all the ingredients well.

◆ Per Tbsp:      Saturated fat: Trace  Total fat: 1gr    Cholesterol: Trace
                  Sodium: 8mg     Calories: 10   Calories from fat: 61%

# VINAIGRETTE CLASSIC

MAKES ABOUT 1-1/3 CUP

This is one of the best dressings for any salad. It can easily take small additions of prepared mustard, dry mustard, lemon juice, herbs and spices, but the classic vinaigrette is very simple.

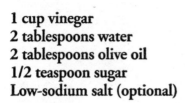

1 cup vinegar
2 tablespoons water
2 tablespoons olive oil
1/2 teaspoon sugar
Low-sodium salt (optional)

Mix all the ingredients.

◆ Per Tbsp:      Saturated fat: Trace  Total fat: 1gr    Cholesterol: 0
                   Sodium: 14mg    Calories: 14    Calories from fat: 79%

# CAESAR SALAD DRESSING

MAKES ABOUT 1/2 CUP

Sometimes you want a Caesar salad dressing even if you aren't having a Caesar salad. You can add as much as 3 tablespoons of olive oil if you wish but you actually don't need any if you spray the lettuce with olive oil spray. An additional tip. If you must have the taste of egg, use a few tablespoons of substitute eggs. They are pasteurized and safe, unlike uncooked fresh eggs that are coddled.

1/2 cup fresh lemon juice
2 tablespoons anchovy paste
1 teaspoon Worcestershire sauce

1 tablespoon minced garlic
1/4 cup grated or slivered Parmesan
Coarse cut black pepper to taste

In a small bowl, mix well with a fork, or if using olive oil, in a blender emulsify the juice, paste, sauce, and garlic and olive oil, if using. Pour on the salad, toss, add the Parmesan and pepper.

◆ Per Tbsp:     Saturated fat: Trace   Total fat: Trace   Cholesterol: Trace
                Sodium: 157mg   Calories: 14   Calories from fat: 8%

## THOUSAND ISLAND DRESSING

MAKES ABOUT 2 CUPS

An old-time favorite with a quarter of the calories of the usual Thousand Island dressing. This makes a fine sandwich spread.

1 cup nonfat mayonnaise
1/4 cup skim milk
3 hard-cooked eggs, yolks discarded, finely chopped
4 tablespoons chunky chili sauce
2 tablespoons chopped parsley
3 tablespoons sweet pickle relish
2 tablespoons chopped green olives
3 tablespoons chopped onion
1/2 teaspoon paprika

Mix all the ingredients by hand.

◆ Per Tbsp:     Saturated fat: Trace   Total fat: Trace   Cholesterol: Trace
                Sodium: 114mg   Calories: 11   Calories from fat: 5%

# CHUTNEY CURRY DRESSING

MAKES ABOUT 1 CUP

Tofu is excellent in dressings because it imparts bulk and a silky feel, but doesn't have much flavor of its own, so whatever else is spicing the dressing shines. It has some fat and lots of protein.

3/4 cup tofu
1 tablespoon sugar
1-1/2 teaspoons curry powder
1/8 teaspoon ground ginger
1 tablespoon fresh lemon juice
1 tablespoon soy sauce
1/2 teaspoon cumin
1/4 cup Hot Bengal Chutney or chutney with a few dashes of
    hot sauce

Combine all the ingredients in a blender or food processor. Serve chilled.

- ◆ Per Tbsp:    Saturated fat: Trace    Total fat: 1gr    Cholesterol: 0
                 Sodium: 66mg    Calories: 20    Calories from fat: 25%

# PASTA, BEANS, RICE & GRAINS

Spaghetti Marinara • Linguine with Tiny Scallops à la
Terry Frantz, or Shells and Shrimp • Fettucine Alfredo
Orzo and Chicken • Pasta Primavera
Dan Dan Noodles • Macaroni and Cheese
White Sauce Macaroni and Cheese • Stuffed Manicotti
Ramen Noodles • Pasta and Spinach • Beans and Rice
Cheese and Bean Burritos • Meatless Meaty Chili
Tacos • Couscous and Tomatoes • Gnocchi
Quinoa Italian Style • Fried Rice • Saffron Rice
Rice Pilaf • Cellophane Noodles

99 LBS. NET WEIGHT
WHOLE BEAN
UNCOATED
TABLE RICE

# Pasta, Beans, Rice & Grains

Z iti, fettucine, manicotti, fusili—red wine, candlelight, classical music. Pasta evokes romantic dining in any setting. Everyone loves pasta and you'll especially love these fast prep recipes. Unexpected guests will marvel as you whip up a very lean and savory spinach and ricotta manicotti. Serve with salad, crusty Italian bread and sorbet for cries of *"Encore, encore."*

Another staple—beans—have finally made it out of the mess tent right into the food pyramid and trendy southwest fare. Legumes are now considered an important source of protein by the USDA. Lucky for our taste buds Tex/Mex cooks knew this all along. But, beans go well in other dishes, too: soups, stews, salads or all alone. Add some steamed carrots, onions, celery, garlic and defatted chicken stock to a can of beans and in 10 minutes those beans go from dull to delicious.

For a lighter touch and more adventure, try couscous, a very fast cooking pasta or the food world's new favorite, quinoa (keen-wah), a South American grain which is reported to contain all necessary amino acids. This one may save the world.

# SPAGHETTI MARINARA

SERVES 4

This is a simple tomato sauce with add-ons. Use sauce from a bottle, jar, or grocer's refrigerator with any type of noodle you wish. The fresh (soft) commercial pasta saves on time because it only takes minutes to cook, but the dry types, such as De Cecco, have a more robust texture.

If the basis of your bottled sauce is mushrooms, add more. If it is olives, add some of your own. If basil, add some fresh. And you can always add chopped green peppers.

1 small onion, coarsely chopped
1 stalk celery, chopped
1/2 carrot, grated
1 tablespoon dried or fresh sweet basil
1 teaspoon dried oregano
1/2 teaspoon brown sugar
1/2 teaspoon low-sodium salt (optional)
1 8-12 ounce jar pasta sauce, or 1 4-ounce can tomato sauce
   mixed with 1 16-ounce can tomato puree
1 pound spaghetti

In a large nonstick skillet, simmer the vegetables in 1/2-inch of defatted stock or water for 5 minutes, adding liquid when necessary. Add the bottled sauce and simmer for another 2 to 3 minutes, covered. Cook the pasta according to directions. Drain. Serve sauce hot over the pasta.

The nutritional values below are for tomato sauce and tomato puree.

◆ **Per Serving:**  Saturated fat: Trace  Total fat: Trace  Cholesterol: 0
            Sodium: 553mg  Calories: 72  Calories from fat: 3%

# LINGUINE WITH TINY SCALLOPS À LA TERRY FRANTZ, OR SHELLS AND SHRIMP

SERVES 4–6

Having friends make dinner for me is always a thrill, especially when the food is low in cholesterol and saturated fat as well as delicious. My longtime friend Terry Frantz whipped this up during one of my thousand or so trips to Virginia Beach. I was so impressed with this busy mother and (then prosecuting) attorney's quick, simple, and delicious dinner (which took about 12 minutes to prepare) I asked her for the recipe, and have made it several times since.

A variation of this can be made with shells and small shrimp.

1 pound fresh linguine or shells
1 clove garlic, minced
1 teaspoon olive oil
1 teaspoon canola/rapeseed oil
1 pound bay scallops or shrimp
1/2 teaspoon red pepper flakes
1/4 teaspoon low-sodium salt (optional)

Garnish:
Chopped parsley
Red pepper strips

Cook the pasta in boiling water until al dente. Drain and set aside. Meanwhile, in a large nonstick skillet, sauté the garlic in the two oils for 1 minute.

Add the scallops and red pepper flakes, and cook over medium heat for about 2 minutes, or until the scallops become opaque. Pour the scallops over the linguine. Season to taste with salt, if using. Serve immediately.

◆ Per Serving:   Saturated fat: 1gr   Total fat: 4gr   Cholesterol: 58mg
                     Sodium: 208mg   Calories: 217   Calories from fat: 16%

# FETTUCCINE ALFREDO

Alfredo sauce is usually made with heavy cheese, cream and butter. My low-fat version achieves a creamy texture by substituting a nondairy cheese.

3/4 pound fettuccine
1/2 cup evaporated skim milk
1/2 cup shredded Dorman's Lo Chol cheese
2 tablespoons grated Parmesan
Black pepper
Low-sodium salt (optional)

Cook the fettuccine until al dente; drain. Meanwhile, combine the milk and shredded cheese and heat until hot but not boiling. Add the cream sauce and Parmesan to the pasta and toss. Sprinkle with pepper. Season with salt, if desired.

◆ **Per Serving:**    Saturated fat: 1gr    Total fat: 3gr    Cholesterol: 2mg
   Sodium: 226mg    Calories: 331    Calories from fat: 7%

WITH HAM AND PEAS
Add 1/2 cup diced lean ham, all fat removed, and 1/4 cup peas to the milk and shredded cheese to warm through.

◆ **Per Serving:**    Saturated fat: 1gr    Total fat: 4gr    Cholesterol: 12mg
   Sodium: 460mg    Calories: 363    Calories from fat: 9%

# ORZO AND CHICKEN

SERVES 4–6

Sounds fancy, but it's simply a delicious mixture of pasta and chicken. The rice-shaped tiny orzo takes only a few minutes to cook, the pieces are so small. The chicken takes much longer, so they are cooked separately. You can add fresh peas, corn, diced tomatoes or the more tiny and slender bean the French prefer called haricot vert, available in most American markets.

1 small onion, coarsely chopped
1 stalk celery, chopped
1/2 carrot, grated
5 cups defatted chicken stock
1/2 pound diced cooked or fresh chicken
1-1/2 cups orzo
1/2 teaspoon low-sodium salt (optional)
2 tablespoons cornstarch
1 teaspoon grated Parmesan

In a large nonstick skillet, simmer the vegetables in 1/2 inch of the defatted stock or water for 5 minutes, adding liquid when necessary. If you are using cooked chicken, add it to the cooked vegetables for the last minute, stirring well.

Bring the remaining stock to a boil. If you are using fresh chicken, cook it in the stock for 3 minutes. Remove with a slotted spoon and add to the vegetables in the skillet. Skim the stock if necessary, bring it back to a boil and add the orzo, testing often as it doesn't take much time. Drain the orzo, reserving 1 cup of the stock, and add the orzo to the vegetables and chicken mixture.

Drop 3 to 4 ice cubes into the reserved cup of stock and let stand, until the stock is cool. Remove the ice cubes and stir in the salt, if using, and the cornstarch, mixing well. Mix the stock into the vegetables and chicken, heat on medium high, stirring until everything is thick, about 1 minute. Transfer to a large platter and sprinkle with cheese. Serve hot.

◆ Per Serving:   Saturated fat: Trace   Total fat: 1gr   Cholesterol: Trace
                 Sodium: 611mg   Calories: 149   Calories from fat: 6%

# PASTA PRIMAVERA

Pasta primavera can be prepared
many ways. It is often made with
a cream sauce, but it doesn't have to be. Many vegetables can be
used. Use sun-dried tomatoes that are packed in olive oil, and let
the oil left on the tomatoes flavor the pasta.

1/2 pound pasta such as small pasta shells
1 Spanish onion, chopped
2 cloves garlic, minced
1 red bell pepper, cored, seeds reserved, cut into 1-inch pieces
1 small eggplant cut into 1-inch cubes
1 small zucchini cut into 1-inch pieces
1 small yellow squash
1 teaspoon fresh basil or 1 teaspoon dried flaked sweet basil
1-1/2 teaspoons fresh oregano or 1/2 teaspoon dried flaked
    oregano
1 bay leaf
2 ripe tomatoes, diced
4 to 6 sun-dried tomatoes, sliced into narrow strips
1 to 2 teaspoons small capers, drained
1 cup small black olives, drained or 1/2 cup sliced kalamata olives
1/2 cup raisins
Low-sodium salt (optional)
1/2 cup store bought nonfat Italian or garlic dressing

Garnish:
2 tablespoons grated Parmesan
2 tablespoons snipped chives
Black pepper
Parsley

Cook the pasta until al dente. When it is finished, drain it and set aside. Meanwhile as it boils, in a large nonstick skillet, over medium heat cook the onion, garlic, peppers, eggplant, zucchini, yellow squash, basil, oregano and bay leaf in 1/4 to 1/2 inch water, stirring often. Add more water whenever necessary. When the vegetables are nearly done, about 8 minutes, remove the bay leaf, and add the fresh tomatoes, sun-dried tomatoes, and capers and cook until heated thoroughly, just a few minutes, letting all excess water evaporate. Season with salt, if using, and add the olives and raisins. Combine the sauce and pasta. Toss with the dressing. Sprinkle with Parmesan, chives, black pepper and parsley. Serve hot.

- ◆ Per Serving: Saturated fat: 1gr    Total fat: 6gr    Cholesterol: 2mg
  Sodium: 398mg    Calories: 372    Calories from fat: 15%

## DAN DAN NOODLES

SERVES 4

Served hot or cold, this Asian dish has become an American favorite. Peanut butter can be substituted for the sesame paste, but it gives it a different flavor. It will be necessary to shop in an Asian market for these ingredients.

The sesame paste is more authentic, but the noodles are delicious both ways. American kids especially like it with peanut butter. Tahini, which is another type of sesame paste doesn't work as well as oriental sesame paste and has a different flavor. Also, regular sesame oil shouldn't be substituted for Asian sesame oil, as it is light colored and too bland for this dish which needs the darker, stronger oriental version of sesame oil. Finally, the vinegar should be Asian black vinegar to give the presentation the proper look and enjoyment. Other types of noodles work, but the perciatelli, a spaghetti length, macaroni style, hollow noodle especially lends itself in texture and type. The sauce in this recipe is cooked for only a minute.

1 pound perciatelli noodles
2 teaspoons chopped fresh ginger
3 tablespoons sesame paste or peanut butter
4 tablespoons defatted chicken broth or water
Several drops Chinese hot oil
3 tablespoons low-sodium soy sauce
1 tablespoon dark sesame oil
1 teaspoon Chinese black vinegar
Pinch sugar
2 cloves minced garlic

Garnish:
1/2 cup chopped scallions
Shredded cucumber
Cilantro

In a large saucepan, boil the noodles until al dente. Meanwhile in a smaller saucepan, add all the other ingredients, heating them thoroughly, and just lightly cooking them for a minute or so. Drain the noodles, add them to a large bowl, stir in the sesame oil, add the sauce, toss, garnish and serve hot immediately, or chill and serve cold.

◆ Per Serving:  Saturated fat: 2gr   Total fat: 12gr   Cholesterol: 0
               Sodium: 64mg   Calories: 541   Calories from fat: 21%

## MACARONI AND CHEESE

SERVES 4

One of the foods I would hate to give up on a low-cholesterol menu would be macaroni and cheese. After experimenting, I found macaroni and cheese can be adapted rather easily to a low-cholesterol, low saturated fat diet. I make several versions of low saturated fat macaroni, and they are all delicious. At one time or another, I have added onions, mushrooms, chopped green olives, sliced, pitted Greek olives, diced red, green and yellow bell peppers with the seeds sprinkled on the top, or such vegetables as a lot of corn and peas, or broccoli and onions, even jalapeño peppers and red pepper flakes. Many of the vegetable additions should be precooked by steaming in 1/4 inch of water for a few minutes.

3/4 pound elbow macaroni
Pinch ground nutmeg
3 tablespoons flour
2 cups skim milk
1 cup nonfat cottage cheese
2 tablespoons shredded cheddar
2 tablespoons chopped parsley
Few shakes paprika
Few shakes red pepper flakes
1 tablespoon grated Parmesan

In a large nonstick pot, boil the macaroni noodles al dente and drain. In a blender, puree the mixture of nutmeg, flour, skim milk, cottage cheese and cheddar until smooth. Add it to the macaroni and heat in the pasta sauce pan until the cheese is melted. Sprinkle with parsley, paprika, pepper flakes and Parmesan. Serve hot.

- ◆ Per Serving:   Saturated fat: 1gr   Total fat: 3gr   Cholesterol: 9mg
  Sodium: 120mg  Calories: 432  Calories from fat: 7%

## WITH DICED HAM
Add 1/2 cup diced very lean ham to the casserole.

- ◆ Per Serving:   Saturated fat: 2gr   Total fat: 4gr   Cholesterol: 18mg
  Sodium: 331mg  Calories: 457  Calories from fat: 8%

# WHITE SAUCE MACARONI AND CHEESE

SERVES 4

It's stovetop cooking, no baking, excellent taste, rich, simple and slick. If you or your family don't like the pale color, call it white cheddar macaroni. If you or they have to have a deep rich orange cheesy look, add 1/8 teaspoon turmeric, which won't bother the flavor, and one half drop red color, which is a very small amount. Some families simply have to have an orange hued cheese sauce or they don't like it. The great flavor and small amount of fat in this one is a trade off for the color.

**3/4 pound elbow macaroni**
**3 tablespoons flour**
**1 cup skim milk**
**1 tablespoon low saturated fat margarine**
**2 tablespoons shredded cheddar**
**2 tablespoons shredded nonfat cheddar**
**Few shakes paprika or few shakes red pepper flakes**

In a large nonstick pot, boil the macaroni noodles al dente and drain. In a nonstick saucepan, whisk together the flour, milk and margarine for 2 minutes over medium high heat. Add the cheeses and continue whisking until thick and smooth. Pour over the macaroni and garnish with paprika or red pepper flakes. Serve hot.

◆ **Per Serving:**   Saturated fat: 2gr   Total fat: 5gr   Cholesterol: 5mg
                    Sodium: 142mg   Calories: 398   Calories from fat: 12%

# STUFFED MANICOTTI

SERVES 4

A stellar dish. You'll need some of your food market's pre-made sauce for this if you want to have dinner on the table in under 20 minutes. Served with a salad and a good bread, this is a great, quick cold-weather dinner.

Manicotti noodles take a while to cook, 12 to 15 minutes, so begin them as soon as possible (water comes to a boil more quickly in a pot with a lid). Use a big pot and stir them during the boiling because, since we use no oil, they can stick together.

Defrost the spinach in the microwave (in its own package) for 5 minutes, while the manicotti is boiling.

Even though ricotta is often labeled "part skim," the percentages of skim milk differ widely, so purchase the one with the lowest amount of saturated fat.

You can make your own sauce for this (page 242).

1 pound manicotti or 8 large noodles for stuffing
1 10-oz package frozen chopped spinach, defrosted
1/2 cup chopped onion
1 6-ounce can sliced mushrooms
1/4 cup chopped green bell pepper
1 pint part-skim ricotta
1/4 teaspoon ground nutmeg
Homemade marinara sauce (page 242) or 1 pint commercial
    refrigerated meatless spaghetti sauce
1/2 teaspoon dried sweet basil
2 tablespoons chopped parsley

Preheat oven to 400° if baking. In a large saucepan, cook the manicotti in boiling water until al dente. Drain and rinse in cold water. Separate and place on wax paper or kitchen towels. Meanwhile, squeeze the spinach completely dry and set aside. In a large nonstick skillet, simmer the onion, mushrooms and peppers in a small amount of water until soft, about 5 minutes, adding more water when necessary. Mix the nutmeg and the spinach into the cheese by hand.

To easily stuff the manicotti, divide the cheese mixture into 8 portions and form each into a roll like a short, narrow hot dog. Hold the manicotti in the palm of one hand with your thumb in the opening. With the other, slide the cheese roll in, squashing both ends of the cheese to conform to the ends of the noodle. Place the filled manicotti side by side in an ovenproof dish. (The stuffing process can extend the time a bit beyond 20 minutes.)

Add the sauce to the onions, mushrooms, and peppers, and heat for 1 minute on high, stirring constantly. Pour over the top of the stuffed manicotti. Bake for 5 to 15 minutes, or heat in a microwave for 5 minutes on high or until bubbly. Serve hot.

◆ **Per Serving:**    Saturated fat: 7gr    Total fat: 15gr  Cholesterol: 127mg
Sodium: 654mg    Calories: 656  Calories from fat: 20%

## WITH CHEESE TOPPING
Sprinkle 2 tablespoons of shredded skim milk mozzarella on top of the sauce and heat as directed.

◆ **Per Serving:**    Saturated fat: 8gr    Total fat: 16gr  Cholesterol: 131mg
Sodium: 687mg    Calories: 674  Calories from fat: 21%

# RAMEN NOODLES

## SERVES 4

Ramen noodles can now be bought in most grocery stores, food markets, and always in Asian or specialty food stores. They come in squares or blocks, about enough for 1 or 2 people (I like a whole block per person if there isn't much other food). They are a curly version of pasta, made from rice. In Asian specialties there are often versions flavored with soy, garlic and sugar. They are quick cooking and can be served as a base or side for a stir fry, soup, lean pork fry or with Tapa Beef, a Filipino specialty. When used as a side, simply cook in boiling water for just a minute or two, and use with the flavoring that is enclosed.

1/2 cup defatted chicken stock
5 scallions or spring onions, coarsely chopped
1/2 clove garlic, minced
2 tablespoons reduced sodium soy sauce
1 teaspoon brown sugar
2 to 4 2-ounce blocks of ramen noodles
2 teaspoons cornstarch
1 to 2 cups cool, defatted chicken stock
Red pepper flakes

Begin boiling 4 cups of water in a large saucepan. In a large, non-stick skillet, add the 1/2 cup of defatted chicken stock, onions and garlic and heat until partially cooked, about 3 to 4 minutes. Add the soy sauce and sugar, stir in and turn off the heat. When the noodle water is boiling, add the ramen noodles, break the block apart with a fork as they begin to separate, boil for about 2 minutes, testing for doneness, drain and add to the skillet and start a low heat under the skillet. In a small bowl, mix the cornstarch in the chicken stock and add to the noodles, stirring until it thickens. Season with the red pepper flakes and serve hot.

◆ Per Serving:  Saturated fat: Trace  Total fat: 1gr  Cholesterol: 0
Sodium: 538mg  Calories: 63  Calories from fat: 22%

## PASTA AND SPINACH

SERVES 4

Using fresh pasta, or commercial pasta that is soft, this takes just a few minutes, but you'll need some vegetable stock or defatted chicken stock (page 17). The pasta has all the vegetables from the stock in it, plus some bright green spinach. It is attractive to look at with the clear sauce. Serve it with a crusty bread, mandarin oranges or peaches, and a small salad. The chicken stock is made with all the chicken trimmings, leeks, celery, and a sprig of thyme and rosemary. After defatting, the herbs are removed but the vegetables stay in, rinsed of any fat. You can dice some cooked chicken for the sauce, or if you are a vegetarian use TVP (textured vegetable protein), a defatted soy protein, which can be found at health food stores or in my catalog (1-800-8-FLAVOR).

**1 pound fresh linguine or spaghetti**
**2 cups defatted chicken or vegetable stock**
**2 teaspoons cornstarch**
**1/2 cup cool, defatted chicken or vegetable stock**
**1/2 pound fresh spinach**
**Lite Salt (optional)**
**Fresh ground pepper**

Begin boiling 4 cups of water in a large saucepan. In a large non-stick skillet with a lid, add the chicken or vegetable stock and heat until simmering. When the water in the saucepan is boiling, add the pasta, and break apart with a fork, and boil for about 2 to 3 minutes, testing for doneness. Drain and set aside. Meanwhile, in a small bowl, mix the cornstarch in the cool chicken stock and add to the heated stock, burner on medium high, stirring until thick. Add the spinach (and the diced chicken or TVP, if using), turn down the heat, season, put on the lid and cook for 2 minutes until the spinach has wilted. Serve hot over the pasta.

◆ Per Serving:   Saturated fat: Trace   Total fat: 1gr   Cholesterol: 0
Sodium: 610mg   Calories: 183   Calories from fat: 6%

# BEANS AND RICE

SERVES 8

Beans and rice are a South American favorite enjoyed throughout the Americas. Together they are the perfect mixture of carbohydrates and protein. Often flavored with bits of ham, this dish can also contain numerous vegetables. The type of bean is usually pinto, however it can vary and different kinds can be used together. The ham or pork stock is always defatted (page 17) before using. Add other vegetables such as chopped canned tomato wedges, coarsely chopped fresh green peppers, or canned corn during the final 5 minutes of cooking. Serve with chopped onions, salsa (page 255), Ecuadorian aji sauce or a commercial hot sauce.

**2 cups canned beans, drained**
**3 cups defatted ham stock**
**1/2 cup rice**

In a large pot, combine the ingredients and cook for 15 minutes. Serve hot.

- ◆ **Per Serving:**    Saturated fat: Trace   Total fat: Trace   Cholesterol: 0
  Sodium: 516mg   Calories: 101   Calories from fat: 4%

WITH HAM
Add 1/2 pound diced, lean ham (from the bone used to make the stock if desired).

- ◆ **Per Serving:**    Saturated fat: 1gr   Total fat: 2gr   Cholesterol: 13mg
  Sodium: 919mg   Calories: 138   Calories from fat: 12%

## CHEESE AND BEAN BURRITOS

SERVES 4

This hearty, flavorful dish can be used for an entree, side dish, lunch or anytime you want a full, rich Tex/Mex fare quickly and easily. This isn't a neat dish covered with mountains of fatty cheese, but is a wonderfully messy combination of robust flavors. The cheese is used judiciously and is showy on top of the beans. Nonfat cheese will not work, but Dorman's Lo Chol and several others will.

Serve it with a lettuce or fruit salad, rice, green vegetable, even corn for a whole meal full of taste and healthy carbohydrates.

1 large onion, coarsely chopped
1 green pepper, coarsely chopped
1 red pepper, coarsely chopped
1/2 clove garlic, minced
2 cups lumpy tomato sauce
Few shakes red pepper flakes or 1/2 teaspoon chopped jalapeño pepper
1/2 teaspoon dried oregano
1-1/2 to 2 tablespoons chili powder
1 teaspoon cumin
4 large flour tortillas
8 tablespoons shredded low-fat mozzarella cheese
Low-sodium salt (optional)
1 cup canned pinto or other beans, drained
4 tablespoons shredded low-fat mozzarella cheese

Garnish:
1 avocado
1/2 cup chopped scallion or onion

In a large, nonstick pan on high heat, add 1/2 inch of water, the onion, peppers and garlic and cook, stirring for about 4 minutes, or until the onions are partially translucent. Add the tomato sauce, red pepper flakes, oregano, chili powder and cumin, stir and cook for 3 to 4 minutes covered on medium heat.

Meanwhile, in the center of the tortilla, make a long row of 2 tablespoons of cheese, and roll it (it will flatten during cooking) and place in a rectangular glass cooking dish. Pour the sauce on top of the tortillas, and the beans on the sauce. Top the beans with the 4 tablespoons mozzarella cheese and microwave on high for 4 minutes. Remove and add the chopped avocado and onion and serve hot.

◆ Per Serving:    Saturated fat: 4gr    Total fat: 16gr    Cholesterol: 10mg
                  Sodium: 663mg    Calories: 455    Calories from fat: 30%

# MEATLESS MEATY CHILI

SERVES 4

This chili is different because it has just a smidgen of chocolate in it which makes it quite exotic. You will love it. When you use Midland Harvest Chili Fixins (page 290), a mixture of soy protein and flavorings, you can prepare chili and beans with lots of taste and texture. Grate a few slices of orange zest, chopped tomatoes, or some slices of avocados for garnish.

1 4-ounce package Midland Harvest Chili Fixins Mix
   (page 290)
1 green pepper cut in 1-inch pieces, seeds reserved
1 red pepper cut in 1-inch pieces, seeds reserved
1 cup coarsely chopped onion
2 cloves garlic, minced
1 teaspoon cumin
1 tablespoon chili powder
1/2 teaspoon cocoa powder
1 8-ounce can tomato sauce
1 16-ounce can dark kidney beans, drained
1-1/2 cups water

In a large nonstick saucepan, add all the ingredients, including seeds, and bring to a boil. Lower heat and simmer for 15 minutes, stirring occasionally. Adjust seasonings. Garnish and serve hot.

◆ Per Serving:   Saturated fat: 1gr    Total fat: 5gr    Cholesterol: 0
                Sodium: 1052mg   Calories: 269  Calories from fat: 23%

# TACOS

These tacos may be made with or without meat or with a combination of meat and taco filling. Midland Harvest Taco Filling 'n Dip is the magic ingredient (page 290) that can go both ways. Adding the beef makes it beefy tasting without compromising cooking with very low fat. You can also add a small amount (1/4 to 1/2 cup) of canned navy beans to this while the mixture is cooking for added protein and flavor. For authentic flavor be sure to garnish.

You can make your own nonfat, nonfried taco shells by draping the 6-inch uncooked corn tortillas over an oven rack and baking for 10 minutes in a 350° oven.

1  onion, chopped
1  garlic clove, minced
1-1/2 cups cool water
1/2 teaspoon chili powder
1 4-ounce package Midland Harvest Taco Filling 'n Dip
    (page 290)
1/4 pound ground, 98% lean top round (optional)
1 package 8 (baked, not fried) taco shells

Garnish:
2 cups shredded lettuce
2 cups finely diced tomatoes
1 cup finely chopped onions
1 cup salsa or taco sauce

Additional garnish suggestions:
Chopped jalapeño
Nonfat sour cream
Chopped avocado
Chopped ripe black olives

In a saucepan, add the onion, garlic, water, chili powder, ground beef, if using, and let rest for 10 to 12 minutes. Bring to a boil and reduce the heat to low and simmer for 12 to 15 minutes. Stir occasionally and cook long enough to remove the liquid. Add a few tablespoons of the taco mixture to each taco shell, fill with lettuce, tomato, onions, top with sauce and serve.

◆ Per Serving:     Saturated fat: Trace    Total fat: 4gr     Cholesterol: 0
                   Sodium: 530mg    Calories: 165   Calories from fat: 23%

## COUSCOUS AND TOMATOES

SERVES 4–6

Couscous is both a grain and a dish. The grain is semolina (the same high quality that's in the best pasta). It is made from durum wheat, a tougher wheat that is widely used in Middle East and North Africa. Almost all couscous available today is pre-made or instant and has a short cooking or steaming time. It is preferable to get the uncooked variety which has a firmer texture, but it can be hard to find unless you know of a health food, specialty or ethnic store which may carry it. Follow the directions on the package of instant, which calls for its own amount of liquid.

This recipe can be a full meal. If you want to add meat, 3 ounces of roasted skinless, lean chicken (page 19), lean broiled lamb, or lightly steamed shrimp work well.

2 cups cooked couscous
1 cup water or defatted chicken stock
1 onion, coarsely chopped
3 cloves garlic, minced
1 carrot, diced
1-1/2 cups shredded cabbage
Black pepper
Cayenne, or Cajun spice
1/2 cup currants or raisins
1/2 cup canned chick peas (garbanzos), drained

1/4 to 1/2 teaspoon saffron
1/2 teaspoon ground turmeric
1 teaspoon grated fresh ginger or 1/4 teaspoon ground ginger
3 tablespoons chopped parsley
4 medium tomatoes, parboiled until warm in the center,
   skins and stems removed, left whole, or diced in 1-1/2 inch
   cubes
Harissa (a hot, spicy Middle Eastern sauce)

If the couscous is cold, heat and set aside. In a large nonstick skillet with 1/4 inch of water or chicken stock (about a half a cup), heat the onion, garlic, carrot, cabbage, a few shakes of pepper and cayenne adding more liquid when necessary, until the vegetables are nearly cooked, about 5 minutes. Add the currants, chick peas and all the spices and cook another 2 to 3 minutes. Mix with the couscous and heat thoroughly. Mound the couscous on each plate and put a whole tomato on top, or mix in while cooking, or place the diced tomatoes around the top of the couscous. Serve hot with harissa.

◆ Per Serving:    Saturated fat: Trace   Total fat: 1gr    Cholesterol: 0
                  Sodium: 26mg    Calories: 187   Calories from fat: 5%

WITH LAMB
Add 1 cup of diced cooked lean lamb with the couscous.

◆ Per Serving:    Saturated fat: 1gr    Total fat: 3gr    Cholesterol: 25mg
                  Sodium: 45mg    Calories: 241   Calories from fat: 12%

# GNOCCHI

SERVES 4–6

Gnocchi, a potato dumpling, is light and filling all at once. This is a Roman recipe, very easy to make, contains no fat, and not counting the potatoes which are pre-boiled, the gnocchi and sauce can be on the table in 15 minutes. This gnocchi is the best I have ever had. The potatoes can be cooked in 10 minutes if cut small enough.

They must be hot when you roll the gnocchi. This is an adaptation from Mrs. Rina DeVita, our TV show's wardrobe mistress.

A dinner of gnocchi and salad is filling, high in fiber, low in saturates and has no fat at all, because there is none in the gnocchi. The potatoes for the gnocchi can be boiled whole or cut up and microwaved.

**3 large russet potatoes, cut in pieces, after boiling or heating**
**2 cups flour (may be more or less)**
**Low-sodium salt (optional)**
**Flour for the board**

Rice (or mash) the cooked, peeled potatoes in a ricer while they are hot. Add about half of the flour and knead, mixing it well into the potatoes, rolling it on a floured counter top or board for a few minutes. Add the other half of the flour and knead again for about 3 minutes. Add more flour if necessary. The dough should not be sticky and the amount is approximately the same as the potatoes—more flour makes the gnocchi harder, less flour, lighter and softer. Also, resist using a processor to mix the dough or mash the potatoes as the gnocchi will be tough and chewy.

In a large pot, boil several quarts of water. Cut off baseball size pieces of the dough. Roll it into several ropes 1/2 to 3/4 inch thick by about 8 to 12 inches long. This takes a few minutes. Cut the ropes with a knife into 1-inch lengths. Poke a depression into each of the gnocchi with your finger (or roll each one with your thumb, indenting it) to make a depression so more sauce gets on each piece. Let the cut gnocchi pieces dry about 5 minutes, separated on several plates, sprinkled very lightly with flour. The gnocchi can now be frozen, or cooked fresh in the following way. Drop the gnocchi into the boiling water and let them cook for 3 to 5 minutes or until each one rises to the top. With a slotted spoon, remove, let drain, and serve hot with a sauce of your choice, with marinara (page 242) being the most popular.

◆ **Per Serving:**   Saturated fat: Trace   Total fat: 1gr   Cholesterol: 0
                     Sodium: 6mg   Calories: 359   Calories from fat: 2%

# QUINOA ITALIAN STYLE

SERVES 6-8

If you haven't eaten quinoa (pronounced keen-wah) you're missing out on a real treat. It contains more protein than any other grain and it is the only grain with all eight amino acids. It looks a little like tiny tapiocas, and it tastes a little like mild rice. It was one of three major foods the Incas ate, along with corn and potatoes three thousand years ago. Like pasta, it can be eaten hot or cold, in casseroles, salads, soups and loaves, and unlike pasta, it can be a dessert when sweetened and served with fruit or baked like a cake. Kids especially like quinoa because of its tiny size and pleasant, mild flavor. The cooking time is about the same as dried pasta, about 10 to 15 minutes on top of the stove, covered, with double the amount of water to quinoa. It can also be baked. One cup of dried quinoa will cook up to be 3 cups.

1 cup minced onion
2 cloves garlic minced
1/2 pound ground 98% lean top round or Harvest Burger and
    water according to package
2 8-ounce cans tomato sauce
1 16-ounce can tomatoes, or 4 tomatoes chopped
1 teaspoon low-sodium salt (optional)
2 teaspoons dried oregano
3 teaspoons chopped fresh sweet basil or 2 teaspoons dried
1/2 teaspoon sugar
3 cups cooked quinoa
1/4 pound part skim ricotta cheese
1/4 pound low-fat mozzarella cheese
Several shakes grated Parmesan cheese

Preheat the oven to 350° if baking.
    In a large nonstick skillet, sauté the onion and garlic until cooked. Add the ground meat or Harvest Burger and water, tomato sauce, tomatoes, salt (if using), oregano, sweet basil, and

sugar and simmer until all the ingredients are just cooked, even slightly underdone.

In a casserole, layer the sauce and quinoa, dollop on some of the ricotta, sprinkle on some of the mozzarella and do another layer so there are two or three with sauce on top. Sprinkle on the Parmesan cheese and microwave for 10 minutes (or bake about 35 minutes). Serve hot.

◆ Per Serving:  Saturated fat: 4gr   Total fat: 11gr   Cholesterol: 22mg
                Sodium: 796mg   Calories: 493   Calories from fat: 20%

## FRIED RICE

SERVES 4–6

Fried rice doesn't have to be actually fried or contain egg yolks to have
the right taste. This is an easy recipe;
the ingredients are flexible and can
vary depending on what you have
available. You can substitute chopped
onions for the scallions, slivered snow
peas for the English peas, or you can add
mushrooms. The last chopped scallion in
the recipe is for garnish. You can also sprinkle sesame seeds on the top for a nice effect. Serve the rice as a main course with mandarin oranges or lychee nuts, broccoli in orange juice (page 146), and green beans with garlic.

1 cup shredded cabbage
1 cup cooked white or brown rice
4 scallions, chopped into 1/4-inch pieces
2 tablespoons low-sodium soy sauce
1 tablespoon minced coriander leaves
1 tablespoon chopped parsley

3 substitute eggs, plain or with green bell pepper and
   onions, or 6 egg whites
1/2 cup frozen peas, defrosted
1 scallion, finely chopped, or 2 tablespoons chopped chives

In a large nonstick skillet over medium heat, cook the cabbage in
1/4 cup of water for several minutes, stirring occasionally, adding
water when necessary, until cooked, letting the water nearly evaporate at the end. Stir in the rice and heat until hot. Add the
chopped scallions, soy sauce, coriander and parsley, and heat until
hot, adding a small amount of water if necessary.

Make a well in the center of the rice mixture and pour in the
eggs. Cover the skillet and turn the heat down very low. When
the eggs are cooked, about 3 to 5 minutes, chop them up in the
well, making crisscrossing cuts with a knife, add the peas, and mix
them into the rice. Sprinkle with chopped scallions. Serve hot.
Serves 4 to 6.

◆ **Per Serving:**  Saturated fat: Trace  Total fat: 2gr   Cholesterol: Trace
                    Sodium: 335mg   Calories: 128  Calories from fat: 12%

## WITH HAM
Add 1/4 cup diced cooked lean ham with the peas.

◆ **Per Serving:**  Saturated fat: Trace  Total fat: 2gr   Cholesterol: 5mg
                    Sodium: 440mg   Calories: 141  Calories from fat: 14%

## WITH SHRIMP
Add 1/2 cup tiny cooked shrimp with the peas.

◆ **Per Serving:**  Saturated fat: Trace  Total fat: 2gr   Cholesterol: 56mg
                    Sodium: 398mg   Calories: 157  Calories from fat: 12%

# SAFFRON RICE

SERVES 4

Popular in the tropics, hot saffron rice is most often served as an accompaniment with chicken or pork. However, it is delicious just as it is. This is a simple flavorful dish that takes little time and adds subtle sophistication for a sweet poultry accompaniment such as chicken and apricots (page 218).

Olive oil spray
1 Spanish onion, finely chopped
1/2 cup short-grain rice
1/4 to 1/3 teaspoon saffron powder, or 1/2 teaspoon of loose
    strands
1/4 teaspoon turmeric
Low-sodium salt, (optional)
1 cup boiling defatted chicken stock or water

Lightly spray a medium size nonstick skillet, add the onion and lightly spray the onion while stirring. Heat the olive oil and the onion, and cook for about 3 minutes. Add the rice, spraying again lightly, coating each piece. Add the saffron, turmeric, salt, if using, and stir into the rice, coloring each piece. Add the stock, cover and cook over low heat for 15 minutes or until the rice is tender. Serve hot.

◆ Per Serving:   Saturated fat: Trace   Total fat: Trace   Cholesterol: 0
                 Sodium: 200mg   Calories: 98   Calories from fat: 3%


# RICE PILAF

SERVES 4

For pilaf, rice is first sautéed in fat or oil, then cooked in flavored water or stock. In my version, the amount of oil is kept to a minimum and the rice is instant. You'll need some flavored cooking spray to give each kernel the least amount of fat possible yet keep the style of the recipe. If you make it with instant white rice, the cooking time is a little less than with instant brown rice.

1 cup instant brown rice
Butter-flavored cooking spray
2-1/2 cups defatted chicken stock
1 chopped onion or 1/2 cup chopped shallots
1/2 pound mushrooms, finely chopped
1 scallion, finely diced (optional)
Low-sodium salt (optional)
2 tablespoons grated Parmesan

Lightly spray a large nonstick saucepan, pour in the rice and heat over low heat for several minutes, stirring constantly. Add either boiling or cold stock, the onion (or shallots), mushrooms and bring to a boil over high heat, reduce the heat and cook, covered, for 10 minutes (rice time varies depending upon brand, size or type of brown rice used). When the rice is finished, add the scallions, salt, if using, and Parmesan cheese. Serve hot.

◆ **Per Serving:** Saturated fat: 1gr    Total fat: 1gr    Cholesterol: 2mg
Sodium: 547mg    Calories: 134    Calories from fat: 9%

## CELLOPHANE NOODLES

SERVES 4

Cellophane noodles, which are clear, take only about 3 minutes to cook in boiling water. They are perfect when you want something fast and filling. They can be purchased in Asian or specialty food stores. Simply boil in hot water for just a minute or two, and use with or without the enclosed packaged flavoring. However they are better with stir-fried vegetables. There are many seasoned Asian sauces such as Szechuan, mushroom soy, and sweet and sour which can be used to further season this dish after it is served.

2 stalks Chinese celery, cut in 1-inch pieces
1 onion, coarsely chopped
2 cloves garlic, coarsely chopped
2 to 3 cups of any mixture of vegetables such as broccoli florets, asparagus, carrots, red, yellow or green bell peppers, snow peas
2 tablespoons shredded ginger
3 tablespoons low-sodium soy sauce
1 package cellophane noodles

Garnish:
Chopped scallions

In a large nonstick skillet cook all the vegetables, garlic, ginger and soy sauce in 1/4 inch of water until they are soft, about 5 minutes. In a large pot of boiling water, add the noodles, boiling for 3 minutes or until soft, stirring continually. Remove and drain. Put the noodles on a plate and add the vegetables on the side. Top with the chopped scallions.

♦ Per Serving:   Saturated fat: Trace   Total fat: Trace   Cholesterol: 0
Sodium: 413mg   Calories: 150   Calories from fat: 2%

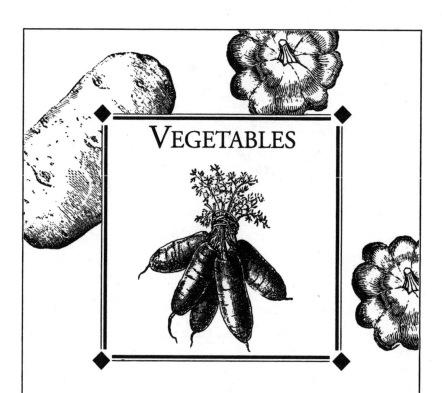

# VEGETABLES

Colorful Vegetable-Filled Baked Potatoes • White Baked
Potatoes • Mashed Potatoes • Hash Browns • Potato Pancakes
Golden Squash • Asparagus • Asparagus and Parmesan Cheese
Cooked Spinach • Creamed Spinach • Spinach with Garlic and
Olive Oil • Lima Beans • Pennsylvania Dutch Beets
Sweet and Sour Red Cabbage • Steamed Bok Choy
Steamed Cauliflower • Broccoli in Orange Juice • Broccoli and
Garlic • Steamed Brussels Sprouts • Orange Brussels Sprouts
Butter-Flavored Carrots • Ginger-Flavored Carrots
Steamed Green Beans • Country Green Beans
Southern Style Green Beans • Spicy Asian Green Beans
(continued)

*English Green Peas • Peas, Carrots and Mushrooms in
Cream Sauce • Fennel • Fennel, Carrots, Peas and Rice
Grilled Summer Vegetables with Shrimp or Chicken on Kebobs
Grilled Onions, Peppers and Zucchini
Steamed Summer Squash • Steamed Zucchini
Fried Zucchini Sticks • Steamed Okra • Eggplant, Asian Style
Creamed Onions • Steamed Whole Onions
Four Onions and Confetti Peppers • Braised Leeks
Stuffed Green and Red Peppers • Sweet and Sour Peppers
Steamed Celery • Natural Corn • Boiled or Steamed Corn
Corn and Pasta • Corn, Squash and Peppers • Sautéed
Mushrooms • Creamed Mushrooms • Easy Stuffed Mushrooms
Harvard Beets*

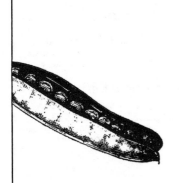

# Vegetables

Tomatoes on the vine, State Fair size zucchini, sweet peas in a pod. Vegetables proclaim the season and they are the cornerstone of low-fat and nonfat meals.

Steam, braise, sauté, boil, poach, grill, broil, microwave, flash-bake or barbecue vegetables.

Vary the cooking time. Onions, peppers and other vegetables have different textures and tastes when they are raw, partially cooked and fully cooked. To lessen cooking time, julienne the longer-cooking vegetables.

Vegetables are cholesterol-free, but all have some trace amounts of fat, even radishes. Avocados have a small amount of saturated fat but most of an avocado's fat is monounsaturated.

When planning your meal look for a balance of heavy and light, dark and pale foods. Use a variety of vegetables, including the more brightly colored ones that are rich in nutrients and vitamins.

New marketing techniques have made so many "new to us" vegetables available year round. Your market's produce manager can help you choose these new items and even provide you with tips on cleaning, storing and cooking them.

When your garden is bountiful, freeze some of your crop for sauces and dishes later in the next season. Cooking with vegetables from last fall's harvest is a most satisfying feeling.

# COLORFUL VEGETABLE-FILLED BAKED POTATOES

SERVES 4

This is an idea for a quick baked potato meal. The vegetables suggested can be substituted with others, but these particular foods
need little pre-cooking. This potato is on the table from start to
finish in 10 minutes. If the potatoes aren't already baked, add
another 10 minutes for microwaving them.

1 cup diced fresh tomatoes
1 cup chopped scallions
1 cup chopped parsley or watercress
4 russet potatoes, baked in a microwave or oven, cut in half
2/3 cup skim milk
Low-sodium salt (optional)
Pepper

Lightly mash each potato half in the skin. In a small dish, add the
tomatoes, scallions, and chopped parsley. Scoop out a large tablespoon or two of the inside of each potato and add to the dish.
Microwave for 1 minute. Divide into 4 parts and pile each potato
with the mixture. Season and serve hot.

◆ **Per Serving:**     Saturated fat: Trace   Total fat: Trace   Cholesterol: 1mg
                        Sodium: 43mg     Calories: 182   Calories from fat: 2%

# WHITE BAKED POTATOES

SERVES 4

Here is a way to bake potatoes that is rather fancy and very pretty
to serve to company or just for yourself. You will need a jar of
sun-dried tomatoes packed in olive oil.

4 long white potatoes
2 tablespoons olive oil from a jar of sun-dried tomatoes
Paprika
Low-sodium salt (optional)
2 tablespoons chopped chives or parsley

Garnish:
Several slivers sun-dried tomatoes

Preheat the oven to 400°. Peel the potatoes and make as many 1/4-inch wide slits crosswise as you can. Slit them almost but not quite through each potato, so a 1/2-inch layer of the potato holds it together at the bottom.

Pour the sun-dried tomato olive oil into a flat dish. Roll the potato in the oil, oiling it well all over, using your hands. Drizzle some oil into the slits. Sprinkle with paprika and salt, if using. Place the potatoes in a baking dish, cover lightly with plastic wrap and microwave for 10 minutes, turning often. Bake uncovered for 5 to 10 minutes, or until lightly browned. Sprinkle with chopped chives and the slivers of sun-dried tomatoes just before serving. Serve hot.

◆ Per Serving:   Saturated fat: 1gr   Total fat: 7gr   Cholesterol: 0
                Sodium: 16mg   Calories: 280   Calories from fat: 22%

## MASHED POTATOES

SERVES 4–6

Mashing potatoes is easier if you have a masher or electric beater. An immersion beater works, but makes the potatoes gooey. If you leave the skins on, the mashed potatoes will have flecks in them, but they taste just as good, and coarse black pepper leaves flecks too.

3 all-purpose, large potatoes such as California Longs or
   California Whites, peeled or unpeeled, cut in eighths
1/4 cup evaporated skim milk

Low-sodium salt (optional)
Pepper, white or freshly ground black

Garnish:
Butter sprinkles
Chopped parsley

In a large saucepan, boil water. Bake the potatoes in a microwave for 8 minutes, remove, cut into small pieces and boil for 5 minutes, or until done. In a large bowl, mash the potatoes, ricing with the skim milk. Season with salt, if using, and pepper and serve hot.

- Per Serving:     Saturated fat: Trace    Total fat: Trace    Cholesterol: 1mg
  Sodium: 34mg     Calories: 115   Calories from fat: 1%

### WITH 2 PERCENT MILK
Substitute 2 percent milk for the evaporated skim milk.

- Per Serving:     Saturated fat: Trace    Total fat: 1gr     Cholesterol: 2mg
  Sodium: 17mg     Calories: 107   Calories from fat: 5%

### WITH MARGARINE
Add 2 teaspoons margarine.

- Per Serving:     Saturated fat: Trace    Total fat: 2gr     Cholesterol: 1mg
  Sodium: 50mg     Calories: 132   Calories from fat: 14%

### WITH COTTAGE CHEESE
Add 1/2 cup pureed, nonfat cottage cheese and chopped parsley.

- Per Serving:     Saturated fat: Trace    Total fat: Trace    Cholesterol: 2mg
  Sodium: 36mg     Calories: 128   Calories from fat: 2%

### WITH GRAVY
Use 1/2 cup defatted chicken (page 246), or beef (page 244) gravy.

- Per Serving:     Saturated fat: Trace    Total fat: Trace    Cholesterol: 1mg
  Sodium: 34mg     Calories: 120   Calories from fat: 1%

# HASH BROWNS

SERVES 4

Hash browns don't need fat because the shredded potatoes thicken and stick together as they cook. You can make them crisper by cooking them longer before turning.

**Vegetable spray (optional)**
**2 large all-purpose potatoes, peeled, shredded or**
   **julienned**
**1 onion, finely chopped**
**Low-sodium salt (optional)**
**Pepper**

Spray (if using) a large
nonstick skillet, and heat
the potatoes, onions, salt,
if using, and pepper in
1/4 inch of water, stirring
occasionally, over medium
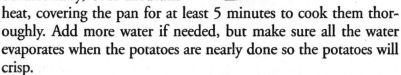
heat, covering the pan for at least 5 minutes to cook them thoroughly. Add more water if needed, but make sure all the water evaporates when the potatoes are nearly done so the potatoes will crisp.

♦ **Per Serving:**   Saturated fat: Trace   Total fat: Trace   Cholesterol: 0
                 Sodium: 8mg     Calories: 162  Calories from fat: 1%

WITH CANOLA/RAPESEED OIL
Sauté the potatoes and onion in 2 teaspoons canola/rapeseed oil.

♦ **Per Serving:**   Saturated fat: Trace   Total fat: 2gr    Cholesterol: 1mg
                 Sodium: 8mg     Calories: 182  Calories from fat: 12%

# POTATO PANCAKES

SERVES 4

There is no cholesterol in these high carbohydrate, high fiber, high nutrient potato pancakes. Since they are virtually greaseless, they are also low in calories. A potato has about the same calories as an apple. You can serve them with fresh applesauce (page 259) or nonfat sour cream, in the tradition of potato pancakes. If potato pancakes are to be the whole meal, you can serve them with a green salad and another vegetable such as a broiled tomato or green beans.

2 to 4 large all-purpose potatoes (not baking)
3/4 to 1 cup grated or shredded onion
2 egg whites, lightly beaten
1 substitute egg
2 to 4 tablespoons flour
Low-sodium salt (optional)
Pepper
Butter-flavored cooking spray

Peel and grate the potatoes, using the larger holes of a four-sided grater or the food processor. Use them immediately, or cover them with water until ready to use (if they get dark or reddish, it can sometimes be washed off). Drain and squeeze the shredded potatoes first with your hands, then more thoroughly with a clean cloth or paper towels. Combine and mix well the potatoes, onion, egg whites, egg, flour, salt, if using, and pepper.

Spray a nonstick skillet with the butter-flavored spray. Using a small ladle or spoon, form 4-inch pancakes. After a few minutes over medium heat, turn to brown. You can make the pancakes smaller. If so, cook for only 10 minutes. If you're making one large pancake that you will then cut into wedges, cover the pan and cook the pancake over very low heat for 15 minutes being careful it doesn't burn, then turn and brown the other side for a few minutes. If you wish a crisper potato pancake, transfer them to a nonstick cookie sheet and place them in a 375° oven to firm and crisp and continue cooking for 10 minutes. Serve hot.

- ◆ **Per Serving:**     Saturated fat: Trace    Total fat: Trace    Cholesterol: 0
                         Sodium: 70mg     Calories: 135   Calories from fat: 2%

### WITH CANOLA/RAPESEED OIL
Fry the pancakes in 2 tablespoons canola/rapeseed oil.

- ◆ **Per Serving:**     Saturated fat: 1gr     Total fat: 7gr     Cholesterol: 0
                         Sodium: 70mg     Calories: 195   Calories from fat: 32%

## GOLDEN SQUASH

SERVES 4

There are several varieties of gold squash. The one I like best is smallish, bright gold, shaped like a pumpkin, and weighs between 1 and 3 pounds and it is exceptionally sweet. It can be baked in the microwave or oven whole (pierce it first), or halved, cut side down. Don't remove the seeds before cooking (see acorn squash, page 173).

1 3-pound golden squash or
   2 1-1/2 pound golden squash
2 tablespoons frozen orange juice, undiluted
1/2 tablespoon fresh lemon juice
1/2 teaspoon ground ginger
Grated orange peel
Pepper

Cut the squash in half and place, cut side down, on a microwavable dish and heat for 8 minutes or until soft. Remove the seeds, wash them and place a few in each squash half. In a cup, mix the orange juice and lemon juice with the ginger, add about 1/2 teaspoon of the mixture back to each squash and sprinkle with grated orange peel. Place the squash under the broiler if you like, to brown. Serve hot.

◆ **Per Serving:**   Saturated fat: Trace   Total fat: Trace   Cholesterol: 0
Sodium: 12mg   Calories: 152   Calories from fat: 2%

## ASPARAGUS

SERVES 4

We are fortunate to have asparagus almost all year round now. Cook it quickly to keep it firm and bright green. Long cooking 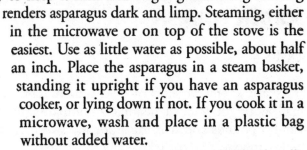 renders asparagus dark and limp. Steaming, either in the microwave or on top of the stove is the easiest. Use as little water as possible, about half an inch. Place the asparagus in a steam basket, standing it upright if you have an asparagus cooker, or lying down if not. If you cook it in a microwave, wash and place in a plastic bag without added water.

Asparagus can be as thick as a broom handle or thin as a reed. Snap or cut off the lower ends where they break easily. Today, with the new varieties, most asparagus doesn't need peeling. Asparagus tastes delicious either hot or cold. Since it requires just a few minutes of cooking and breaks apart easily, asparagus in soups or pasta should be cooked separately and added just before serving.

1-1/2 pounds asparagus
Low-sodium salt (optional)
Pepper
Grated lemon

Heat the asparagus in a steamer, a skillet with a steaming rack, or in a small amount of water and steam the asparagus until tender, 2 to 8 minutes, depending on thickness of stalks. Drain, season and serve immediately.

- ◆ **Per Serving:**   Saturated fat: Trace   Total fat: Trace   Cholesterol: 0
  Sodium: 3mg   Calories: 38   Calories from fat: 7%

## WITH HOLLANDAISE
Serve with 2 tablespoons Hollandaise sauce (page 241) per serving.

- ◆ **Per Serving:**   Saturated fat: 2gr   Total fat: 9gr   Cholesterol: Trace
  Sodium: 144mg   Calories: 129   Calories from fat: 56%

## WITH CHEESE SAUCE
Serve with 2 tablespoons cheese sauce per serving.

- ◆ **Per Serving:**   Saturated fat: 1gr   Total fat: 2gr   Cholesterol: Trace
  Sodium: 266mg   Calories: 86   Calories from fat: 25%

## WITH MARGARINE
Serve with 1 teaspoon margarine per serving.

- ◆ **Per Serving:**   Saturated fat: 1gr   Total fat: 5gr   Cholesterol: Trace
  Sodium: 121mg   Calories: 95   Calories from fat: 50%

## WITH BUTTER SPRINKLES
Serve with 1/2 teaspoon butter sprinkles per serving. After sprinkling on the butter sprinkles, cover briefly, then serve.

- ◆ **Per Serving:**   Saturated fat: Trace   Total fat: Trace   Cholesterol: 1mg
  Sodium: 68mg   Calories: 42   Calories from fat: 6%

# ASPARAGUS AND PARMESAN CHEESE

SERVES 4

Slightly undercook this northern Italian classic, since the asparagus will continue to cook as you transfer it to the broiler.

**1-1/2 pounds asparagus, hot but lightly cooked and drained**
**4 teaspoons Parmesan cheese**
**Coarsely ground black pepper**

Preheat the broiler. Place the asparagus on an ovenproof platter, sprinkle with the Parmesan and pepper place under the broiler until the cheese has melted. Serve immediately.

◆ **Per Serving:**   Saturated fat: Trace   Total fat: 1gr   Cholesterol: 1mg
                    Sodium: 34mg   Calories: 46   Calories from fat: 14%

## COOKED SPINACH

SERVES 4

Spinach can be hard to clean. If the supplier or packager hasn't already done it for you, then rinse each leaf under a strong spray in several changes of cold water. If you want to use the stems, cut them into 1-inch pieces. One pound of spinach looks like a lot, though it cooks down dramatically, so use a very large pot. You can chop it, cut or tear it into 3 or 4-inch pieces or leave it whole. Serve it with malt vinegar or fresh lemon juice.

**1 pound loose spinach or 1 10-ounce Cellophane pack, washed**
**Malt vinegar or fresh lemon juice**

In a large pot, cook the spinach only in the water clinging to the leaves, just until it wilts. Pour into a colander and cover for a few minutes (it will keep cooking while it drains so be careful not to overcook). Drain well and serve hot with vinegar or lemon juice.

◆ **Per Serving:**   Saturated fat: Trace   Total fat: Trace   Cholesterol: 0
                    Sodium: 89mg   Calories: 25   Calories from fat: 10%

WITH MARGARINE
Serve with 2 teaspoons margarine.

◆ **Per Serving:**   Saturated fat: Trace   Total fat: 2gr   Cholesterol: 0
                    Sodium: 111mg   Calories: 42   Calories from fat: 42%

## WITH MARGARINE AND CRUMBLED BACON

Serve with 2 teaspoons margarine and 1/4 cup of cooked, defatted crumbled bacon.

◆ **Per Serving:**  Saturated fat: 1gr    Total fat: 3gr    Cholesterol: 3mg
Sodium: 201mg   Calories: 53    Calories from fat: 42%

## CREAMED SPINACH

SERVES 4

This tastes like the fanciest creamed spinach you've ever had, full of flavor and without the fat. Green onion, parsley and a hint of nutmeg blend with the garden freshness of spinach for an unbeatable taste. It's versatile enough for dinner parties or for family. Garnish with tiny leaves placed on a slice or wedge of lemon and sprinkle them with a pinch of nutmeg. The spinach must be very dry or the combination will become watery.

1 10-ounce package frozen chopped spinach, thawed and
squeezed almost dry, or 1 pound fresh spinach, washed and
trimmed, wilted and chopped (1-1/2 cups)
1/2 cup substitute egg
1 cup nonfat cottage cheese, pureed in a blender
1 cup finely sliced scallions, including green parts
1/2 cup chopped parsley
1/4 teaspoon grated nutmeg
1/2 teaspoon low-sodium salt (optional)
Pepper
Vegetable cooking spray

Preheat the oven to 325° degrees if baking.

In a medium bowl, combine the spinach and substitute egg. Beat with a large whisk to blend well, then beat in the pureed cottage cheese, scallion, parsley, nutmeg, salt, if using, and pepper. Spray a 1-quart baking dish with vegetable oil. Transfer the spinach mixture to the dish. Microwave for 10 minutes, turning once, or bake for 45 minutes or until bubbly at the edges. Let stand for 5 minutes. Serve hot.

◆ Per Serving:  Saturated fat: 1gr  Total fat: 4gr  Cholesterol: 3mg
Sodium: 160mg  Calories: 114  Calories from fat: 30%

## SPINACH WITH GARLIC AND OLIVE OIL

SERVES 4

This Sicilian-style spinach is very good. Cut the spinach leaves in half if they are more than 5 inches wide. The garlic is cooked separately in water allowing you to use less olive oil but still giving the full flavor of the oil on the spinach.

Olive oil spray
1 clove garlic, minced
1 pound loose spinach, washed and trimmed
1 tablespoon olive oil
Low-sodium salt (optional)

Spray a very large nonstick skillet lightly, combine a few teaspoons of water and the garlic and cook the garlic lightly without burning it, stirring often, about 2 minutes. Add the olive oil, swirl around the garlic over medium heat for 30 seconds, then add the spinach (it will spatter). Stir well to mix the garlic oil on all the spinach, turn the heat down, cover, and cook just until the spinach wilts. Season with salt, if using, and serve hot.

◆ Per Serving:  Saturated fat: 1gr  Total fat: 4gr  Cholesterol: 0
Sodium: 89mg  Calories: 56  Calories from fat: 53%

# LIMA BEANS

SERVES 4

This simple method of cooking brings out the flavor of lima beans. The baby limas don't take quite as long to cook as Fordhooks.

3 cups shelled baby or Fordhook limas
1 tablespoon fresh orange juice
1/2 teaspoon fresh lemon juice
3/4 cup water
Low-sodium salt (optional) or butter sprinkles (optional)
Pepper

In a saucepan, combine all the ingredients except the butter sprinkles and pepper in 1/4 inch of water. Cover and cook over medium heat for 15 to 20 minutes, or until the beans are soft, adding more water if necessary. Or microwave in a loosely covered dish for 10 minutes, turning once. Add salt, if using, or butter sprinkles. Cover briefly, and sprinkle with pepper. Serve hot.

- **Per Serving:**     Saturated fat: Trace   Total fat: Trace   Cholesterol: 0
  Sodium: 25mg      Calories: 184   Calories from fat: 2%

## WITH YOGURT
Add 1/2 cup nonfat yogurt to the cooked limas.

- **Per Serving:**     Saturated fat: Trace   Total fat: Trace   Cholesterol: Trace
  Sodium: 47mg      Calories: 200   Calories from fat: 2%

## WITH MARGARINE AND CRUMBLED BACON
Serve with 2 teaspoons margarine and 1/4 cup of cooked, defatted crumbled bacon.

- **Per Serving:**     Saturated fat: 1gr     Total fat: 3gr     Cholesterol: 5mg
  Sodium: 132mg   Calories: 217   Calories from fat: 12%

# PENNSYLVANIA DUTCH BEETS

SERVES 4

This is originally a Pennsylvania Dutch dish. The beets can be peeled. They will take about 15 minutes to cook when steamed or covered in boiling water.

1-1/2 pounds raw beets, sliced or quartered, and cooked
1 onion, sliced into wafer-thin rings, separated
2 tablespoons sugar
1/2 teaspoon grated lemon rind
1/2 teaspoon grated orange rind
2 tablespoons cornstarch or arrowroot
2 tablespoons fresh orange juice
1 tablespoon lemon juice
2 tablespoons cider vinegar

In a saucepan, add the cooked beets and onion rings and a few tablespoons of water and heat for 3 to 4 minutes, until the onions are soft, adding more water and covering for a minute if necessary. In a small bowl, add the sugar, lemon and orange rinds, the juices, vinegar and cornstarch or arrowroot and blend. Add to the hot beets and stir over medium high heat until thickened. Serve immediately.

◆ **Per Serving:**   Saturated fat: Trace   Total fat: Trace   Cholesterol: 0
Sodium: 71mg   Calories: 92   Calories from fat: 1%

# SWEET AND SOUR RED CABBAGE

SERVES 4

Red cabbage is high in fiber and minerals, good raw in salads or cooked German style. If you can, serve the cabbage after just 15 minutes of cooking, it has a fresher flavor. You can also braise it for up to 1 hour, adding more water when necessary. This has a more "settled" and rich taste when it is refrigerated overnight and reheated the next day.

1 small head red cabbage, finely shredded
1 small onion, finely chopped
1 Granny Smith apple, diced
1/4 cup red-wine vinegar
1/4 cup brown sugar

In a large saucepan, combine the cabbage, onion, apple, vinegar, and brown sugar with 1/2-inch water, and cook, covered, for 15 to 20 minutes, adding small amounts of water, when necessary. Or microwave covered loosely for 12 minutes, turning once. Serve hot.

- ◆ Per Serving:   Saturated fat: Trace   Total fat: Trace   Cholesterol: 0
                   Sodium: 7mg       Calories: 96     Calories from fat: 2%

# STEAMED BOK CHOY

SERVES 4

Bok choy, a vegetable used in oriental cooking, resembles celery, but is closer to the cabbage family. It is mild, crunchy and delicious. Prepare it in a variety of ways. This recipe uses a bottled oyster sauce, available in oriental markets. Many vegetables can be substituted for the bok choy including romaine or napa cabbage.

1 pound bok choy, chopped in large, 1 to 2-inch, pieces
2 tablespoons chopped or grated fresh ginger
1 clove minced garlic
1 16-ounce jar oyster sauce

In a large skillet with several tablespoons water, steam the bok choy, ginger and garlic for about 5 minutes, adding more water when necessary, but never enough so there is more than a few scant tablespoons in the pan. Cover briefly to contain the heat. In a small saucepan, heat the oyster sauce. Drain the bok choy, mound on a serving plate or divide into individual servings onto plates and drizzle the oyster sauce over the vegetable. Serve hot.

◆ **Per Serving:** Saturated fat: Trace Total fat: 1gr Cholesterol: 0 Sodium: 5568mg Calories: 140 Calories from fat: 4%

## STEAMED CAULIFLOWER

SERVES 4

You can steam the cauliflower whole, cut it in wedges (cutting away the stem) or cut off bite-size florets.
The whole cauliflower takes longest to cook.

1 cauliflower, washed and
   trimmed
1 slice of lemon
Low-sodium salt (optional)
Pepper

In a large saucepan steam the cauliflower in a small amount of boiling water,
adding more if necessary, along with the lemon slice, until the head is barely tender, about 15 minutes. Drain and add the salt, if

using. For florets, the cooking time is much less, about 5 minutes. Serve hot.

◆ **Per Serving:** Saturated fat: Trace    Total fat: Trace    Cholesterol: 0
                      Sodium: 9mg      Calories: 35    Calories from fat: 6%

## WITH MARGARINE

Add 1 teaspoon margarine with canola as the first ingredient.

◆ **Per Serving:** Saturated fat: Trace    Total fat: 1gr    Cholesterol: 0
                      Sodium: 17mg    Calories: 43    Calories from fat: 21%

## WITH PARMESAN CHEESE

Add 1 tablespoon Parmesan cheese to the cooked cauliflower and toss.

◆ **Per Serving:** Saturated fat: Trace    Total fat: 1gr    Cholesterol: 1mg
                      Sodium: 38mg    Calories: 40    Calories from fat: 14%

## WITH NONFAT SOUR CREAM

Add 1 teaspoon nonfat sour cream per serving.

◆ **Per Serving:** Saturated fat: Trace    Total fat: Trace    Cholesterol: 0
                      Sodium: 12mg    Calories: 39    Calories from fat: 5%

## WITH CHEDDAR CHEESE

Shred 2 ounces of cheddar cheese. In a separate pan, mix 1 cup of cool skim milk and 2 tablespoons flour, heat, stirring, and add the cheese and when hot, pour over the cauliflower.

◆ **Per Serving:** Saturated fat: 3gr    Total fat: 5gr    Cholesterol: 16mg
                      Sodium: 128mg    Calories: 128    Calories from fat: 35%

# BROCCOLI IN ORANGE JUICE

SERVES 4

This is so simple, it is easy to underestimate how completely satis-fying it tastes. There is no extra fat or flavor needed, including salt, and it takes about 3 minutes. Steamed fresh broccoli, sprin-kled with fresh lemon juice also works nicely.

1/4 cup orange juice
1/4 cup water
1 pound broccoli florets, washed

In a nonstick saucepan, combine the water, orange juice and broccoli and cook, covered, for 7 to 10 minutes, or just until the broccoli is bright green. Drain. Serve hot.

♦ **Per Serving:**    Saturated fat: Trace    Total fat: Trace    Cholesterol: 0
                Sodium: 31mg    Calories: 45    Calories from fat: 7%

# BROCCOLI AND GARLIC

SERVES 4

Cooked Italian style with garlic and olive oil, broccoli's flavor is enhanced by both. The garlic is cooked separately in water to allow for less olive oil, but still keeps the full flavor.

1 pound broccoli florets
1 clove garlic, minced
1 tablespoon olive oil
Red pepper flakes
Low sodium salt (optional)
Pepper

In a large nonstick skillet, heat the garlic in 1/2 inch of water for about 2 minutes. Add the broccoli and olive oil and mix well. Cover and let steam for a couple of minutes, just until the broccoli is very green. Season with red pepper flakes, salt, if using, and pepper. Serve hot.

◆ Per Serving:   Saturated fat: Trace   Total fat: 4gr   Cholesterol: 0
Sodium: 31mg   Calories: 62   Calories from fat: 47%

### WITH ROMANO CHEESE
Add 2 tablespoons grated Romano cheese just before removing the broccoli from the skillet. Cover to melt the cheese.

◆ Per Serving:   Saturated fat: 1gr   Total fat: 5gr   Cholesterol: 7mg
Sodium: 74mg   Calories: 76   Calories from fat: 49%

## STEAMED BRUSSELS SPROUTS

SERVES 4

These tiny spheres, which look like miniature cabbages, can be very mild and sweet. They are practically a staple in England, where they are usually cooked about ten times longer than we cook them here. I like to add some sugar and herbs to the cooking water. Sprouts can also be steamed in water with little or no flavoring, like cabbage.

**20 Brussels sprouts**
**Low-sodium salt (optional)**
**1 teaspoon margarine, with canola or safflower oil as the first**
   **ingredient**

Wash the Brussels sprouts, remove any wilted outer leaves, cut the stems flat and slice into 4 wedges or lengthwise slices. In a saucepan, add the sprouts, 1 inch of water and steam until tender, about 8 to 10 minutes, adding more water if necessary. Pour out the water, add the salt, if using, and the margarine. Serve hot.

◆ Per Serving:   Saturated fat: Trace   Total fat: 1gr   Cholesterol: 0
Sodium: 26mg   Calories: 40   Calories from fat: 24%

# ORANGE BRUSSELS SPROUTS

SERVES 4

Cooked whole, Brussels sprouts can make delicious additions to winter meals. Serve with potatoes, as a side, or as an addition to other carbohydrates and meats. Brussels sprouts can be tasty and delicious, even cold in salads.

20 Brussels sprouts
2 teaspoons fresh lemon juice
2 tablespoons fresh orange juice
1 teaspoon cider vinegar
1 tablespoon chopped fresh dill
1/2 teaspoon sugar

Wash the Brussels sprouts, remove any wilted outer leaves and cut the stems flat. In a saucepan, combine the sprouts, juice, vinegar, dill and sugar with 1 cup of water, cover and cook until barely tender, about 10 to 15 minutes. Add more water if necessary. Serve hot.

◆ **Per Serving:**    Saturated fat: Trace   Total fat: Trace   Cholesterol: 0
                      Sodium: 29mg     Calories: 54     Calories from fat: 5%

WITH MARGARINE
Add 1 teaspoon margarine to the cooking water.

◆ **Per Serving:**    Saturated fat: Trace   Total fat: 1gr    Cholesterol: 0
                      Sodium: 40mg     Calories: 62     Calories from fat: 16%

# BUTTER-FLAVORED CARROTS

SERVES 4

Simple preparation brings out the best in carrots. As the basic flavor can be very different from one time to another, sometimes very sweet, sometimes almost tasteless, they need to be tasted first so you know how to complement its basic flavor. Best are freshly dug carrots with tops; next best, loose carrots with no blemishes or new growth around the stalk end.

Cooking carrots is very easy. If small enough, they can be cooked whole, which takes between 20 and 30 minutes; quartered, about 15 to 20 minutes; thick rounds, about 5 to 10 minutes; and thin rounds or julienne sticks, just a few minutes.

**6 to 8 medium carrots, sliced into 1/4-inch thick rounds**
**1 tablespoon honey**
**1/2 teaspoon low-sodium salt (optional)**
**1 tablespoon butter sprinkles**
**1 tablespoon chopped fresh parsley or 1 teaspoon chopped fresh rosemary**

In a saucepan combine the carrots and honey and steam or boil in 1/2-inch of water, covered, for 4 to 5 minutes. Drain and add the parsley or rosemary, the butter sprinkles, swirling to coat, cover for 1 minute, stir again and serve hot.

◆ **Per Serving:**     Saturated fat: Trace   Total fat: Trace   Cholesterol: 1mg
                 Sodium: 136mg   Calories: 77   Calories from fat: 3%

## WITH MARGARINE
Add 1 tablespoon margarine to the pan after draining, swirling to coat.

◆ **Per Serving:**     Saturated fat: Trace   Total fat: 3gr       Cholesterol: 1mg
                 Sodium: 159mg   Calories: 102   Calories from fat: 26%

# GINGER-FLAVORED CARROTS

SERVES 4

Carrots are a favorite for many. They are usually sweet, they taste delicious cooked in soups, stocks, stews, raw in salads, marinated, as a dipping vegetable, used as a side dish, and even for dessert in carrot cake or carrot bread. Select small, sweet carrots.

12 to 16 sweet carrots, sliced into 1/4-inch thick diagonal
   rounds
2 tablespoons honey
1/8 teaspoon ground ginger
1/2 teaspoon fresh lemon juice
1/2 teaspoon low-sodium salt (optional)
1 tablespoon chopped fresh parsley

In a saucepan combine all the ingredients except the parsley with 1/2-inch of water, and cook, covered, for 4 to 5 minutes. Drain and add the parsley or rosemary, swirling to coat. Serve hot.

◆ Per Serving:  Saturated fat: Trace  Total fat: Trace  Cholesterol: 0
                Sodium: 76mg    Calories: 96    Calories from fat: 2%

WITH MARGARINE
Add 1 tablespoon margarine to the pan after draining, swirling to coat.

◆ Per Serving:  Saturated fat: 1gr   Total fat: 3gr   Cholesterol: 0
                Sodium: 103mg  Calories: 126  Calories from fat: 18%

# STEAMED GREEN BEANS

SERVES 4

Most of us are able to buy fresh green beans almost all year round. The most popular is a hybrid of the old string bean with the strings bred out. Sometimes you find tiny haricots verts or huge flat romano beans, about 1 inch wide (cut these on the diagonal in bite-size pieces). Yellow or wax beans are available in spring and early summer.

1 pound green beans, washed and tipped
1 tablespoon chopped parsley or 2 teaspoons chopped fresh tarragon (optional)
Low-sodium salt (optional)
Pepper

In a saucepan, steam the beans in a small amount of water until they are as tender as you like. Season with parsley and salt, if using, and pepper. Serve hot.

◆ **Per Serving:**  Saturated fat: Trace   Total fat: Trace   Cholesterol: 0
Sodium: 7mg      Calories: 35    Calories from fat: 3%

WITH MARGARINE
Add 1 tablespoon margarine to the pan after draining, swirling to coat.

◆ **Per Serving:**  Saturated fat: 1gr    Total fat: 3gr    Cholesterol: 0
Sodium: 40mg    Calories: 61    Calories from fat: 39%

# COUNTRY GREEN BEANS

SERVES 4

Fresh snap beans with a splash of vinegar and a touch of sugar are memory food for folks who grew up on country cooking in the

South and some parts of the Midwest. This adaptation combines the best of an old-time seasoning trick with beans that are cooked 1990s style—crisp-tender and bright green. Add the vinegar just before serving, so the beans don't turn gray-green.

**1 pound green beans, washed and tipped**
**1/2 teaspoon low-sodium salt (optional)**
**1 teaspoon sugar**
**1 teaspoon cider vinegar**
**1 tablespoon butter sprinkles**

If large, cut the beans into 2-inch pieces; cook small beans whole. In a saucepan, cook the beans in 2 cups of water, with salt, if using, and sugar, until tender, about 10 minutes. Drain. Sprinkle with vinegar and butter sprinkles. Serve hot.

♦ **Per Serving:**   Saturated fat: Trace   Total fat: Trace   Cholesterol: 0
                     Sodium: 105mg   Calories: 45   Calories from fat: 2%

## WITH MARGARINE
Add 1 teaspoon margarine with the vinegar.

♦ **Per Serving:**   Saturated fat: Trace   Total fat: 1gr   Cholesterol: 1mg
                     Sodium: 116mg   Calories: 54   Calories from fat: 16%

## WITH HAM
Add 1 ounce diced cooked 95% fat-free ham to the cooked beans.

♦ **Per Serving:**   Saturated fat: Trace   Total fat: 1gr   Cholesterol: 5mg
                     Sodium: 200mg   Calories: 56   Calories from fat: 16%

## WITH ALMONDS
Add 1 ounce slivered almonds to the cooked beans. Season with margarine or butter.

♦ **Per Serving:**   Saturated fat: Trace   Total fat: 4gr   Cholesterol: 1mg
                     Sodium: 105mg   Calories: 87   Calories from fat: 36%

# SOUTHERN STYLE GREEN BEANS

SERVES 4

These really have the flavor of beans as they were traditionally served in the old South. The stock takes some time when you don't want the saturated fat. The rest of the defatted stock can, of course, be used as a soup base. Use the same method for spinach, broccoli, collards, or okra.

**1 smoked ham hock or 1/4 pound salt pork**
**1 pound green beans, washed and tipped**
**Pepper**

In a large pot with 2-1/2 cups water, boil the ham hock or salt pork for 15 minutes. Remove and discard the pork. Defat the broth completely with a defatting cup (see page 17). If using a ham hock, remove the meat from the bone, discard all the fat, and dice the meat. Defat the broth. You should have about 2 cups.

In a small saucepan, combine 2 cups defatted liquid, the meat, beans, and cook, covered, until the beans are as tender as you like. Season with pepper and serve hot.

◆ **Per Serving:**  Saturated fat: Trace  Total fat: Trace  Cholesterol: 4mg
Sodium: 107mg  Calories: 44  Calories from fat: 9%

# SPICY ASIAN GREEN BEANS

SERVES 4

These are the beans you will make again and again. They are very similar to the restaurant fried version, but because they are nearly nonfat, they have more flavor. Serve with a large mound of rice, and some lychees or mandarin oranges, to make a perfect vegetarian, Asian-style meal.

Vegetable spray
1 teaspoon minced garlic
3 tablespoons low-sodium soy sauce
1/2 to 1 teaspoon Szechuan or hot sauce
2 packages frozen green beans or 1 pound fresh, tipped and cut
   into thirds

Spray a large nonstick skillet. Add the garlic and soy sauce.
   Cook over medium high heat for 2 minutes, being careful not
to brown the garlic. Stir in the hot sauce and add the beans, coating each well with the mixture. Lower the heat, cover and cook
for 5 minutes. Uncover for another minute or two until all the
moisture is evaporated. Serve hot.

◆ **Per Serving:**    Saturated fat: Trace    Total fat: Trace    Cholesterol: 0
                     Sodium: 372mg    Calories: 44    Calories from fat: 3%

## ENGLISH GREEN PEAS

SERVES 4

Green peas are always an American favorite. They can be served
simply or with chopped onions which need to be steamed in a
tablespoon of water a few seconds first.

1 pound shelled fresh English green peas
Butter sprinkles
Low-sodium salt (optional)

Garnish:
Chopped red pepper

In a small, nonstick saucepan, add 1/4-inch water and boil or
steam the peas covered until tender, about 2 minutes if frozen, 10
minutes if fresh. Undercook them slightly. Sprinkle on the imita-

tion butter, cover for a few minutes, stir, salt, if using, and serve hot.

◆ Per Serving:    Saturated fat: Trace   Total fat: Trace   Cholesterol: 0
                    Sodium: 3mg     Calories: 59   Calories from fat: 4%

## PEAS, CARROTS AND MUSHROOMS IN CREAM SAUCE

SERVES 4

Peas, mushrooms and onions are wonderful companions, and they can be creamed easily.

1 cup finely chopped onions
3/4 cup sliced mushrooms
1 cup diced carrots
1-1/2 cups fresh peas
1/2 teaspoon sugar
Low-sodium salt (optional)
Pepper
1 cup evaporated skim milk
2 tablespoons cornstarch or arrowroot
1/2 cup skim milk

In a large nonstick skillet, heat the onions, mushrooms and carrots in 1/4-inch of water, over medium heat, adding more water if necessary, until the vegetables are cooked, about 4 minutes. Add the peas, and stir in the seasonings. Add the evaporated skim milk and heat below the boiling point for 2 to 3 minutes. In a small bowl, mix the cornstarch or arrowroot and skim milk, add it to the skillet and stir over low heat until the mixture thickens, about 30 seconds. Serve hot.

◆ Per Serving:    Saturated fat: Trace   Total fat: 1gr   Cholesterol: 3mg
                    Sodium: 95mg    Calories: 142  Calories from fat: 3%

# FENNEL

SERVES 4

Fennel is a flavorful vegetable, much like celery with a mild licorice or anise-type taste. Use uncooked in salads or cooked. Trim off the stalks and foliage and, like celery, the tough base, leaving just the bulbous root.

**1 pound fennel root, slivered or julienne**
**1/2 cup water or defatted chicken stock**
**Low-sodium salt (optional)**
**Pepper**

In a saucepan, cook the fennel in the water or stock for about 7 minutes, adding more liquid if necessary. Season and serve hot.

- **Per Serving:**   Saturated fat: Trace   Total fat: Trace   Cholesterol: 0
  Sodium: 98mg   Calories: 18   Calories from fat: 7%

WITH OLIVE OIL
Add 1 tablespoon olive oil to the cooked fennel.

- **Per Serving:**   Saturated fat: Trace   Total fat: 4gr   Cholesterol: 0
  Sodium: 98mg   Calories: 48   Calories from fat: 61%

# FENNEL, CARROTS, PEAS AND RICE

SERVES 4

This is a colorful way to serve several vegetables and it can be a vegetarian main course. Cooked pasta can be substituted for the rice.

**1/2 pound fennel root, sliced thinly**
**1/2 cup defatted chicken stock**
**1/2 cup shredded carrots**
**1/3 cup peas, fresh or frozen**

2 cups cooked rice, hot
Low-sodium salt (optional)
Pepper
Chopped parsley or sweet basil

In a large nonstick skillet, heat the fennel in 1/2-inch of stock or water over medium heat, adding more water if necessary, for about 5 minutes. Add the carrots. Cook for another 2 minutes, then add the peas. Cook 4 minutes for fresh peas, an additional 2 minutes for frozen. Make a nest in the rice and spoon in the vegetables. Season to taste. Serve hot.

◆ Per Serving:   Saturated fat: Trace   Total fat: Trace   Cholesterol: 0
                 Sodium: 155mg   Calories: 158   Calories from fat: 3%

## GRILLED SUMMER VEGETABLES WITH SHRIMP OR CHICKEN ON KEBOBS

SERVES 4

Grilling vegetables on built-in or stove top grills or on the outdoor grill is yet another way to enjoy many different foods. Use a basting sauce or a light brush of olive oil, or better yet, a quick spray over the vegetables. Use slices of bell peppers, zucchini, onion, mushrooms, celery, leeks, carrots, pattypan, eggplant, turnips, parsnips, sweet potatoes, and anything else you like. Wooden skewers work better if soaked first in water. If you have more time, marinate the meats and vegetables covered in the refrigerator for 3 hours and skip the microwave stage.

1/4 cup brown sugar
2 tablespoons low-sodium soy sauce
2 tablespoons sherry
1/4 cup lemon juice
1/2 teaspoon grated ginger
6 cloves crushed garlic

12 chunks fresh pineapple
Vegetables for 4, such as 2 carrots, 2 stalks celery,
    1 sweet potato, 1 small eggplant, sliced diagonally in
    1/4-inch slices, and 12 mushrooms
1/2 pound shelled, deveined shrimp, or
    skinned defatted chicken, turkey or duck nuggets
Vegetable spray

Heat the grill. In a microwavable dish, add the sauce ingredients and stir. Add the vegetables, fruit and meat, coating each well. Heat the longer-cooking vegetables such as mushrooms, onions, peppers, eggplant, sweet potatoes, etc., covered in the microwave for 2 to 3 minutes on high, turning once or twice, covering the food with the sauce (foods should be partially cooked). Add the shrimp and shorter-cooking vegetables, stir and heat for 2 minutes. Remove and alternate foods on a metal or wood skewer, brush with sauce, spray each very lightly, and place on the grill. Close the lid, turn up the heat if possible and heat for 4 to 6 minutes, then turn and heat for another 4 minutes or until done. Serve hot.

◆ **Per Serving:**    Saturated fat: Trace   Total fat: 1gr   Cholesterol: 111mg
                      Sodium: 406mg   Calories: 255   Calories from fat: 3%

## GRILLED ONIONS, PEPPERS AND ZUCCHINI

SERVES 4

Grilling can be a delicious way to cook many vegetables, and this combination, served with chicken, fish, smoked turkey, rice or pasta and a fresh garden tomato salad is an ideal summer meal. You can heat the zucchini alone with cheese for one meal, and the onions and pepper for another meal, or all of them together.

1 pound zucchini, ends discarded, sliced 1/4-inch thick
2 large onions sliced in 1/4-inch rounds
1 red bell pepper sliced in 1/4-inch pieces

1 green bell pepper sliced in 1/4-inch pieces
1 yellow bell pepper sliced in 1/4-inch pieces
1/8 cup grated Parmesan cheese or olive oil spray
Lite Salt (optional)
Pepper

Heat grill. Lightly dust the vegetables with Parmesan or lightly spray with olive oil, salt and pepper, place on the grill, close lid (if you haven't got a lid, double the cooking time) and heat for 5 minutes, turn the vegetables and heat for another 5 minutes until tender but al dente.

◆ Per Serving:   Saturated fat: 1gr   Total fat: 1gr   Cholesterol: 2mg
                 Sodium: 67mg   Calories: 63   Calories from fat: 18%

## STEAMED SUMMER SQUASH

SERVES 4

All summer squash—yellow, zucchini, pat-typan can be cooked this easy, nonfat way. To be sure the vegetables aren't too watery when served, let the water evaporate as you cook them, or add just a minimum.

1 pound zucchini, pattypan or yellow
   squash, cut in rounds or sticks
1 small onion, coarsely chopped
Low-sodium salt (optional)
2 tablespoons chopped parsley
2 tablespoons chopped fresh summer savory
   or basil
Pepper

In a large nonstick skillet, heat the squash and onion in 1/4-inch of water over medium heat, adding more water if necessary until the vegetables are cooked, about 6 minutes. Season with salt, if using, and pepper, sprinkle with herbs and serve.

- ◆ **Per Serving:** Saturated fat: Trace  Total fat: Trace  Cholesterol: 0
  Sodium: 5mg  Calories: 27  Calories from fat: 6%

WITH MARGARINE
Add 1 tablespoon margarine to the cooked squash.

- ◆ **Per Serving:** Saturated fat: 1gr  Total fat: 3gr  Cholesterol: 0
  Sodium: 38mg  Calories: 53  Calories from fat: 44%

## STEAMED ZUCCHINI

SERVES 4

This uses all your wild, baseball bat sized zucchini grown by either you or the neighbors. Vary by cutting the vegetable into julienne strips with your food processor.

**Olive oil spray**
**1/2 teaspoon minced garlic**
**2 tablespoons low-sodium soy sauce**
**1 pound zucchini, julienned or cut into 1/4-inch wide sticks**

Spray a large, nonstick skillet, add the garlic and soy sauce and heat with a few teaspoons of water for 1 or 2 minutes, stirring. Add the zucchini, spray the vegetable lightly with olive oil, mix into the sauce and cover over low heat for 4 minutes, stirring occasionally.

- ◆ **Per Serving:** Saturated fat: 1gr  Total fat: Trace  Cholesterol: 0
  Sodium: 27mg  Calories: 22  Calories from fat: 7%

# FRIED ZUCCHINI STICKS

SERVES 4

Zucchini, like eggplant, is one of those vegetables that absorbs oil. This recipe needs the time to give it enough attention to continue with the turning to ensure even browning. They taste as good as the old variety fried in oil.

1 cup egg white
1 cup bread crumbs
Olive oil spray
4 cups zucchini sticks
Salt and pepper

Preheat oven to 375°. In a small bowl beat the egg white. In a plastic bag add the crumbs. Dip the sticks in the egg white and shake in the bag. Spray the covered sticks, place on an oven tray and bake for 10 to 15 minutes, turning once. Season and serve hot with dip of choice.

◆ Per Serving:  Saturated fat: Trace  Total fat: 1gr  Cholesterol: 1mg
Sodium: 201mg  Calories: 121  Calories from fat: 10%

# STEAMED OKRA

SERVES 4

For this dish, select only okra pods that are the smaller variety, about finger length in size. You can tell if they are tough by gently squeezing them. The bigger or tougher okra will feel tough. If they are hard, don't buy them. Cut off only the stem or conical-shaped ends.

1 pound okra
1 tablespoon fresh lemon or lime juice
Low-sodium salt (optional)
Pepper

In a large saucepan cook the okra in 1/2-inch of water until tender and bright green, about 3 minutes. Remove immediately from the heat and drain (they keep on cooking) or plunge into ice water and drain if using them in a salad. Add the lemon juice, season and serve hot or cold.

◆ Per Serving:     Saturated fat: Trace   Total fat: Trace   Cholesterol: 0
                   Sodium: 5mg        Calories: 37   Calories from fat: 4%

WITH MARGARINE
Add 1 tablespoon of margarine to the cooked okra.

◆ Per Serving:     Saturated fat: 1gr    Total fat: 3gr    Cholesterol: 0
                   Sodium: 39mg      Calories: 63    Calories from fat: 39%

# EGGPLANT, ASIAN STYLE

SERVES 4

Try to find the long skinny oriental eggplants for this dish as they have a distinctive, sweet, flavor. Snow peas and sliced water chestnuts can be added for extra flavor, texture and color. Asian or Chinese hot oil is found is most specialty food markets and fine food stores.

3/4 pound oriental eggplants
1 large onion, coarsely chopped
2 cloves garlic, minced
3 to 5 teaspoons low-sodium soy sauce
1 to 2 tablespoons brown sugar
Several drops Asian hot oil
Low-sodium salt (optional)
1/2 cup snow peas
1 can water chestnuts
2 tablespoons cornstarch or arrowroot
1/2 cup chopped scallions

Quarter the eggplants and cut them into 2-inch long by 1/2-inch wide sticks. In a large nonstick skillet, heat the eggplant, onion and garlic in 1/4-inch of water, adding more if necessary. After 4 or 5 minutes, add the soy sauce, sugar, and hot oil to taste. Add more water, if necessary, to make about 1 cup in the pan. Heat for another 8 to 10 minutes, stirring, until the eggplant is nearly cooked. Add the snow peas and water chestnuts the last 2 minutes. Cover and let them steam until heated and the snow peas are bright green. In a small bowl, mix the cornstarch or arrowroot with a 1/2 cup of water, and, moving the vegetables aside to reveal the liquid in the pan, add the cornstarch or arrowroot mixture to the skillet over medium heat, stirring until the sauce thickens, about 30 seconds. Sprinkle the scallions over the top. Serve hot.

- **Per Serving:**  Saturated fat: Trace  Total fat: Trace  Cholesterol: 0
  Sodium: 8mg  Calories: 69  Calories from fat: 2%

WITH PEANUTS
Sprinkle with 2 tablespoons finely chopped, unsalted peanuts before serving.

- **Per Serving:**  Saturated fat: Trace  Total fat: 2gr  Cholesterol: 0
  Sodium: 8mg  Calories: 96  Calories from fat: 21%

## CREAMED ONIONS

SERVES 4

This is an update of the old classic. For a true onion lover, this dish is pretty to look at, smells wonderful and tastes delicious. It also works well with large onions quartered or sliced. It is slightly different but delicious using large spring onion or scallion ends. The dish works best with fresh, pearl or small onions, but can work with canned onions (these taste different than fresh) or pearl onions in a jar. Fresh pearl onions are hard to peel unless they are parboiled first. The rest is easy.

1 pound pearl onions, parboiled and peeled
2 tablespoons sherry
1 cup skim milk
1 cup evaporated skim milk
3 tablespoons flour
Low-sodium salt (optional)
White pepper
Freshly grated nutmeg

Garnish:
Paprika
Chopped parsley

In a medium saucepan, cook the onions in 1/2-inch of water with the sherry over medium heat, adding more water if necessary, until they are cooked, about 8 minutes. Drain and peel. In a medium nonstick saucepan, whisk the flour into the milk, add salt, if using, pepper, and nutmeg to taste and cook until the mixture thickens. Add the onions and heat thoroughly but not to the boiling point. Sprinkle with paprika. Serve hot.

◆ Per Serving:    Saturated fat: Trace    Total fat: Trace    Cholesterol: 3mg
                  Sodium: 109mg    Calories: 142    Calories from fat: 3%


## STEAMED WHOLE ONIONS

SERVES 4

Steamed whole onions go with anything—meat, pasta, fish, or other vegetables. Leave the onions unpeeled. Use large sweet onions, red, yellow or white or Vidalia.

4 large onions
2 teaspoons margarine
2 tablespoons honey
Low-sodium salt (optional)
White pepper

Garnish:
**Parsley**

Cut a 1/2-inch slice off the top of the onions and place the onions in a microwave safe dish. Put a small dollop of margarine on top of each, drizzle on a little honey, cover with plastic wrap, poke a few holes in the wrap, and microwave for about 12 minutes, turning once or twice.

◆ **Per Serving:**   Saturated fat: Trace   Total fat: 2gr   Cholesterol: 0
Sodium: 25mg   Calories: 68   Calories from fat: 26%

# FOUR ONIONS AND CONFETTI PEPPERS

SERVES 4

Cooking several kinds of onions and peppers together makes a colorful accompaniment to any meal. Use four or five kinds of onions: shallots, scallions, Vidalias, leeks, Spanish onions, yellow onions, even pearl onions. Cut the larger onions into chunks so they are all approximately the same size as the smaller ones. Cut up the peppers, and mix some of the seeds into the mixture. This dish can be served with hot pasta or rice.

**3/4 pound mixed onions, peeled and left whole or cut into chunks**
**1/2 red bell pepper, diced**
**1/2 green bell pepper, diced**
**1/2 yellow bell pepper, diced**
**1 bay leaf**
**Low sodium salt (optional)**
**Pepper**
**Pinch sugar**
**1/4 cup chopped scallions**
**1/4 cup chopped chives**

In a large nonstick skillet, cook the onions for 2 minutes, then add the peppers, bay leaf, salt, if using, pepper and sugar in 1/2-

inch of water, adding more water if necessary, and cook for 4 to 6 minutes. Add the scallions and cook for another 6 to 8 minutes until all the big onions and peppers are cooked. Discard the bay leaf. Sprinkle with chives. Serve hot.

◆ **Per Serving:**   Saturated fat: Trace   Total fat: Trace   Cholesterol: 0
                      Sodium: 6mg     Calories: 52   Calories from fat: 4%

## WITH MARGARINE
Add 1 tablespoon margarine to the skillet.

◆ **Per Serving:**   Saturated fat: 1gr   Total fat: 3gr   Cholesterol: 0
                      Sodium: 39mg   Calories: 77   Calories from fat: 34%

## BRAISED LEEKS

SERVES 4

Leeks are a milder member of the onion family, and look something like a big thick scallion. Leeks are very versatile and perfect as a vegetable side dish, in soups or even stuffed.

Leeks are difficult to clean since sand hides in the layers. Trim away all but 4 inches of the green part, cut the leeks lengthwise almost but not quite to the root end and rinse well under running water. Leeks cut this way should be placed close together so they don't fall apart.

Steam or poach the leeks in a small amount of flavored liquid such as wine, stock or broth. The leeks can be steamed with small cherry tomatoes and pieces of Greek olives, capers or herbs for extra flavor.

12 medium leeks, trimmed and washed
1 cup water or defatted stock
1 teaspoon low-sodium salt (optional)
2 tablespoons chopped parsley

In a skillet or saucepan with a vegetable steaming rack, place the leeks in the water or stock and cook, covered, for 12 to 15 minutes, adding more liquid if necessary. Season with salt, if using, and sprinkle with parsley. Serve hot.

◆ Per Serving:     Saturated fat: Trace   Total fat: Trace   Cholesterol: 0
                   Sodium: 25mg     Calories: 70     Calories from fat: 4%


## WITH MARGARINE
Add 2 teaspoons margarine to the cooking liquid.

◆ Per Serving:     Saturated fat: Trace   Total fat: 2gr     Cholesterol: 0
                   Sodium: 48mg     Calories: 87     Calories from fat: 22%

## WITH OLIVE OIL
Add 2 tablespoons of olive oil to the cooking liquid.

◆ Per Serving:     Saturated fat: 1gr    Total fat: 7gr     Cholesterol: 0
                   Sodium: 25mg     Calories: 129   Calories from fat: 47%


# STUFFED GREEN AND RED PEPPERS

SERVES 4

For traditionalists, nothing beats the savory taste of ground meat in stuffed peppers. Select peppers that are more round than long, and that will stand up by themselves, or else pack them in a high-sided baking dish so they won't fall over. If you use elongated peppers, you will serve them on their side, which is also attractive. However, you should cut the top off at an angle, so when they are on their side, the stuffing faces up. You can also stuff green peppers vegetarian style, with fresh corn kernels or a meat substitute taking the place of the meat. Other vegetables can also be used, as can orzo, or another small pasta.

**4 to 6 large bell peppers, green, red and/or yellow or mixed**
**1 small onion, finely chopped**

1/2 pound 98% lean top round, ground
1 cup cooked white rice
Low-sodium salt (optional)
Pepper
1 teaspoon Worcestershire sauce
3/4 cup ketchup or tomato sauce (optional)

Preheat the oven to 400°. Cut off the tops of the peppers with a flat cut, going down about an inch, and remove the ribs and pith, and set aside. In a large nonstick skillet, heat the onion and top round in a few teaspoons of water for 5 minutes. Add the rice, salt, if using, pepper and Worcestershire sauce, and stir over the heat for 1 or 2 minutes, until everything is hot. Stuff the mixture into the peppers. Spoon the ketchup or tomato sauce, if using, on top, place the peppers in a baking dish, cover with plastic wrap with a few holes poked in the top and microwave for 10 to 12 minutes, turning once or twice, then bake uncovered for 10 minutes more. Serve hot.

◆ Per Serving:    Saturated fat: 1gr    Total fat: 3gr    Cholesterol: 38mg
                  Sodium: 499mg   Calories: 210   Calories from fat: 12%

## SWEET AND SOUR PEPPERS

SERVES 4

Colorful, sweet, tangy and delicious is this blend of green, red and yellow peppers, onions and pineapple. Add some rice to make a meal, or serve as a side dish. Chopped fresh ginger can be added for extra zest.

1 green pepper, cut into 1-inch squares, seeds reserved
1 red pepper, cut into 1-inch squares, seeds reserved
1 yellow pepper, cut into 1-inch squares, seeds reserved
1 large onion, coarsely chopped

1 clove garlic, minced

1-1/2 cups fresh pineapple chunks or 1 cup canned chunks, drained

2 tablespoons cornstarch or arrowroot

1/4 cup cider vinegar

1/3 cup white sugar

1/2 cup chopped scallions

In a large nonstick skillet, cook the peppers, onion and garlic in 1/2-inch of water over medium heat, adding more water if necessary, about 6 minutes. Stir in the pineapple and pepper seeds. There should be at least 1 cup water in the skillet; add more if necessary. In a small bowl, mix the cornstarch or arrowroot, vinegar and sugar and add to the skillet, stirring over medium-high heat until the mixture thickens, about 1 minute. Garnish with chopped scallions. Serve hot.

◆ **Per Serving:** Saturated fat: Trace  Total fat: Trace  Cholesterol: 0
Sodium: 6mg  Calories: 137  Calories from fat: 3%

WITH PEANUTS
Add 1/4 cup unsalted chopped peanuts or peanut butter to the skillet.

◆ **Per Serving:** Saturated fat: 1gr  Total fat: 5gr  Cholesterol: 0
Sodium: 6mg  Calories: 183  Calories from fat: 23%

## STEAMED CELERY

SERVES 4

Celery is one of the vegetables most people like in almost anything—as a side dish, raw in salads, cooked in soups, casseroles and stews, but seldom serve cooked and alone. This is a simple steamed or braised version.

1 pound celery, washed and cut into 2-inch pieces, with tops
    coarsely chopped
1/2 cup defatted chicken stock
Low-sodium salt (optional)
Pepper
2 tablespoons chopped parsley

In a saucepan, steam the celery in the stock, adding more if necessary, for about 5 minutes. Season with salt, if using, and pepper.
Sprinkle with parsley and serve.

◆ Per Serving:     Saturated fat: Trace   Total fat: Trace   Cholesterol: 0
                    Sodium: 170mg   Calories: 20    Calories from fat: 89%

WITH MARGARINE
Add 1 teaspoon margarine to the stock.

◆ Per Serving:     Saturated fat: Trace   Total fat: 1gr     Cholesterol: 0
                    Sodium: 204mg   Calories: 29    Calories from fat: 32%

## NATURAL CORN

SERVES 4

Corn cooked in the husk
has a different, more true
corn flavor. You need a microwave for this recipe.

4 ears of corn still in the husk
1 tablespoon margarine (optional)
Low-sodium salt (optional)

Examine the corn to be sure there are no worms. Cut both ends
off and remove some but not all the silk. Microwave on high for
about 10 minutes, changing the positions and turning the corn
once. With a paper towel to protect your hands, pull back and cut

off the husk, twist with another paper towel to remove the silk, and season with margarine, salt and pepper, if using.

◆ **Per Serving:**    Saturated fat: 1gr    Total fat: 4gr    Cholesterol: 0
                    Sodium: 46mg    Calories: 108  Calories from fat: 20%

## BOILED OR STEAMED CORN

SERVES 4

The second easiest way to cook corn is the old-fashioned way (the easiest is in the microwave, unshucked), covered in boiling water (some people add a little milk and a teaspoonful of sugar). It is easier to use only an inch of water, however, add the sugar if you like.

**4 ears shucked corn**
**Butter sprinkles (optional)**

In a large pot with a lid, heat the corn on high heat with 1 inch of water for about 7 minutes. Remove, shake on the sprinkles, if using, and cover for one minute. Serve hot.

◆ **Per Serving:**    Saturated fat: Trace  Total fat: 1gr    Cholesterol: 0
                    Sodium: 13mg    Calories: 83    Calories from fat: 9%

WITH MARGARINE
Substitute 1 teaspoon margarine instead of butter sprinkles for each ear of corn.

◆ **Per Serving:**    Saturated fat: 1gr    Total fat: 5gr    Cholesterol: 0
                    Sodium: 58mg    Calories: 117  Calories from fat: 33%

# CORN AND PASTA

SERVES 4

Two starchy foods, one crisp, the other soft, work quite well together. If you like a color contrast in foods, add some chopped black olives, or for a stronger flavor, chopped, pitted Greek olives or chopped sun-dried tomatoes. All alone, the dish is delicately pale. The red pepper flakes add enough color and heat, if you like that.

1 onion, finely chopped
4 ears corn, kernels removed
2 cups cooked pinwheel pasta
1 tablespoon grated Parmesan or other cheese
Low-sodium salt (optional)
Pepper or red pepper flakes

In a nonstick skillet, heat the onion in a small amount of water until slightly undercooked, about 4 to 5 minutes, adding more water if necessary. Add the corn kernels and the pasta and heat for just a few minutes, adding a little more water if necessary. Sprinkle on the cheese, mix and serve hot.

◆ Per Serving:   Saturated fat: Trace   Total fat: 2gr   Cholesterol: 1mg
                 Sodium: 38mg   Calories: 197   Calories from fat: 8%

WITH MORE CHEESE
Add an additional 3 tablespoons cheese.

◆ Per Serving:   Saturated fat: 1gr   Total fat: 3gr   Cholesterol: 5mg
                 Sodium: 109mg   Calories: 214   Calories from fat: 12%

# CORN, SQUASH AND PEPPERS

SERVES 4

This is the famous triad of vegetables
that all came from the Americas, and
make a complete food when
combined. It is especially good
when you use fresh corn that
has been stored for several
days, any sweet squash such as
golden, butternut or acorn, and a
mixture of green and red peppers.
Onions can be added for extra flavor.
It can be baked, microwaved, pre-boiled or
cooked on the stove top; each way imparts a
slightly different flavor.

The quickest way is to cook all the vegetables separately. Boil
the squash, microwave the corn and add the peppers and spices
to the cooked vegetables, but if you like short prep, long cook,
let them all cook together inside the squash halves, in the oven
for an hour.

To speed up the cooking time of the squash, julienne it in
your food processor and heat everything at once in the skillet.

2 pounds sweet squash, acorn or butternut,
   halved and scooped, some seeds reserved,
   cut into small chunks
2 cups fresh or frozen corn kernels
1 large, chopped Spanish onion
1 red pepper, coarsely slivered, seeds reserved
1 green pepper, coarsely slivered, seeds reserved
Low-sodium salt (optional)
1/2 teaspoon maple syrup
Pepper
Chopped fresh parsley

In a large covered pot, boil the squash for about 10 minutes. In a nonstick skillet with 1/2-inch water, heat the corn, onions and peppers. Season and serve hot.

◆ **Per Serving:**   Saturated fat: Trace   Total fat: 1gr   Cholesterol: 0
Sodium: 23mg      Calories: 213   Calories from fat: 6%

### WITH CANOLA MARGARINE
Add 1 teaspoon margarine, with canola as the first ingredient.

◆ **Per Serving:**   Saturated fat: Trace   Total fat: 2gr   Cholesterol: 0
Sodium: 34mg      Calories: 222   Calories from fat: 8%

## SAUTÉED MUSHROOMS

SERVES 4

Mushrooms sautéed in olive oil can be served as an appetizer, as a side dish, a main dish or in a salad. You can add some Madeira if you desire a rich wine taste.

2 tablespoons olive oil
1 pound mushrooms, cleaned and sliced
2 tablespoons chopped shallots or onions
Low-sodium salt (optional)
Pepper

In a large nonstick skillet, heat the olive oil and add the mushrooms and onions. Cook until tender, adding the seasonings during or after cooking. Serve hot or cold.

◆ **Per Serving:**   Saturated fat: 1gr   Total fat: 7gr   Cholesterol: 0
Sodium: 5mg      Calories: 91   Calories from fat: 65%

# CREAMED MUSHROOMS

SERVES 4

Creamy and thick with lots of mushrooms, vegetables and herbs, this dish is luscious. The fennel instead of celery is just as good but has a slightly different flavor. Serve over potatoes, rice, pasta or toast, or on its own.

1 pound mushrooms, cleaned and sliced
2 tablespoons finely chopped leeks
2 tablespoons finely chopped shallots
2 tablespoons grated carrot
2 tablespoons finely chopped celery or fennel
Low-sodium salt (optional)
Pepper
1 tablespoon chopped fresh basil
1 teaspoon oregano
1 bay leaf
1/4 cup white wine
1/4 cup defatted chicken stock
1 cup skim milk
1 cup evaporated skim milk
2 tablespoons flour
2 tablespoons chopped parsley

In a large nonstick skillet, cook the mushrooms, leeks, shallots, carrot, celery, salt, if using, pepper, basil, oregano, and bay leaf in the wine and stock until the mushrooms are tender. Remove and discard the bay leaf. In a small bowl, mix the skim milk, evaporated skim milk and the flour, whisking it well. Add this to the cooking mushrooms, stirring and whisking over medium low heat at least 2 minutes until the mixture thickens. Return the mushrooms to the pan, and heat thoroughly, but do not boil. Sprinkle with parsley and serve hot.

♦ Per Serving:  Saturated fat: Trace  Total fat: 1gr  Cholesterol: 3mg
Sodium: 216mg  Calories: 144  Calories from fat: 9%

# EASY STUFFED MUSHROOMS

SERVES 4

I often make this just for myself, or as a showy vegetable for company. It is always elegant and delicious. Select very large mushrooms (2 to 3 inches in diameter) since they shrink when cooked.

12 large mushrooms
1 Spanish onion, finely chopped
1/2 cup herbed bread crumbs (optional)
Chopped parsley
Low-sodium salt (optional)
Pepper

Wipe or wash the mushrooms, remove and finely chop the stems. In a large nonstick skillet, cook the mushroom stems and onion in 1/4-inch of water for about 4 minutes. Remove any excess water, mix the crumbs and parsley and season to taste with salt, if using, and pepper. Spoon the mixture into the shells. Put the stuffed shells in the skillet, cover and cook over very low heat for 15 minutes. Serve hot.

◆ Per Serving:    Saturated fat: Trace   Total fat: 1gr    Cholesterol: Trace
Sodium: 96mg    Calories: 81    Calories from fat: 11%

## WITH PARMESAN CHEESE
Sprinkle 1/2 teaspoon Parmesan cheese on each stuffed mushroom before putting them back into the pan.

◆ Per Serving:    Saturated fat: 1gr    Total fat: 2gr    Cholesterol: 3mg
Sodium: 144mg   Calories: 92    Calories from fat: 16%

# HARVARD BEETS

Harvard beets are bright and shiny, tangy and flavorful. They really don't need any garnish, but you can add some thinly sliced onions, slivers of lemon peel, or a sprinkling of chopped parsley.

1-1/2 pounds beets, cooked, peeled, and julienned,
   1/4 cup cooking liquid reserved
3/4 cup cider vinegar
1/3 cup sugar
3 tablespoons cornstarch or arrowroot

Microwave the beets in 1 or 2 inches of water for 8 minutes (or boil in a large saucepan 10 minutes, adding more water if necessary). Reserve 1/2 cup beet water. In a small saucepan, combine the vinegar, sugar and cornstarch or arrowroot. Over medium heat, add the reserved water, stirring until it begins to thicken. Add the beets, and stir until the mixture is thick and shiny. Serve hot.

◆ **Per Serving:**   Saturated fat: Trace   Total fat: Trace   Cholesterol: 0
                     Sodium: 85mg   Calories: 171   Calories from fat: 0%

# FISH & SEAFOOD

Creamed Tuna (or Salmon) and Noodles
Steamed Fish and Vegetables • Trout Amandine
Filet of Sole • Tuna Steaks with Orange/Soy Sauce and
Red Grapes • Flounder Pecan • Cajun Fish • Halibut on
Watercress Sauce • Halibut with Sherry • Monkfish with
Mustard • Tuna or Orange Roughy on the Grill
Baked Salmon • Poached Salmon or Tuna Steaks
Broiled Orange Roughy • Pollock, Oriental Style
Swordfish with Watercress Sauce • Steamed Shrimp
Shrimp Teriyaki • Scallops on Spinach
Steamed Soft Shell Clams

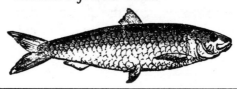

# Fish & Seafood

Clambakes, shipboard buffets, campfire cooking by the lake. These delicious times all share the same healthy element—fresh fish.

Today, no matter where we live, we can enjoy fresh fish. Modern fish-processing techniques and faster modes of transportation bring the day's catch to our neighborhoods right from the sea, lake or fish farm.

Regardless of how quickly the fish arrives at your grocer's case, you'll still want to check its freshness for yourself. Remember to use your eyes and your nose to check it. Ask to smell the fish before it is wrapped. Look for a clear, plump eye when buying a whole fish.

Health experts are investigating the omega-3 fatty acids contained in fish. They believe these may help reduce triglycerides.

As nutritious as fish may be, it is still animal protein. So, most fish contain as much cholesterol as chicken or beef. However, most fish does have less total fat and saturated fat.

Shellfish, such as shrimp, lobster and crab, are very low in fat but fairly high in cholesterol. Keep portions under 3-1/2 ounces.

Bivalves, such as clams, oysters, and mussels, are the shellfish lowest in fat and cholesterol but like all other animal protein they should be eaten sparingly about six per serving. If you want clams or oysters as an appetizer at a restaurant, ask your server if you can have just 2 or 3. New York's famous Grand Central Station's Oyster Bar serves them by the piece.

Unless you are an expert, leave the sushi making to the cook-san in a trusted Japanese restaurant or the seviche to the Mexican cocinero who really knows the quality and freshness of the fish. I love both of these but eating them can be chancy.

# CREAMED TUNA (OR SALMON) AND NOODLES

SERVES 4

Leftover vegetables and pasta or rice make a great new dish when tuna is added. Or start fresh with a quick rice, or with quick ramen or soba-style noodles, available in most food markets and all Asian markets. You can substitute canned salmon for the tuna.

**1 12-ounce can water-packed tuna or salmon, drained and broken into 1-inch pieces**
**2 cups skim milk white sauce (page 249)**
**1/2 cup frozen peas**
**Low-sodium salt (optional)**
**Pepper**
**2 cups cooked noodles or rice**
**Paprika or cayenne**

Preheat oven to 375°. Mix all the ingredients except the paprika or cayenne. Be careful not to overly mash the fish. Place in a ovenproof glass or ovenproof dish. Sprinkle the top with paprika or cayenne, and bake, uncovered, for 15 minutes (or lightly covered in the microwave for 10 minutes). Serve immediately.

♦ Per Serving:   Saturated fat: 1gr   Total fat: 3gr   Cholesterol: 38mg
                Sodium: 435mg   Calories: 311   Calories from fat: 9%

WITH LOW SATURATED FAT CHEESE
Add 1/4 cup shredded Dorman's Lo Chol cheese.

♦ Per Serving:   Saturated fat: 1gr   Total fat: 3gr   Cholesterol: 38mg
                Sodium: 441mg   Calories: 313   Calories from fat: 9%

# STEAMED FISH AND VEGETABLES

SERVES 4

I first tasted this dish in a restaurant in Portland, Oregon, and it is a fine example of how delicious steamed fish can be. Almost any mild-flavored fish that isn't over 1/2-inch thick can be used, including salmon, orange roughy, catfish or monkfish. Serve the fish and vegetables either plain with lemon slices, or dress it up with any Asian-style sauce or a tartar sauce (page 257).

1/2 teaspoon low-sodium salt (optional)
1-1/2 pounds firm-fleshed fish, cut into 4 filets
1 head iceberg lettuce
1 cup shredded or julienned carrots
1 cup shredded cabbage
1 cup shredded onions
1 cup Asian-style or tartar sauce (page 257)

Salt the fish slightly on both sides, if desired. Using a bamboo steamer (or any other kind), place several lettuce leaves on the bottom, then half of the carrots, cabbage and onions, all the fish, and the rest of the vegetables on top. Cover and steam over high heat, boiling the water vigorously for 5 to 10 minutes, or until the fish is cooked. Serve from the bamboo steamer or on a platter.

◆ Per Serving:    Saturated fat: Trace   Total fat: 2gr    Cholesterol: 52mg
                  Sodium: 248mg   Calories: 102   Calories from fat: 11%

# TROUT AMANDINE

SERVES 4

There is something about eating trout that makes you feel like you are dining at a rustic lodge. Substitute other mild white fish, such as turbot, sole, monkfish, halibut, flounder and scrod for your catch of the day. I like to use unpeeled almonds that are sliced wafer thin.

**4 pounds fresh rainbow trout**
**1/2 cup white wine**
**1/4 cup thinly sliced almonds**
**3 tablespoons lemon juice**
**1/2 cup defatted fish stock or chicken stock**
**2 tablespoons cornstarch**
**1 tablespoons flour**
**Low-sodium salt (optional)**
**1 tablespoon chopped parsley**

In a large nonstick skillet, heat the fish in 1/2-inch of white wine, adding more wine if necessary. Turn the fish to continue cooking. Add the almonds and 2 tablespoons of lemon juice when the fish is half cooked. In a saucepan, mix the fish or chicken stock with the cornstarch, flour and salt, if using, and heat. Add the remaining tablespoon of lemon juice as the sauce thickens and pour the hot sauce into the pan with the fish. Sprinkle with parsley and serve immediately.

◆ Per Serving:     Saturated fat: 1gr     Total fat: 8gr     Cholesterol: 64mg
                   Sodium: 57mg     Calories: 224   Calories from fat: 31%

## WITH MORE ALMONDS
Use 1/2 cup slivered almonds instead of 1/4 cup.

◆ Per Serving:     Saturated fat: 1gr     Total fat: 11gr     Cholesterol: 64mg
                   Sodium: 58mg     Calories: 266   Calories from fat: 38%

## BATTER-FRIED WITH MARGARINE AND CANOLA OIL
Dredge the fish in flour, dip into 2 egg whites mixed with 1/4 cup of skim milk, then coat again with more flour. In a nonstick skillet, melt 2 tablespoons of canola margarine with 2 tablespoons of canola/rapeseed oil and sauté the fish. Turn the fish, and when cooked, add the lemon juice and almonds, spooning them over the fish. Serve hot with the sauce.

◆ Per Serving:     Saturated fat: 1gr     Total fat: 15gr     Cholesterol: 64mg
                   Sodium: 126mg     Calories: 351   Calories from fat: 42%

# FILET OF SOLE

SERVES 4

A classic fish dish, mild in flavor and popular when most fish wasn't. It takes little time, has few ingredients and is an outstanding taste treat. Sole can be fish other than sole, let alone Dover sole, so don't be surprised if you order sole from your fishmonger and get something that looks more like flounder—it probably is. Dover sole is flown fresh from England and is more expensive than the regular "sole." Both (or all) are a mild, non-fishy-tasting white fish. If you have real Dover sole, which is thicker than flounder, break it in half by hand so each piece is 4 ounces, or about the size of man's palm.

**2 8-ounce sole filets, broken in half to make 4 filets**
**2 to 4 tablespoons fresh lemon juice**
**1/2 cup white wine**
**1/4 teaspoon low-sodium salt (optional)**
**1/2 cup coarsely chopped parsley**
**2 tablespoons drained capers (optional)**

In a large nonstick skillet over medium heat, cook the filets with the lemon juice, wine, salt, if using, and 1 or 2 tablespoons of the parsley for just a few minutes, occasionally spooning the sauce onto the fish, until the fish goes from translucent to opaque, which takes about 3 to 4 minutes. Sprinkle with the capers, if using, seasoning and the remaining parsley and serve.

♦ **Per Serving:**    Saturated fat: Trace   Total fat: 1gr    Cholesterol: 54mg
Sodium: 103mg   Calories: 128   Calories from fat: 10%

WITH MARGARINE
Add 1 tablespoon of margarine with the lemon juice.

♦ **Per Serving:**    Saturated fat: 1gr     Total fat: 4gr     Cholesterol: 54mg
Sodium: 136mg   Calories: 153   Calories from fat: 25%

# TUNA STEAKS WITH ORANGE/SOY SAUCE AND RED GRAPES

SERVES 4

Tuna steaks can cook exceptionally fast, right on the stovetop. Served with an orange/soy sauce and seedless red grapes, they make a very glamorous and tasty meal. Tuna can be cooked several ways: broiled, grilled or poached, which is how I do it here.

Olive oil spray
30 to 50 red seedless grapes
4 4-ounce tuna steaks, 1/2-inch thick
1 teaspoon olive oil
1/2 cup orange juice
1/4 cup lemon juice
1/3 cup white wine

Orange-soy sauce:
2 tablespoons cornstarch
1 cup orange juice
1/2 teaspoon soy sauce
Parsley

Lightly spray a large nonstick frying pan. Take half the grapes and squeeze them by hand or mash with a fork, collecting juice in the pan. You should have 1/2 cup of juice. Put the squeezed grapes in the pan and add the tuna steaks. Pour in the 1/2 cup orange juice, lemon juice and wine. Cook until just done, 2 to 3 minutes on each side. Add the remaining whole grapes to the pan.

In a small dish, mix the cornstarch, 1 cup orange juice and soy sauce. Tilt the frying pan so the juice is at one end, and with the heat on high, add the cornstarch mixture and stir until thick, about 1 minute.

Remove the fish to serving plates, pour the orange/soy sauce and remaining whole grapes over the fish, or serve the sauce on the side. Garnish and serve hot.

- **Per Serving:** Saturated fat: Trace   Total fat: 3gr      Cholesterol: 51mg
  Sodium: 284mg   Calories: 195   Calories from fat: 12%

### WITH OLIVE OIL
Use 2 teaspoons of olive oil along to the cooking liquid to cover the fish.

- **Per Serving:** Saturated fat: 1gr     Total fat: 5gr      Cholesterol: 51mg
  Sodium: 284mg   Calories: 215   Calories from fat: 20%

## FLOUNDER PECAN

SERVES 4

Lightly toast pecans, then cook the fish with them for an elegant main course. For more color, serve it with broccoli steamed in half water and half orange or lemon juice, and potatoes cooked in their jackets. Other fish, such as sole, snapper or sea trout, also work well.

Butter-flavored cooking spray
2 tablespoons finely chopped pecans
1 pound flounder filet or 4 4-ounce filets
2 tablespoons lemon juice
1 tablespoon chopped parsley
Several shakes imitation butter sprinkles

Spread the pecans on a cookie sheet, spray with butter-flavored cooking spray and broil 3 minutes, stirring twice, until the pecans are golden. Spray the fish lightly with the cooking spray and arrange in a single layer over the pecans. Pour the lemon juice over the fish and broil 3 to 4 minutes until the thickest part is opaque. Place the fish on individual plates or a large platter and sprinkle with parsley, butter sprinkles, and the pecans. Serve immediately.

◆ **Per Serving:**    Saturated fat: 1gr    Total fat: 4gr    Cholesterol: 54mg
                     Sodium: 92mg    Calories: 130   Calories from fat: 28%

## WITH MARGARINE
Use 3 tablespoons pecans and place 1/2 tablespoon soft-light or diet tub margarine instead of butter sprinkles on each portion of fish, return the fish to the broiler for 1 minute, then sprinkle with parsley.

◆ **Per Serving:**    Saturated fat: 2gr    Total fat: 9gr    Cholesterol: 54mg
                     Sodium: 163mg   Calories: 181   Calories from fat: 47%

## WITH OLIVE OIL
Use 3 tablespoons pecans and pour 1/2 tablespoon olive oil instead of dotting with butter sprinkles over each filet.

◆ **Per Serving:**    Saturated fat: 2gr    Total fat: 12gr    Cholesterol: 54mg
                     Sodium: 92mg    Calories: 202   Calories from fat: 53%

# CAJUN FISH

SERVES 4

Celebrate Mardi Gras any time of the year with fish and a spicy Cajun seasoning. It's simple and fast. You can purchase Cajun spice already prepared.

**Vegetable spray**
**1-1/4 pounds snapper, flounder, monk fish or other mild fish**
**Lemon juice**
**Cajun spice**

Coat the filets with lemon juice and sprinkle with seasoning. Lightly spray a large nonstick skillet and fry the fish, turning once. Serve immediately.

◆ **Per Serving:**    Saturated fat: Trace    Total fat: 2gr    Cholesterol: 52mg
                     Sodium: 91mg    Calories: 144   Calories from fat: 13%

# HALIBUT ON WATERCRESS SAUCE

SERVES 4

You won't know how delicious this dish is until you taste it. The sauce is so wonderful that you'll want to try it on other dishes too, because you just can't get enough of it.

2 cups defatted fish broth (can be bought)
10 scallions, trimmed and chopped
2 green peppers cored and chopped
2 bunches fresh watercress, remove stems
2 anchovy filets, rinsed and patted dry
Freshly ground white pepper
2 cups plain nonfat yogurt cheese (page 14)
Olive oil spray
4 4-ounce halibut steaks

Garnish:
Watercress sprig
Chopped almonds
Lemon zest
Lemon wedges
Black olives
Small bit of black caviar

In a saucepan, boil the fish stock. Then, blanch the scallions and peppers in it for 2 minutes. Add the watercress for 30 seconds. Turn off the heat, and add the anchovies and pepper. Then, process with an immersion blender or in a food processor until pureed. Gently whisk in the yogurt cheese.

Lightly spray a nonstick skillet and brown the fish on one side for 3 to 5 minutes, then turn and brown on the other side. Cut the fish and remove the bone. Pool the sauce on plates and add the fish. Garnish and serve.

♦ Per Serving:    Saturated fat: 1gr    Total fat: 4gr    Cholesterol: 54mg
                  Sodium: 506mg    Calories: 310    Calories from fat: 12%

# HALIBUT WITH SHERRY

SERVES 4

This way of preparing halibut produces a very mellow flavor. It looks especially pretty when garnished with watercress, and whole or chopped mandarin oranges or tangerines.

4 scallions, chopped
1 very small clove garlic, minced
1/2 to 1 cup defatted fish or chicken stock
1-1/4 pounds halibut, cut into 4 serving pieces
1/3 cup very low saturated fat sour cream (nonfat varieties work
    well too)
2 tablespoons cornstarch
3 tablespoons cream sherry

In a nonstick skillet, cook half the scallions and all the garlic in a few tablespoons of water or stock, adding more when necessary, for about 4 minutes. Add the fish, several more tablespoons of the fish stock or chicken stock, and cook the fish for 3 minutes on each side, or until it is done. Remove the fish and cover with foil to keep warm. Stir the sour cream and the fish stock or chicken stock into the skillet and heat but do not boil. Mix the cornstarch with the sherry, and stir it in over medium heat, until the sauce thickens, about 30 seconds. Pour over the fish. Sprinkle the rest of the scallions on top, garnish and serve immediately.

◆ Per Serving:     Saturated fat: 1gr     Total fat: 5gr     Cholesterol: 59mg
                   Sodium: 140mg   Calories: 253   Calories from fat: 53%

# MONKFISH WITH MUSTARD

SERVES 4

If you've never had monkfish you are in for a treat. It is sweet and tender. The mustard gives it a nice little kick. The dish takes less than 10 minutes to prepare. It can also be made with halibut, orange roughy, scrod, flounder, sole or any mild-flavored fish. The taste of the mustard is important, so use one you really love because it is the only discernible flavoring.

**Olive oil spray**
**1 pound monkfish cut into 4 equal pieces**
**1/2 cup nonfat sour cream**
**1 tablespoon skim milk**
**1-1/2 tablespoons Dijon-style mustard**
**2 tablespoons chopped chives**

Spray a nonstick skillet with olive oil spray and sauté the fish until done, about 3 minutes on each side. Either remove the fish or push it aside, and, tipping the pan, heat the sour cream, milk and mustard, mixing them well with a whisk until hot, but not boiling. Pour this sauce over the fish, and sprinkle with the chives. Serve immediately.

◆ Per Serving:    Saturated fat: Trace    Total fat: 2gr    Cholesterol: 44mg
                  Sodium: 195mg    Calories: 134    Calories from fat: 12%

# TUNA OR ORANGE ROUGHY ON THE GRILL

SERVES 4

Grilling in foil makes this orange roughly especially tender. Onions and lemons give this a special flavor. It needs no sauce; however, tartar sauce (page 257) or a mustard sauce (page 258) can be added for extra flavor.

**1-1/4 pounds tuna or orange roughy cut into 4 pieces or 4 filets**
**1 large onion sliced thinly**
**2 lemons sliced thinly**

Preheat the grill. Place each fish filet on a piece of aluminum foil large enough to be thoroughly sealed without crushing the fish. Put a quarter of the onion slices on top and several lemon slices on top of the onion. Wrap and seal the foil around the fish and place on the grill for about 8 minutes, turning once for another 8 minutes. The time varies depending on how far the foil is from the heat. Serve hot with the sauce of your choice or without sauce.

♦ Per Serving: Saturated fat: Trace   Total fat: 2gr   Cholesterol: 34mg
Sodium: 1mg   Calories: 137   Calories from fat: 11%

# BAKED SALMON

SERVES 4

This is a flavorful and tender salmon that is simple and fast to prepare. The fresh herbs add just the right amount of color. It can also be microwaved instead of baked.

**1 tablespoon olive oil or olive oil spray**
**1 pound salmon slab**
**2 tablespoons chopped fresh thyme**
**2 tablespoons chopped fresh basil**

3 tablespoons chopped fresh parsley
3 tablespoons chopped chives
Creole spices

Preheat oven to 350°.

In an ovenproof baking dish, add the olive oil and place the salmon in the dish, rubbing the salmon into the oil on both sides. Add the herbs to the dish. Rub the herbs into the salmon on both sides. Then shake the creole spices over the salmon. Bake uncovered for 7 to 10 minutes or until flaky. Serve hot.

◆ Per Serving:  Saturated fat: 2gr   Total fat: 11gr   Cholesterol: 63mg
Sodium: 185mg   Calories: 205   Calories from fat: 48%

## POACHED SALMON OR TUNA STEAKS

SERVES 4

You don't need a special pan to poach. A nonstick skillet will do. For sauce, try the wasabe, a Japanese green horseradish, which is spicy and different. Or heat the cooking juices in cornstarch mixed with wine and simmer briefly until the sauce thickens. Garnish the fish with parsley sprigs, lemon slices or a few shakes of paprika.

1/4 cup white wine
1/4 cup lemon juice
1/4 cup finely chopped onion
4 salmon or tuna steaks, no thicker than 1 inch

In a large nonstick skillet big enough for the 4 steaks, combine the wine, lemon juice and onion and heat to simmer. Add the steaks, cover and simmer gently for 2 to 3 minutes. Turn and cook for another 2 to 3 minutes. When the flesh turns opaque, the steaks are done. Serve hot.

◆ Per Serving:  Saturated fat: 1gr   Total fat: 9gr   Cholesterol: 78mg
Sodium: 64mg   Calories: 232   Calories from fat: 35%

# BROILED ORANGE ROUGHY

SERVES 4

Orange roughy is a mellow, mild fish, somewhat on the fragile side. It can be broiled, poached, fat-free fried, grilled, steamed, or microwaved. There are many good sauces for this fish, from creole to salsa (page 255) to honey mustard (page 258). Or just garnish with lemon or lime wedges.

**1/2 teaspoon low-sodium salt (optional)**
**1 pound orange roughy cut into 4 pieces**

Rub the fish with the salt, if using, and broil for just a few minutes on each side. Serve with the sauce of your choice.

- **Per Serving:**  Saturated fat: 0  Total fat: 1gr  Cholesterol: 23mg
  Sodium: 69mg  Calories: 79  Calories from fat: 12%

# POLLOCK, ORIENTAL STYLE

SERVES 4

Pollock is a mild, white-fleshed fish that is very versatile. It is most often used in imitation shrimp and crab, which are sold in nearly all supermarkets. These ersatz products are very popular because they look like shellfish but are lower in price. This pollock, however, is steamed in a classic oriental style. If you don't have a steamer, place it on a rack about 2 inches above the boiling water.

**10 ounces pollock filets**
**1 cup white wine**
**2 tablespoons low-sodium soy sauce**
**2 tablespoons sherry**
**1/2 teaspoon brown sugar**

1/4 cup fresh ginger, grated or julienned
2 scallions, chopped
1/4 cup cilantro, chopped
Strips of lemon zest for garnish

Set the pollock on the steamer rack. In the bottom of the steamer, boil 2 cups of water and the white wine. In a small bowl, mix the soy sauce, sherry, sugar, ginger, scallions and cilantro and spoon it carefully on the fish. Lower the fish into the steamer and steam, covered, for about 5 minutes, or until the fish is done. Garnish and serve hot.

- ◆ Per Serving:   Saturated fat: Trace   Total fat: 1gr   Cholesterol: 50mg
  Sodium: 72mg   Calories: 98   Calories from fat: 8%

## SWORDFISH WITH WATERCRESS SAUCE

SERVES 4

Swordfish has a wonderful flavor of its own, but it is good with many kinds of sauces. Watercress sauce has the tang that suits this fish.

4 swordfish steaks, 1/2-inch thick
1 tablespoon olive oil
Watercress sauce (page 188)
Several slices of lemon or lime

Brush the steaks with the olive oil. In a nonstick skillet, quickly cook the fish on both sides, about 2 minutes per side. Meanwhile, heat the sauce. Pour some sauce over the middle of each fish or serve it on the side. Place lemon or lime slices next to the fish and serve immediately.

- ◆ Per Serving:   Saturated fat: 2gr   Total fat: 11gr   Cholesterol: 71mg
  Sodium: 163mg   Calories: 250   Calories from fat: 40%

## STEAMED SHRIMP

SERVES 4 (Three shrimp each)

Shrimp cooks in as little as 1 to 2 minutes when steamed in a small amount of boiling water. Overcooking makes shrimp tough. Steam in the shell, serve hot or cold, and peel at the table. Good dipping sauces for hot or cold shrimp include cocktail sauce (page 252), wasabe (a Japanese horseradish sauce), nonfat mayonnaise, or any other sauce. The shrimp can also be peeled and served cold in a shrimp cocktail or as part of a salad, or hot on a bed of rice or with vegetables.

**12 medium to large shrimp**
**1 cup wine**
**1 cup water**
**1/2 teaspoon Old Bay seasoning**

Wash the shrimp well. In a large saucepan, bring the wine, water and seasoning to a boil. Add the shrimp. Cover and steam just until they turn pink and the flesh turns opaque, about 2 to 3 minutes. Drain and rinse with cold water to stop the cooking. Serve immediately, or refrigerate and serve cold.

◆ **Per Serving:**   Saturated fat: Trace   Total fat: 2gr   Cholesterol: 131mg
Sodium: 166mg   Calories: 132   Calories from fat: 11%

## SHRIMP TERIYAKI

SERVES 4

This is a Japanese and American favorite. Teriyaki sauce can be made at home, but there are many excellent bottled sauces on the market. Instead of shrimp, you can use fish, such as tuna, shark or swordfish, or chicken or lean pork strips. Skewering the shrimp and grilling them is particularly attractive. If you are serving this on a large platter, garnish it with some chopped chives or scallions. Shrimp teriyaki is delicious plain, but there are sauces that go well with it, such as oriental chili paste, available in Asian markets. Serve shrimp teriyaki with lots of rice, snow peas and Chinese vegetables.

2 cloves garlic, minced
1 teaspoon grated fresh ginger
3 tablespoons sherry
Few drops Tabasco sauce
1/2 cup teriyaki sauce
12 ounces shrimp, peeled and deveined

In a small bowl, mix all the ingredients and add the shrimp. Let the mixture stand for 30 minutes at room temperature. With a slotted spoon or your fingers, remove the shrimp (reserving the marinade) and place on a broiler rack. Brush on more marinade and broil close to the heat for 1 or 2 minutes, being careful they don't burn. Turn the shrimp over and brush them again with the marinade and broil for 1 minute. Serve immediately.

◆ Per Serving:    Saturated fat: Trace   Total fat: 2gr   Cholesterol: 129mg
                  Sodium: 1507mg  Calories: 136  Calories from fat: 11%

MORE SHRIMP
Use 1 pound of shrimp for 4 people.

◆ Per Serving:    Saturated fat: Trace   Total fat: 2gr   Cholesterol: 172mg
                  Sodium: 1349mg  Calories: 216  Calories from fat: 11%

# SCALLOPS ON SPINACH

SERVES 4–6

Green vegetables, scallops and sauce are wonderful for impromptu entertaining or as a spicy appetizer over toasted French bread, or even a "home alone" meal just for you. To use this recipe as a topping for pasta, add some tomato sauce and chop the spinach.

2 cloves garlic, minced
1 pound fresh spinach, washed and destemmed
1/8 teaspoon red pepper flakes
1/2 teaspoon low-sodium salt (optional)
1/2 pound bay scallops or sea scallops cut in half
Olive oil spray
1 tablespoon chopped chives

In a large nonstick skillet, cook the garlic in a few teaspoons of water, adding more water if necessary, until the garlic is cooked but not browned, about 2 minutes. Add the spinach, pepper flakes and salt, if using, and a few more tablespoons water. Cover and cook over moderate heat until the spinach begins to wilt, about 3 to 4 minutes, checking the water periodically, letting it evaporate until it is all gone. Remove from heat and set aside. Spray another nonstick skillet with olive oil spray and cook the scallops a few seconds on each side, until they are opaque. Mound a serving platter with the spinach, add the scallops and sprinkle with the chives. Serve hot.

♦ Per Serving:  Saturated fat: Trace  Total fat: 1gr  Cholesterol: 9mg
Sodium: 207mg  Calories: 52  Calories from fat: 10%

WITH OLIVE OIL
Cook the garlic and scallops with 1 teaspoon olive oil.

♦ Per Serving:  Saturated fat: Trace  Total fat: 3gr  Cholesterol: 9mg
Sodium: 207mg  Calories: 72  Calories from fat: 33%

# STEAMED SOFT SHELL CLAMS

SERVES 4

Soft shell clams don't really have soft shells, but they are easily removed from their shells. Some areas of the country call these long neck clams. Use the neck for holding and dipping but not for eating! Be sure to buy extra clams because you must discard the ones that don't open after steaming. Keep an eye on your cooking time because tough clams are the result of cooking too long.

**20 to 30 clams, depending upon how many you want to serve each guest**
**1/2-inch mixture of half white wine and half water**
**1/2 to 1 teaspoon Old Bay seasoning**

Scrub the clams well. In a large kettle or pot with a lid, boil the wine, water and seasoning. Add the clams. Cover, and steam for 3 to 5 minutes, or just until they open. Serve immediately.

◆ **Per Serving:** Saturated fat: Trace   Total fat: 1gr   Cholesterol: 18mg
Sodium: 30mg   Calories: 40   Calories from fat: 12%

# RED MEAT

Hamburgers • Hamburgers with Stretchers
Earth Bounty Burgers • Nutty Burgers • Beef Hash
Filet Mignon au Poivre • Beef Stroganoff
Beef Sukiyaki • Swedish Meatballs with Tomato
Romantic Lamb and Mushrooms • Sweet and Sour Pork
Glazed Ham Slices with Pineapple
Hot Dogs and Beans • Meatloaf

# Red Meat

**B**arbecues, weddings, Sunday dinners—gatherings where red meat's presence was once a status symbol. Times and tastes change but almost all of us remember with nostalgia those rich occasions. We can still bring back those moments and share those dishes with our guests. The trick to enjoying them in today's healthier diet is in choosing extremely lean cuts, removing any visible fat and serving smaller portions.

And if you want to start a new tradition, try serving mouth-watering Nutty Burgers or Earth Bounty Burgers. Open the bun and pile on the onions, lettuce and tomatoes for a not-to-be forgotten picnic delight.

# HAMBURGERS

SERVES 4 (3-1/2 oz each serving)

This tasty hamburger is made with the lowest fat content possible. To keep it from falling apart while cooking, add a bit of canola oil. If you like plain hamburgers omit the other ingredients.

3/4 pound ground 98% lean top round, all fat trimmed
2 tablespoons canola/rapeseed or safflower oil
4 tablespoons grated onion (optional)
Low-sodium salt (optional)
1/2 teaspoon Worcestershire sauce
4 to 8 leaves lettuce
4 slices tomato
4 hamburger buns split and toasted, cut side down on a griddle

Mix the meat, oil, onion, salt, if using, and Worcestershire. Form 4 hamburgers and grill or broil medium well. Add the lettuce and tomato to the bun, add the meat and serve hot.

◆ **Per Serving:**   Saturated fat: 2gr    Total fat: 13gr    Cholesterol: 59mg
                    Sodium: 319mg    Calories: 329    Calories from fat: 29%

# HAMBURGERS WITH STRETCHERS

SERVES 4

You can make a tasty hamburger with little or no fat and less meat by using stretchers such as TVP (textured vegetable protein), which is a vegetable protein. You get lots of meat taste without a lot of meat or oil.

1/2 pound ground 98% lean top round, all fat trimmed
1/4 pound or 1 cup Harvest Burger
1 cup water

4 tablespoons grated onion (optional)
Low-sodium salt (optional)
1/2 teaspoon Worcestershire sauce
4-8 leaves lettuce
4 slices of tomato
4 hamburger buns split and toasted, cut side down on a griddle

In a small bowl, mix the meat, Harvest Burger, water, onion, salt, if using, and Worcestershire. Let sit undisturbed for 12 minutes. Then form 4 hamburgers. Grill or broil until medium well. Add the lettuce and tomato to the buns, and place the meat on top. Serve hot.

◆ Per Serving:    Saturated fat: 3gr    Total fat: 9gr    Cholesterol: 48mg
                  Sodium: 599mg    Calories: 344   Calories from fat: 33%

## EARTH BOUNTY BURGERS

SERVES 6–8

These contain no meat. Try them with or without a bun, and add onions, tomatoes and nonfat mayonnaise. Instead of frying, you can bake the patties in a 350° oven for 20 minutes.

1/2 cup chopped onions
1/2 cup finely chopped celery
1 tablespoon canola oil
1 cup canned soybeans, drained, mashed or coarsely chopped
1 cup cooked brown rice
1/4 cup grated low-fat cheese
1/3 cup whole wheat flour
2 substitute eggs
2 tablespoons low-sodium soy sauce
1/2 teaspoon basil
Sesame seeds for sprinkling
Vegetable spray

In a nonstick skillet, sauté the onions and celery in oil for a few minutes. Add the remaining ingredients except the sesame seeds. When the mixture is cool enough, shape into patties and cook on a griddle or in the same skillet that is sprayed lightly with cooking spray if needed. When finished, sprinkle on sesame seeds.

◆ Per Serving:    Saturated fat: 1gr    Total fat: 6gr    Cholesterol: 3mg
                          Sodium: 199mg   Calories: 159  Calories from fat: 35%

## NUTTY BURGERS

SERVES 4

These are high in protein and have moderate fat. Purchase unroasted nuts for less fat and salt.

2 egg whites
1 cup finely chopped walnuts or almonds
1/2 cup nonfat cottage cheese
1/2 cup toasted wheat germ, bread crumbs, or crushed crackers
1 clove garlic, minced
2 tablespoons sesame seeds
1 tablespoon chopped fresh parsley
1 tablespoon chopped onion
1 teaspoon low-sodium soy sauce
1/2 teaspoon thyme leaves
1/4 cup skim milk
1 tablespoon nonfat dry milk
Vegetable spray

In a medium-size mixing bowl, combine all the ingredients except the spray. Mix well. Form the mixture into 4 patties, each 1/2-inch thick. Spray a large nonstick skillet and cook the patties over medium heat on both sides until lightly browned, about 2 minutes on each side.

◆ Per Serving:    Saturated fat: 2gr    Total fat: 21gr   Cholesterol: 5mg
                          Sodium: 281mg  Calories: 328  Calories from fat: 56%

# BEEF HASH

SERVES 4 (3-1/2 oz each serving)

Heating leftover beef with potatoes and onions has always been a favorite. This recipe uses green and red peppers but they can be omitted, and fresh or canned sliced or chopped mushrooms can be added.

2 potatoes, diced
2 Spanish onions, sliced thinly
1 clove garlic, minced
1 green pepper, cut into 1-inch pieces, seeds reserved
1 red pepper, cut into 1-inch pieces, seeds reserved
1-1/4 cups diced cooked (medium well) lean beef, all fat
    trimmed
Low-sodium salt (optional)
Pepper

In a large, nonstick skillet, heat the vegetables and seeds in 1/2-inch of water, adding more water when necessary, over medium heat until the vegetables are cooked, about 12 to 15 minutes. Stir often. Add the beef near the end of the vegetable cooking time, when most of the water has evaporated. Add the salt, if using, and the pepper. Serve hot.

- **Per Serving:**    Saturated fat: 1gr    Total fat: 5gr    Cholesterol: 71mg
Sodium: 58mg    Calories: 238   Calories from fat: 18%

# FILET MIGNON AU POIVRE

SERVES 4

Filet mignon, the tenderloin section in a T-bone steak, is moderate in saturated fat and cholesterol according to USDA figures. Occasionally you will see a filet that has no visible fat in the muscle, and that is the one you will want to purchase. Although small, it is tasty and makes a perfect meal when served with a large baked potato, and two or more green vegetables, a Caesar salad (page 76) and a fruit tart. Plenty of food, yet all have little fat.

1/2 cup whole black peppercorns
1 teaspoon low-sodium salt (optional)
4 4-ounce filet mignons
2 tablespoons canola/rapeseed or safflower oil
1 teaspoon Worcestershire sauce
1 tablespoon brandy or lemon juice
Vegetable spray

Pour the peppercorns on a large cookie sheet. With the bottom of a flat heavy pan, crush them well. Add the salt, if using, to the crushed pepper. Push the meat pieces into the pepper hard, so both sides are covered with pepper. In a small bowl, mix the oil, Worcestershire and brandy and set aside. Heat a large nonstick skillet on high, spray it, and brown the filets on both sides. Reduce the heat and cook until medium done, about 7 minutes, turning once and cooking for another 7 minutes. Remove the meat from the heat and set it on a serving plate. In the same skillet, add the oil, Worcestershire sauce and brandy mixture, heating for just a minute. The sauce will be served on the side. Serve the meat and sauce hot.

◆ Per Serving:    Saturated fat: 5gr    Total fat: 18gr    Cholesterol: 95mg
                      Sodium: 72mg    Calories: 309   Calories from fat: 53%

## BEEF STROGANOFF

SERVES 4 (3-1/2 oz each serving)

By using the leanest beef tenderloin and then zero trimming it, the meat in this Beef Stroganoff recipe is nearly fat-free. The new fat-free sour creams still make this a sumptuous meal served over noodles or pasta.

1 large sweet onion, sliced into 1/4-inch slices
1 clove garlic, minced
1 pound mushrooms, sliced thick
12 ounces lean beef, cut into 1-1/2 by 1/2-inch strips
1 cup defatted beef stock (page 17)
3 tablespoons flour
1 cup nonfat sour cream
1 pound linguine or noodles made without egg yolks
Pepper
2 tablespoons chopped parsley

In a nonstick skillet cook the onions, garlic and mushrooms in 1/2-inch of water, adding more water if necessary, heating over medium heat until they are partially cooked, about 4 minutes. Meanwhile, cook the pasta until al dente.

Add the beef strips and salt, if using, to the onions and mushrooms and cook for another few minutes, until the meat is done to the desired degree. In a small bowl, add the beef stock and whisk in the flour until there are no lumps (or shake them up in a covered jar). When the meat is cooked, put the burner on low, add the stock and flour mixture and stir in until it thickens. Add the sour cream and stir in until just heated. Serve hot over the pasta and sprinkle on the pepper and parsley.

◆ **Per Serving:**     Saturated fat: 3gr     Total fat: 10gr     Cholesterol: 59mg
                           Sodium: 347mg     Calories: 715     Calories from fat: 12%

## WITH MORE BEEF
Use 1 pound of lean beef strips.

◆ **Per Serving:**     Saturated fat: 4gr     Total fat: 11gr     Cholesterol: 77mg
                           Sodium: 365mg     Calories: 749     Calories from fat: 14%

# BEEF SUKIYAKI

SERVES 4

This Japanese "friendship dish" is pretty and healthy with very lean beef and lots of vegetables. You can substitute sherry for the soy sauce, or use them half and half. The raw food is arranged on one or two large platters, with an electric skillet in the center. Each person cooks a portion, taking some of the onions and cabbage as it is ready. Have a pitcher on the table with the soy, stock and sugar mixture and keep adding it to the cooking food. Serve with cooked rice.

4 scallions, 8 inches long, shredded or sliced lengthwise
1 tablespoon canola/rapeseed or safflower oil
3/4 pound lean top round, all fat removed, sliced 1/8-inch thick
    by 1/2-inch wide and 2 inches long
1 cup thinly sliced onions
1/2 cup canned sliced bamboo shoots, well drained
2 cups thinly sliced mushrooms
1 cup Chinese cabbage, shredded
1/2 cup diced tofu
4 tablespoons low-sodium soy sauce
1-1/2 cups defatted beef stock or water
1 teaspoon sugar

Place one shredded scallion on the side of each individual plate, which is in front of each person. Spread the oil around in a large, nonstick skillet, placed in the center of the table. On two platters, one on each side of the table, place mounds of beef, onions, bamboo, mushrooms, cabbage and tofu. Mix the soy, stock and sugar in a pitcher and add the mixture as the food is steaming, pouring small amounts into the skillet. Guests put what they want into the skillet, stir, heat and serve themselves. Serve hot.

◆ Per Serving:   Saturated fat: 2gr   Total fat: 9gr   Cholesterol: 59mg
                 Sodium: 406mg   Calories: 231   Calories from fat: 35%

# SWEDISH MEATBALLS WITH TOMATO

SERVES 4

Everyone adores meatballs. This version is modified for healthy eating. Rice, which if instant, can be prepared in 5 minutes, lightens the meatballs. For fresh flavor and texture often lacking in long-cooked sauces, try adding 1/2 cup of chopped plum tomatoes.

**10 ounces ground 98% lean top round beef**
**1/2 medium onion, grated**
**3/4 cup instant brown rice, cooked**
**1/4 cup water**
**Low-sodium salt, optional**
**1/2 teaspoon freshly ground pepper**
**4 ounces mushrooms, sliced thin**
**1 (15-ounce) can tomato sauce**
**1 (6-ounce) can tomato paste**
**1 teaspoon Worcestershire sauce**
**2 drops hot pepper sauce**
**1 teaspoon nutmeg**
**4 tablespoons chopped parsley**

Preheat oven to 350°. In a food processor, place all the ingredients. Mix well and shape into 1-inch balls. Fry the meatballs in a nonstick pan, discarding any fat, or arrange the meatballs one layer deep in a baking dish and bake for 15 minutes until browned, turning once.

◆ **Per Serving:**    Saturated fat: 2gr    Total fat: 5gr    Cholesterol: 55mg
Sodium: 1056mg  Calories: 242   Calories from fat: 19%

# ROMANTIC LAMB AND MUSHROOMS

SERVES 2

Make any evening romantic with this special meal. The small amount of cream is a treat and adds to the flavor. Serve this with large mounds of steamed green beans, asparagus or broccoli, cooked noodles or rice, sliced tomatoes for the salad, and fresh raspberries for dessert.

Vegetable spray
2 cups chopped mushrooms
1/2 cup minced shallots
1/2 pound lean lamb tenderloin, cut in strips or small medallions
1 teaspoon Worcestershire sauce
1 teaspoon low-sodium soy sauce
Several shakes garlic powder
1/4 cup dry red wine
2 tablespoons heavy cream
Freshly ground pepper

Spray a nonstick skillet, heat the mushrooms, shallots, lamb, Worcestershire sauce, soy sauce and sprinkle lightly with garlic powder. Cook until lamb is done to your desire, about 3 to 5 minutes. Move meat and vegetables to one side, turn off heat, tip skillet, stir in the wine, cream and any meat and vegetable juices. Place the lamb on a plate, and spoon the creamed juices over it. Season to taste with pepper and serve hot.

◆ Per Serving:   Saturated fat: 8gr   Total fat: 24gr  Cholesterol: 127mg
                 Sodium: 233mg   Calories: 427   Calories from fat: 50%

# SWEET AND SOUR PORK

SERVES 4

This is considered Asian in origin,
but it has become an American favorite.
Other foods such as red pepper, snow peas,
water chestnuts or mandarin oranges can be successfully added.
To add some spicy heat, sprinkle on some red pepper flakes. Serve
it with rice or Asian noodles to keep the Chinese theme.

1 clove garlic, minced
1 large onion, chopped coarsely
1 green pepper cut into 1-inch pieces, seeds reserved
2 carrots julienned
12 ounces lean pork tenderloin, all fat trimmed, cut into 1-inch
    cubes
3 tablespoons flour
3 tablespoons cornstarch
1/4 cup brown sugar
1 fresh pineapple or 1 20-ounce can pineapple chunks, syrup
    reserved
1/4 cup cider or rice wine vinegar
2 teaspoons low-sodium soy sauce

In a large, nonstick skillet, heat the vegetables and pork in 1/2-
inch of water, adding more water if necessary, over medium heat
for 4 to 5 minutes, stirring constantly. Cover, lower the heat and
cook for another 8 to 10 minutes, until the pork is cooked. In a
small bowl add the flour, cornstarch and sugar, mixing well. Set
the pineapple aside. Into the bowl add the syrup, if using, or 3/4
cup of cool water. Mix in the vinegar and soy sauce. Add it to the
skillet, stirring until it begins to thicken. Add the pineapple to the
skillet, stirring and heating thoroughly. Serve hot.

◆ Per Serving:     Saturated fat: 1gr     Total fat: 4gr     Cholesterol: 75mg
                   Sodium: 81mg     Calories: 337   Calories from fat: 11%

# GLAZED HAM SLICES WITH PINEAPPLE

SERVES 4 (3-1/2 oz each serving)

Purchase a large center cut of a very lean ham and trim all fat. Serve it with ham sauce (page 251) or applesauce (page 259), plenty of corn, potatoes, broccoli or peas, green salad and cornbread for a filling traditional ham meal. This ham can be baked, or microwaved covered in a bag to keep it moist, or heated on top of the stove.

1/4 cup maple syrup
3/4 pound lean, fully cooked center cut ham, all fat removed
1 16-ounce can drained pineapple rings or chunks

Brush the meat on both sides with the syrup. Using an oven bag place the ham on a rack or an overturned ovenproof dish so any excess fat will drain. Wrap up the bag well. Microwave on a turntable (or turn a couple of times for 4 minutes). Serve with the pineapple. Serve hot.

◆ Per Serving:     Saturated fat: 2gr     Total fat: 6gr     Cholesterol: 54mg
                   Sodium: 617mg    Calories: 306   Calories from fat: 17%


# HOT DOGS AND BEANS

SERVES 4

These old family favorites are easy and quick to cook. Look for the lowest fat hot dogs possible, which are not always from poultry. Check the saturated fat grams on the label. Healthy Choice has a 98 percent fat-free hot dog made of turkey, but pork hot dogs can be low too. It isn't the type of meat, but the amount of fat that is important.

2 Healthy Choice hot dogs, sliced and boiled for 7 minutes
1 16-ounce can vegetarian beans
1 green pepper, chopped

1 small onion, chopped
1 tablespoon molasses or brown sugar
2 tablespoons tomato sauce or tomato paste
1 teaspoon prepared mustard

In a microwave loaf dish, combine the hot dog slices, beans, pepper, onion, molasses or brown sugar, tomato sauce or paste and the mustard, cover and microwave for 8 to 10 minutes. Serve hot.

◆ Per Serving:  Saturated fat: Trace   Total fat: 2gr   Cholesterol: 10mg
Sodium: 696mg   Calories: 164   Calories from fat: 9%


## MEATLOAF

SERVES 4

Meatloaf can be made quickly when several of the ingredients are lightly pre-cooked, then microwaved. This meatloaf has an extender of TVP which is soy flour. You can buy it in a health food store. You can also make this without the meat. It is delicious made with Harvest Burger (page 290).

1/2 pound ground defatted lean choice top round, or Harvest
    Burger 'n Loaf prepared according to directions
6 ounces TVP
1-1/4 cup water
1 onion, chopped finely
1 stalk celery, chopped
2 inches carrot, shredded
1/2 cup tomato ketchup

In a small bowl, mix all the ingredients except the ketchup and let sit for 10 minutes. In a glass microwave loaf pan, press in the meat mixture, top with ketchup and heat on high for 10 minutes, turning twice. Serve hot.

◆ Per Serving:  Saturated fat: 2gr   Total fat: 5gr   Cholesterol: 76mg
Sodium: 1376mg  Calories: 356   Calories from fat: 32%

# POULTRY

*Juicy Roasted Chicken • Fried Chicken*
*Chicken à la King • Chicken and Apricots*
*Chicken and Mushrooms*
*Onion & Herb Chicken for One or Two*
*Sweet and Sour Chicken • Chicken, Turkey or Duck Curry*
*Chicken, Duck or Pork Stir-Fry*
*Turkey Burgers*

# Poultry

T hanksgiving, Christmas, Easter—turkey, chicken, Cornish hen and duck. Holidays and foods abound with traditions. You can enjoy all poultry on a low-fat, low-cholesterol diet.

Although the cholesterol remains the same (75 milligrams for every 3-1/2 ounces), poultry's fat can be reduced by skinning and trimming off all fat—even on a duck. When duck is skinned and defatted, it is nearly the same as chicken in fat and cholesterol content.

Like all animal products, you may wish to eat poultry in 3-1/2 ounce servings, which is about the size of a deck of cards. This will help keep your intake of fat low because most domestic poultry has fat even when you remove all that is visible. With your new love of vegetables, pasta, rice and beans, animal protein is no longer the center of your meal, it's just a delicious accompaniment now.

When preparing any poultry, act as if you know for sure that it has the bacteria salmonella. Much of it may in fact be contaminated. So, rinse all raw birds and bird parts. Be particularly careful not to cross-contaminate by using the same dish, plate, marinating brush, knives and cutting boards for both the raw bird and the cooked bird. Wash your hands often with soap whenever you handle raw poultry—especially if you will be fixing something else like a salad next. Salmonella is only killed by thorough cooking. So follow some simple precautions and enjoy all poultry.

# JUICY ROASTED CHICKEN

SERVES 6

I often use this recipe with only two ingredients, chicken and seasonings on my "Low Cholesterol Gourmet" TV show and in my cooking classes and it is always a hit. It takes just 12 minutes. Serve on a large platter with grapes and other fruits, asparagus and hot rolls. You'll need an oven bag, but plain plastic bags also work if your microwave doesn't cook at too high a temperature.

1 whole frying chicken, skinned
Spice mixture such as Mrs. Dash, Spike, or Cajun-style
    spices
2 sprigs fresh rosemary (optional)
1 sprig fresh thyme (optional)

Completely defat the bird and cut off the wing ends and tail. The defatted gizzard and heart can be stuffed back into the bird. The skin, wing ends and neck and fat can be used for stock (page 17). Shake and pat the spices on both the outside and inside of the skinned, fat-free chicken, coating every part. If you are using rosemary and thyme, stuff them loosely into the bird cavity.

Put the chicken in a roasting bag, tie to seal, pierce at the top, put the bag on a small inverted ovenproof saucer (so any extra fat will drip off) and in an ovenproof pie plate or dish and microwave for 12 minutes (depending upon your microwave), turning once after 7 minutes. If there is any red visible in the joints, microwave the bird in the bag for an additional 2 to 3 minutes. Serve hot or cold.

◆ Per Serving:   Saturated fat: 1gr   Total fat: 3gr   Cholesterol: 77mg
                Sodium: 85mg   Calories: 131  Calories from fat: 24%

# FRIED CHICKEN

SERVES 4–6

This is real fried chicken, fried in oil, but there is very little oil, and the canola/rapeseed or safflower oil is less saturated than any other. You can make it spicy by adding a teaspoon of your favorite brand of Cajun spice to the bag.

**1/2 cup flour**
**Low-sodium salt (optional)**
**Pepper**
**1 chicken, skinned and defatted, cut up, or 2 whole breasts**
  **skinned and defatted, split**
**2 tablespoons canola/rapeseed or safflower oil**

Put the flour, salt, if using, and pepper to taste in a bag, add the chicken and shake the bag, coating each part well.

In a large, nonstick skillet heat the oil, but don't burn it. Add the chicken, turning the pieces over immediately to lightly coat them. Brown each side until golden. Cover the pan and cook for 12 minutes, turning once, then cook uncovered to crisp for 5 minutes. Serve immediately.

♦ **Per Serving:**   Saturated fat: 1gr   Total fat: 10gr   Cholesterol: 92mg
                     Sodium: 102mg   Calories: 250   Calories from fat: 36%

MORE OIL
Use 3 tablespoons of canola/rapeseed or safflower oil.

♦ **Per Serving:**   Saturated fat: 2gr   Total fat: 12gr   Cholesterol: 92mg
                     Sodium: 102mg   Calories: 275   Calories from fat: 42%

# CHICKEN À LA KING

Chicken à la king used to be a very popular luncheon, brunch or light supper dish. It can be made very low in cholesterol and saturated fat with no loss in taste or appeal. This is an updated, thick, rich, chicken-based repast with all the traditional tender chicken, pimentos and hard cooked egg whites, but without the yolks, cholesterol and fat. It is usually served over biscuits which are usually too high in fat, so we use English muffins or even a microwave-baked potato. A green salad, tomatoes and avocados, for instance, plus some cooked vegetables would complete this banquet staple. If you don't have hard cooked egg whites on hand, begin boiling them when you start the recipe and add them last, stirring them in. If you are using uncooked chicken, cook an extra 2 to 3 minutes.

1/2 pound fresh mushrooms, chopped, or
   1 8-ounce can chopped mushrooms, drained
1/2 red bell pepper, diced into 1/4-inch pieces,
   seeds included
2 tablespoons sherry or lemon juice
1 cup diced cooked, defatted and skinned chicken
5 hard cooked egg whites, coarsely chopped
1/2 cup coarsely chopped canned pimentos, drained
2 cups evaporated skim milk
1 teaspoon Worcestershire sauce
2 tablespoons cornstarch
Low-sodium salt (optional)
White pepper
Toast triangles, English muffins, pasta or rice

In a large nonstick skillet, heat the mushrooms and red peppers with a few tablespoons of water for about 5 minutes, stirring occasionally and adding more water as necessary. Add the sherry, chicken, hard cooked egg whites and pimento, stirring and cooking until thoroughly heated. In a small bowl, whisk the milk, Worcestershire sauce and cornstarch well and add it to the chicken mixture, stirring with a very large whisk over medium heat, until the mixture becomes thickened, about 3 minutes. Season to taste with salt, if using, and pepper. Serve hot over hot toast, muffins, baked potato, pasta or rice.

◆ Per Serving:   Saturated fat: 1gr    Total fat: 3gr    Cholesterol: 34mg
                 Sodium: 247mg    Calories: 226    Calories from fat: 12%

## CHICKEN AND APRICOTS

SERVES 6

Simple and quick, tasty and satisfying—the way chicken should be. Using a large, thick nonstick skillet that affords a higher heat without burning helps speed up the cooking time. Pitted prunes can be substituted for the apricots.

1 chicken, skinned, defatted, and cut up
1/2 cup coarsely chopped onions
1/2 cup white wine or water
1/4 cup apricot preserves
1 cup canned pitted apricots, drained
1/3 cup diced dried apricots
2 tablespoons lemon juice
1/4 teaspoon cinnamon
1/4 teaspoon turmeric
1 teaspoon low-sodium salt (optional)

Garnish:
Chopped and whole fresh mint or fresh lemon mint
Chopped or whole parsley
Chopped dried apricots

In a large nonstick skillet, combine the chicken, onions and wine, cover and cook over medium-low heat for 15 to 18 minutes, stirring occasionally. Add the remaining ingredients and cook for another 3 to 4 minutes, stirring occasionally, or until the chicken is completely done. Serve immediately.

◆ **Per Serving:**     Saturated fat: 1gr     Total fat: 3gr     Cholesterol: 77mg
                       Sodium: 90mg     Calories: 235   Calories from fat: 14%


## CHICKEN AND MUSHROOMS

SERVES 4

This classic dish is hearty and delicious and is very similar to the original version prepared by chefs in San Francisco a generation ago. This can be served with noodles or rice.

Olive oil spray
4 defatted and deboned chicken breast filets
1/2 cup defatted chicken stock
1/3 cup all-purpose or unbleached flour
1 onion, coarsely chopped
1 large clove garlic, minced
1/2 pound button mushrooms, sliced
1/4 cup dry white wine
1/2 teaspoon low-sodium salt (optional)
Freshly ground pepper
2 tablespoons minced parsley

Spritz a large nonstick skillet with cooking spray, then heat. Dust the chicken lightly with flour. Brown the chicken in the hot pan, cooking it in two batches, if necessary, until it is golden brown on both sides, about 5 minutes. Add the onion, garlic, mushrooms, wine, seasonings, cover, turn the heat low and cook for 12 minutes. Sprinkle with parsley and serve.

- **Per Serving:**    Saturated fat: 1gr    Total fat: 4gr    Cholesterol: 73mg
  Sodium: 86mg    Calories: 220   Calories from fat: 15%

## WITH OLIVE OIL
Use 2 tablespoons of olive oil to skillet for sautéing the chicken and mushrooms.

- **Per Serving:**    Saturated fat: 2gr    Total fat: 10gr    Cholesterol: 73mg
  Sodium: 86mg    Calories: 279   Calories from fat: 34%

# ONION & HERB CHICKEN FOR ONE OR TWO

## SERVES 1 OR 2

This is chicken that is perfect when you want something richly flavored and uncomplicated to prepare that you can have on the table in under 20 minutes. If you are using the thigh, cut out the fat 'almonds' between the muscles when you remove the skin. For a whole meal with foods that take about the same amount of time to prepare, serve with rice or ribbon noodles, and a large salad or slightly cooked green or yellow vegetable.

If you wish to hurry the cooking time more, remove the chicken from the skillet after 6 or 7 minutes, and microwave on high, uncovered, for 3 to 4 minutes. A small amount of white wine could also be added to the pan for taste. No moisture is really necessary because the onions supply more than enough.

1/2 teaspoon olive oil
1 or 2 pieces of completely skinned and defatted chicken
   breasts, thigh and leg or both, about 3-1/2 ounces for each
   person
1/4 teaspoon anise seed
1/2 teaspoon Cajun spice

1 large red or Spanish onion, halved and sliced
1 bay leaf
Low-sodium salt (optional)
Pepper

In a small, nonstick skillet, heat the olive oil on medium high, add the chicken and brown it well on both sides. Sprinkle on the anise seed and the small amount of Cajun spice, turning the chicken so some of the spice and seeds are on both sides. Top with the sliced onion, then the bay leaf, cover, turn the heat on low and simmer for 15 minutes. Serve hot.

- Per Serving:    Saturated fat: 1gr    Total fat: 3gr    Cholesterol: 65mg
                 Sodium: 75mg    Calories: 155   Calories from fat: 16%

## SWEET AND SOUR CHICKEN

SERVES 6

This pungent dish can bring the Orient right to your kitchen. Garnish with finely chopped scallions and sesame seeds and serve it with lots of white or brown rice.

1 small onion, sliced
4 scallions, cut diagonally into 1-inch
    pieces
1 clove garlic, minced
6 ounces canned or fresh mushrooms, sliced
    1/2-inch thick
1 green bell pepper, cut into 1-inch pieces
1/2 red bell pepper, cut into 1-inch pieces
1/2 yellow bell pepper, cut into 1-inch pieces
2 carrots, peeled and sliced into narrow,
    diagonal slices
1 tablespoon grated fresh ginger or 1 teaspoon
    ground ginger

2 tablespoons low-sodium soy sauce
1 chicken, skinned and defatted, cut into small pieces
   (thigh in half, breast in fourths, etc.), or 2 whole breasts,
   skinned and defatted, cut into 1-inch by 3-inch pieces
2/3 cup defatted chicken stock
1-1/2 cups fresh or canned pineapple chunks,
   drained, juice reserved
1 8-ounce can sliced water chestnuts, drained
2 teaspoons vinegar
2 teaspoons brown sugar
2 tablespoons cornstarch
2 tablespoons chopped scallions
1/2 teaspoon sesame seeds

In a large nonstick skillet, combine everything up to the pineapple, simmer, turning often, until all are cooked, about 12 to 15 minutes. Add the drained pineapple and the water chestnuts.

   In a small bowl, mix the pineapple juice, vinegar, and sugar with the cornstarch and pour it in the skillet. Cook, stirring, until the liquid thickens, about 30 seconds. Transfer everything to a serving platter. Sprinkle the scallions and sesame seeds over the top. Serve immediately.

◆ Per Serving:    Saturated fat: 1gr    Total fat: 4gr    Cholesterol: 77mg
                  Sodium: 145mg    Calories: 221    Calories from fat: 16%

WITH OIL
Fry the vegetables and chicken in 2 tablespoons canola/rapeseed or safflower oil.

◆ Per Serving:    Saturated fat: 1gr    Total fat: 9gr    Cholesterol: 77mg
                  Sodium: 145mg    Calories: 261    Calories from fat: 29%

# CHICKEN, TURKEY OR DUCK CURRY

SERVES 6

Guests love this extravagant-looking dinner. In separate ramekins or custard cups, offer a variety of condiments such as dried apricots, raisins or currants, fresh seedless grapes, chopped preserved or candied ginger, chopped chutney, chopped chilies, fresh South American finger or apple bananas or dried bananas, chopped walnuts, chopped scallions or onions, chopped apples, chopped hard-boiled egg whites, chopped coriander or watercress.

6 scallions, cut into 2-inch pieces
2 green peppers, cut into narrow strips, seeds reserved
1 tart apple, cored and coarsely chopped
2 whole chicken breasts (4 halves), skinned and defatted, cut
    into 1/2-inch strips
2 teaspoons mild curry powder
1/2 teaspoon low-sodium salt (optional)
3/4 teaspoon sugar
1/2 cup skim milk
1 tablespoon flour

In a large nonstick skillet, simmer the scallions, green peppers and apple in a very small amount of water for 4 minutes. Push the vegetables and fruit aside and add the chicken to the pan. Cook over very low heat for 2 minutes, turning often.

Add the curry powder, salt, if using, and sugar and cook, covered, for 2 to 3 minutes, stirring until it is blended. Stir in the milk, sprinkle the flour on top, add a little more water, and whisk or stir until well blended. Cover and cook on low heat for 5 minutes. Serve with the condiments and rice immediately.

◆ Per Serving:    Saturated fat: 1gr    Total fat: 2gr    Cholesterol: 49mg
                Sodium: 139mg   Calories: 132   Calories from fat: 15%

# CHICKEN, DUCK OR PORK STIR-FRY

SERVES 8

This is a flashy and delicious one-dish meal. It looks and tastes as if it were actually fried in fat, but it has none, unless you count the few drops of Chinese hot oil seasoning.

You can use chicken or duck (which when skinned and defatted is as low in fat as chicken) solo, or you can combine the poultry with lean pork, which is very low in saturated fat. In fact it is the lowest of all of the red meats. If you combine it, use half as much poultry.

Since it is so colorful, I've often prepared it on television shows, and it always causes quite a stir, nice comments, and hunger pangs among the crew. So I am more than confident that you, your family or guests will also find it spectacular and delicious.

For the best and most attractive results, it is important to cut the vegetables into larger, rather than smaller pieces; say 2 inches by 2 inches, with none smaller than 1 inch by 1 inch. Other vegetables can be substituted, but try and keep them bright and of different colors. For example, if you are using primarily green vegetables, add some diagonally sliced carrots, chunks of yellow bell or banana peppers, fresh or bottled roasted red peppers or pimentos, some wax beans, or even sweet potato slices.

1 carrot, cut into 1/4-inch slices
1 large onion, coarsely cut
1 stalk bok choy or celery, sliced
6 tablespoons low-sodium soy sauce
1 whole chicken or duck breast (or lean pork), skinned, boned and defatted, cut into 1-1/2- by 1/2-inch strips (about 1-1/2 cups)

1 red bell pepper, cut into 1-inch pieces
1 green bell pepper, cut into 1-inch pieces
1 yellow bell pepper, cut into 1-inch pieces
8 to 10 florets broccoli or 2-inch asparagus pieces
1 4-ounce can sliced water chestnuts, drained
3/4 pound snow peas, strings removed
Optional small amounts of cut asparagus spears, English peas,
    roasted red pepper slices, yam slices, green or wax beans
2 to 3 tablespoons cornstarch
2 to 4 teaspoons brown sugar
4 to 10 drops Chinese hot oil (available at Asian markets)

In a wok or large nonstick skillet, heat the carrot, onion, and bok choy in 3 tablespoons of the soy sauce and a few tablespoons of water, stirring often, for about 5 minutes. Add the chicken and peppers and cook for another 5 minutes. Add the broccoli, water chestnuts and snow peas and cook, stirring continually, until the broccoli and peas turn green, about 4 minutes. Make sure there is about a cup of liquid in the vegetables at all times. In a small bowl, mix the cornstarch, remaining soy sauce, brown sugar and hot oil. Add the mixture to the vegetables, stirring constantly, until the sauce thickens, about 30 seconds. Serve immediately.

### WITH CHICKEN

◆ **Per Serving:**  Saturated fat: Trace   Total fat: 1gr   Cholesterol: 18mg
                 Sodium: 29mg   Calories: 100  Calories from fat: 10%

### WITH DUCK

◆ **Per Serving:**  Saturated fat: 2gr   Total fat: 5gr   Cholesterol: 38mg
                 Sodium: 42mg   Calories: 150  Calories from fat: 32%

### WITH PORK

◆ **Per Serving:**  Saturated fat: 1gr   Total fat: 2gr   Cholesterol: 37mg
                 Sodium: 42mg   Calories: 131  Calories from fat: 16%

# TURKEY BURGERS

SERVES 4

Purchase turkey breast with the skin and bones and have the meat cutter remove all the skin, fat and bone. Look at it before you let it be ground into hamburger to be sure there is no fat. This insures more moist, flavorful turkey that has the least amount of fat since most ground turkey contains more fat than you want.

These go well on buns with all the trimmings. If the meat cutter won't grind it, process the defatted, skinned meat along with the onions and celery.

3/4 pound fat-free ground turkey breast
1/2 cup onions, finely chopped
1/2 cup celery, finely chopped
1 teaspoon Worcestershire sauce
1 teaspoon low-sodium soy sauce
1/2 teaspoon garlic salt or minced garlic
Vegetable spray

In a large bowl, mix all the ingredients well and make into 4 large, flat burgers. Spray a large, nonstick skillet with vegetable spray and fry the burgers until well done (no pinkness), covering for a few minutes. Serve hot.

◆ Per Serving:   Saturated fat: 1gr   Total fat: 2gr   Cholesterol: 49mg
                   Sodium: 109mg   Calories: 118   Calories from fat: 19%

# EGGS & EGG DISHES

Scrambled Eggs or Scrambled Eggs and Cheese
Italian Garden Frittata • Curry-Chutney Omelet
Ham and Cheese Eggs with Peppers
Huevos Rancheros • Tomato-Ricotta Omelet
Guacamole Omelet & Tomato Hot Sauce
French Toast

# Eggs & Egg Dishes

**F**luffy omelets are always a satisfying meal. And today there are many brands of both fresh and frozen substitute egg products available. Try several brands to find out which suits your taste or cooks up the fluffiest for omelets and scrambled eggs, and use the other brands for baking. Read the labels. Some egg substitutes contain small amounts of fat, but it is usually minimal. If you are on a restricted cholesterol eating plan, the reduced-cholesterol eggs in a shell will most likely still be too high in cholesterol for you.

Egg substitutes, besides tasting great, are pasteurized. This makes them safer than eggs in a shell to eat, especially in Caesar salads, egg nogs and hollandaise where the eggs aren't thoroughly heated.

# SCRAMBLED EGGS OR SCRAMBLED EGGS AND CHEESE

SERVES 4

With so many new low saturated fat cheeses and nonfat cheeses to select from, you can vary the taste of the eggs easily. So, choose from swiss to cheddar, mozzarella to muenster, cream cheese to pot, hoop or nonfat cottage cheese. The cheese can be shredded and cooked with the eggs, or added to the top of the uncooked eggs. If you wait until the eggs are cooked, cover briefly to melt. For fluffier eggs, beat the egg whites until stiff and blend into substitute eggs.

3 egg whites
4 substitute eggs
2 tablespoons water
Low-sodium salt (optional)
Cayenne or pepper

Garnish:
Chopped parsley
Cooked mushrooms

In a small bowl, beat the egg whites until frothy and mix in the substitute eggs and water, blending well. Add low-sodium salt, if using, and cayenne or pepper.

In a medium-hot, large nonstick skillet, pour in the mixture, lower the heat and cook until partially firm, mixing occasionally. Sprinkle on the parsley and serve immediately.

◆ Per Serving: Saturated fat: Trace   Total fat: Trace   Cholesterol: 0
Sodium: 123mg   Calories: 43   Calories from fat: 2%

## WITH POTATOES
Add 1 cup of hot, cooked, sliced potatoes to the eggs.

◆ Per Serving: Saturated fat: Trace   Total fat: Trace   Cholesterol: 0
Sodium: 129mg   Calories: 136   Calories from fat: 1%

# ITALIAN GARDEN FRITTATA

SERVES 4

Prepare this typical Italian omelet and topping in an attractive skillet that can be used for presentation. Frittatas can be made with any mixture of precooked vegetables, plain mushrooms, onions, or olives. A frittata can also be cooked in a 350° oven for 15 minutes.

Vegetable spray
1 cup sliced fresh mushrooms
1 cup sliced zucchini
1/2 sweet red pepper, cut into julienne strips
1/2 green bell pepper, cut into julienne strips
1 scallion, chopped
1 clove garlic, minced
4 substitute eggs, lightly beaten
1/4 cup freshly grated Parmesan cheese
Dash of freshly ground black pepper
3 tablespoons water
Dash of basil
Dash of oregano

Garnish:
Paprika
Black or green olive slices

Spray a large nonstick skillet and heat the mushrooms, zucchini, peppers, scallion and garlic in 1/4-inch of water. Stir occasionally, cooking until the vegetables are tender, about 5 minutes.

Meanwhile, in a medium-size bowl, combine the eggs with 1/2 cup of the Parmesan cheese. Add remaining seasonings and water. In the serving skillet, pour in the eggs and the vegetable mixture, cooking over medium low heat, being very careful not to burn the eggs until they are set, about 4 minutes. Serve from skillet or loosen around edges with a rubber spatula and slide onto a warmed serving plate. Sprinkle with remaining Parmesan cheese. If large, slice into wedges, garnish and serve immediately.

◆ **Per Serving:**   Saturated fat: 1gr    Total fat: 3gr    Cholesterol: 5mg
Sodium: 237mg   Calories: 74    Calories from fat: 30%

## CURRY-CHUTNEY OMELET

MAKES 4 SERVINGS

There is something satisfying about the mixture of curry and chutney. There are several kinds of curry and several kinds of chutney. Hot Bengal chutney is a liquid-like spicy blend, others, like the traditional Major Grays will need chopping. Serve with a salad and toasted bread or a lavosh.

Curry Sauce:
Vegetable spray
1 cup sliced mushrooms
1 carrot, grated
1/4 cup chopped onion
1 tablespoon curry powder
1/4 teaspoon black pepper
1/4 teaspoon ground cumin
1 cup nonfat milk
1/4 cup apple juice
1 tablespoon cornstarch
6 tablespoons commercial fresh fruit chutney, chopped

Eggs:
4 frozen substitute eggs
2 tablespoons water

Garnish:
Fresh parsley sprigs
Raisins or currants

Spray a medium-size nonstick saucepan with vegetable spray and add a few tablespoons of water. Sauté the mushrooms, carrot, onion, and curry powder until the onion is tender, stirring often, adding more water if necessary, about 4 minutes. Stir in the pepper, cumin, and milk and lightly simmer for 3 minutes, stirring occasionally.

In an unheated nonstick saucepan, combine the apple juice and cornstarch and mix well and add into the curry mixture. Turn the heat to medium high, stirring constantly, and heat until just thickened, about 2 minutes.

For the omelet, spray a large nonstick skillet, and heat to medium. Add the eggs and water and mix well. Lower the heat, stir with a fork, tilting the pan occasionally so the uncooked eggs can flow to the bottom. Make sure the omelet doesn't burn. Reduce the heat to low, cover and allow to heat for 1 minute or until solid.

Fill omelet with mixed fruit chutney. Top with curry sauce. Garnish.

◆ **Per Serving:**   Saturated fat: Trace   Total fat: Trace   Cholesterol: 2mg
Sodium: 127mg   Calories: 192   Calories from fat: 3%

## HAM AND CHEESE EGGS WITH PEPPERS

SERVES 4

You can't tell the difference between these eggs and eggs from a shell. Melted cheese and diced ham help give that lazy Sunday morning feeling.

1/4 cup chopped scallions
1/4 cup diced green bell pepper
1/4 cup diced red bell pepper
4 substitute eggs
3 egg whites, stiffly beaten
1/4 cup nonfat sour cream
1/4 teaspoon crushed red pepper flakes

1/3 cup diced (1/4-inch), low saturated fat cheese such as
   Dr. Cheddar, Dorman's Lo Chol Cheddar
1/4 cup lean ham, diced
Lite Salt (optional)

In a large nonstick skillet, cook the scallions and peppers in 1/4 inch of water, adding more water if necessary, until the vegetables are nearly cooked, about 3 minutes. Fold the egg substitutes into the egg whites, add the sour cream and blend. Add together the pepper flakes, cheese, ham and salt to the skillet, add the egg mixture, stir well, and heat over medium-high heat (taking care not to burn the eggs), until it is cooked. Serve hot.

◆ Per Serving:   Saturated fat: Trace   Total fat: 1gr   Cholesterol: 5mg
                 Sodium: 246mg   Calories: 69   Calories from fat: 10%

WITH MORE HAM
Use 1 cup of diced lean ham.

◆ Per Serving:   Saturated fat: 1gr   Total fat: 2gr   Cholesterol: 19mg
                 Sodium: 562mg   Calories: 107   Calories from fat: 19%

## HUEVOS RANCHEROS

SERVES 4

Huevos Rancheros (ranch eggs) are a Mexican omelet. They have a hot, spicy salsa-type sauce covering the eggs. You can use a combination of 4 substitute eggs and 4 fresh egg whites, or all substitute eggs.

1 clove garlic, minced
1 large onion, coarsely chopped
1 green pepper, cut in 3/4-inch squares, seeds reserved
1 cup hand-squeezed canned tomatoes, or diced fresh tomatoes,
   juice reserved
2 teaspoons chili powder

1/2 teaspoon ground cumin
1/2 teaspoon dried oregano
1/2 teaspoon chopped cilantro (optional)
Lite Salt (optional)
Black pepper
Several drops Tabasco sauce or 1/8 teaspoon finely chopped
    jalapeño peppers
4 egg whites
4 substitute eggs
Vegetable spray

In a large nonstick skillet, cook the garlic, onion and pepper in
1/4 inch of water, adding more water if necessary, until the vegetables are cooked, about 5 minutes. Add the tomatoes, 1/2 cup
of the reserved tomato juice, pepper seeds, and seasonings and
cook over medium heat for 10 minutes, stirring occasionally until
the sauce has thickened. Adjust seasonings. In a small bowl, beat
the egg whites until frothy, add the egg substitutes and beat them
both. In a large nonstick skillet sprayed with vegetable spray, cook
the eggs, scrambling them, stirring often. Remove the eggs to a
serving plate. Pour the sauce over the eggs. Serve immediately.

◆ Per Serving:    Saturated fat: Trace   Total fat: 2gr    Cholesterol: 1mg
                  Sodium: 105mg    Calories: 96    Calories from fat: 22%


## TOMATO-RICOTTA OMELET

SERVES 4

Tomatoes and ricotta are satisfying whether eaten hot or cold.
Serve with cooked green beans, sliced cooked eggplant or other
vegetables, a small dinner salad and a crusty bread for a full meal.

Ricotta filling:
3/4 cup part skim ricotta cheese
1 tablespoon nonfat milk

1 teaspoon fresh chopped parsley
1 teaspoon tarragon
1/2 teaspoon black pepper

Omelet:
Vegetable spray
8 substitute eggs
3 tablespoons cold water
Commercial or homemade salsa (page 255)

Garnish:
Pine nuts
Fresh basil leaves
Few slivers of Parmesan or low-fat mozzarella cheese

In a small bowl, mix the filling ingredients well.

For the omelet, spray a large nonstick skillet, and heat to medium. Add the eggs and water and mix well. Lower the heat and stir with a fork, tilting the pan occasionally so the uncooked eggs can flow to the bottom. Make sure the omelet doesn't burn. Reduce the heat to low, cover and allow to heat for 1 minute or until solid.

While the eggs are still moist, spread the center third with the filling at an angle that is perpendicular to the handle of the pan. Using a spatula, turn a third of the omelet over the filling to cover. Cover the pan and heat over low for about 1 minute.

Turn out onto serving dish. Top with tomato hot sauce (see recipe on following page). Garnish. Serve hot.

◆ Per Serving:   Saturated fat: 3gr   Total fat: 6gr   Cholesterol: 16mg
                 Sodium: 412mg   Calories: 137   Calories from fat: 34%

# GUACAMOLE OMELET & TOMATO HOT SAUCE

SERVES 4

This is an omelet with flair. It's a festival on a plate.

Tomato hot sauce:
1 15-ounce can unsalted tomato sauce
3/4 teaspoon hot pepper sauce
1 teaspoon ground coriander
1/4 teaspoon black pepper
1/2 teaspoon ground cumin
Dash of crushed red pepper flakes

Guacamole filling:
2 avocados, at room temperature
2 tablespoons lemon or lime juice
1/2 small onion
1 bunch cilantro
Dash of hot pepper sauce

Omelet:
8 substitute eggs
4 tablespoons cold water
Vegetable spray

Garnish:
Tomato slices
Alfalfa sprouts
Parsley
Orange wedges
Corn or tortilla chips

In a small saucepan, combine sauce ingredients; cover and simmer over low heat. While it simmers prepare the filling. Peel and halve avocados. Remove the pits. Place the avocados in a food processor fitted with steel blade along with remaining filling ingredients.

Process until partially smooth. Leave the filling somewhat chunky. Cover and set aside.

To prepare the omelet, beat the eggs with water in a medium size bowl. Lightly spray a large nonstick skillet with vegetable spray. Pour in the egg mixture. Cook over medium heat. Stir occasionally so the uncooked eggs can flow to the bottom. While the top still looks moist and creamy, spread the avocado mixture down the center of omelet. Fold the two edges of the omelet over, reduce heat to low, and allow to heat for 1 minute.

Slice into 4 portions; remove each with a spatula.

Pour one quarter of the tomato hot sauce over each serving. Top with one or a combination of the suggested garnishes.

◆ **Per Serving:**     Saturated fat: 2gr     Total fat: 15gr     Cholesterol: 0
                              Sodium: 286mg     Calories: 307     Calories from fat: 49%


## FRENCH TOAST

SERVES 4

Imagine inch-high slices of French bread topped with pure maple syrup and a lean slice of Canadian bacon, orange juice and coffee. A perfectly delicious and healthy way to start the day. For something different and aromatic, try nutmeg syrup, essence of nutmeg in a thick base of dark cane syrup. It can be bought in fine food markets.

**3 substitute eggs**
**1 fresh egg white (optional)**
**Vegetable spray**
**8 slices thick or thin, white or whole grain bread**

Topping suggestions:
**Powdered sugar**
**Maple syrup**
**Nutmeg syrup**
**Heated brown sugar**

Berry sauce or preserves
Fresh berries

In a large, shallow dish or bowl, combine the substitute eggs and egg white and whisk together. Lightly spray a large, nonstick skillet and heat on medium high. Dip the bread in the egg liquid and fry until lightly browned, turning once, until both sides are fully cooked. Cut diagonally. Serve hot with a sweet topping.

◆ **Per Serving:**   Saturated fat: Trace   Total fat: 3gr      Cholesterol: 0
Sodium: 396mg   Calories: 194   Calories from fat: 18%

# SAUCES, SALSAS, RELISHES & GRAVIES

Hollandaise Sauce

Gnocchi or Pasta Marinara Sauce Romano

Spaghetti Sauce • Beef Gravy

Chicken or Turkey Gravy • Clear White Sauce

Thick White Sauce • Curry Sauce • Ham Sauce

Cranberry Sauce • Cocktail Sauce

Barbecue Sauce • Chicken or Fish Sauce

Asian Zesty Stir-Fry Flavoring and Thickening Sauce

Garlic Salsa • Salsa • Yogurt Cheese Tartar Sauce

Mayonnaise Tartar Sauce • Sweet Tartar Sauce

Hot and Spicy Barbecue Sauce

Honey Mustard Sauce • Applesauce

# Sauces, Salsas, Relishes & Gravies

**T**asty and innovative low-fat and nonfat sauces, salsas, relishes and gravies transform ordinary meals into festive occasions.

The Asian thickening sauce (page 254) makes flavoring any stir-fry very simple. Just cook all the vegetables (and any meat or poultry) and when they are within 30 seconds of being done, add the thickening sauce for restaurant taste without the oil.

With ingredients from peaches and mangoes to tomatoes and jalepeños, salsas are refreshing to taste and have lots of eye appeal. They add a fresh new approach to fish, chips, meats, rice, and beans. They're even a treat alone.

Once relishes were thought of as condiments, little additions of flavor for some foods. Now, relishes are part of a meal, adding fresh vegetables and fruits to scaled-down meat portions.

Holidays wouldn't be the same without thick, rich gravy for our mashed potatoes. With easy to prepare defatted recipes, your turkey or roast dinner will still garner raves.

To top off all these great tastes, try one of the dessert sauces for a splendid conclusion to any feast.

# HOLLANDAISE SAUCE

MAKES ABOUT 1-1/2 CUPS

This is an absolutely delicious sauce that substitutes nicely for the butter-and-yolk-filled version. It is not totally low in fat, however, so use it sparingly. It can be used over asparagus and on many other foods. Today's substitute eggs are pasteurized, so you can use them without the concern of salmonella, a bacteria that should be treated as if it is in all partially cooked eggs. This is called finger cooking, and you'll see why.

**1/2 cup margarine, with canola as the first ingredient on the label**
**2 tablespoons lemon juice**
**6 substitute eggs, at room temperature**
**1/2 teaspoon flour**
**Few sprinkles cayenne**

In a small nonstick skillet, heat the margarine until it is melted and very hot. Add the lemon juice to the margarine and mix. In another larger nonstick skillet, very gently heat the eggs until they are lukewarm. In a food processor with a beater, add the warmed eggs. Drizzle the hot margarine very slowly into the eggs and beat well. Add the mixture back to the skillet, and with very low heat, and putting a clean finger to the side of the cooking eggs (to be sure the temperature is low), constantly whisk the eggs. Remove the mixture and process again. Sprinkle the flour on top, mix in the cayenne, and add back to the pan slowly, in increments of 30 seconds, raise the temperature one notch four times, whisking continually, until the mixture thickens. When your finger gets very warm, you know the sauce is about to get thick. Remove from heat. Serve hot.

♦ **Per Tbsp:**   Saturated fat: 1gr   Total fat: 5gr   Cholesterol: Trace
               Sodium: 83mg   Calories: 52   Calories from fat: 81%

# GNOCCHI OR PASTA MARINARA SAUCE ROMANO

SERVES 4

This is a classic Italian marinara sauce as they do it in Rome. It can be made two ways, same ingredients. I fell in love with the aroma of this sauce at the home of Mrs. Rina DeVita in Washington, DC. Mrs. DeVita removes the vegetables and leaves and serves a smooth sauce. I have done that and I have also left all the vegetables in, processing them after cooking. The sauce takes only 15 minutes, about as long as it takes to boil pasta or make gnocchi.

1 28-ounce can tomato sauce
1 large onion, quartered
1 large carrot, quartered
Tops of 4 to 6 stalks celery
4 to 5 sprigs fresh sweet basil
1 bay leaf
1 teaspoon margarine (optional)
Pinch sugar

In a large nonstick pot, add all the ingredients and simmer on medium low heat for 15 minutes, stirring occasionally. Remove the bay leaf. Place an immersion blender in the pot and partially puree, or if the sides are too low, blend in the immersion blender cup for a smoother version. Serve hot.

♦ Per Tbsp:    Saturated fat: Trace   Total fat: 1gr    Cholesterol: 0
Sodium: 82mg    Calories: 91    Calories from fat: 12%

# SPAGHETTI SAUCE

SERVES 4–6

This is a hearty, spicy spaghetti sauce, good for pizza, lasagna, pasta, ravioli or eggplant. Since it is so textured, it works just as well with or without meat. It is important to keep the pieces of food large, rather than tiny. If you have a processor, grind your own meat by cutting it into large chunks. Then, pulse the blade on and off two or three times, for a coarse cut. If not, have the meat cutter grind the lean cuts coarsely. Different brands of tomato sauce and paste are used to balance a sometimes bitter harvest with one brand.

1 onion, coarsely cut
3 cloves garlic, minced
1/2 pound mushrooms, cut into 1/4-inch slices
1 green pepper, cut into 1-inch chunks, seeds reserved
1 stalk celery, cut into 1/2-inch slices
1 28-ounce can tomatoes, liquid reserved, or 5 fresh tomatoes, chopped
1 6-ounce can tomato paste
1 10-ounce can tomato sauce
1 teaspoon sugar
1 teaspoon dried oregano
2 teaspoon dried sweet basil or 2-1/2 teaspoons chopped fresh sweet basil
2 teaspoons chopped fresh parsley
1/8 teaspoon crushed red pepper
1/2 teaspoon Lite Salt (optional)

In a large nonstick skillet, heat on medium the onion, garlic, mushrooms, pepper and celery in several tablespoons of water until partially tender, about 5 minutes, adding more water if necessary.

In a bowl, hand squeeze the tomatoes to break them up, then whisk the tomatoes, juice, and the seeds from the pepper. Add the paste and sauce, sugar, oregano, basil, parsley and crushed pepper with 1/2 cup of water and blend. Add the mixture to the skillet and heat for 10 minutes. Puree in the pot with an immersion blender. Serve hot.

◆ **Per Serving:**     Saturated fat: Trace    Total fat: 1gr     Cholesterol: 0
                         Sodium: 176mg    Calories: 107   Calories from fat: 8%

## WITH MEAT

Use 1/4 pound 98 percent lean beef (top round) coarse ground and 1/4 pound very lean pork (tenderloin) coarse ground, heating in a separate nonstick skillet. Rinse in a colander after cooking and add to the sauce just before adding the tomatoes.

◆ **Per Serving:**     Saturated fat: 1gr      Total fat: 6gr     Cholesterol: 39mg
                         Sodium: 204mg    Calories: 183   Calories from fat: 16%

## BEEF GRAVY

### MAKES JUST OVER 1 CUP

Gravy never has to have fat in it to be delicious. Nonfat beef gravy can be thick or thin, creamy or glistening. It all depends upon the ingredients and the thickener used.

Remove all the fat from the meat juices using a defatting cup, or cool it in the freezer so the fat congeals and you can easily remove it. Decide whether you wish to have a water- or milk-based gravy. Substituting skim milk or evaporated milk creams the gravy. The gravy can be thickened with cornstarch or flour. Gravy made with cornstarch may become thin if reheated. To reheat you can then substitute flour for the original cornstarch, heating it long enough to cook the flour, or you can add more cornstarch mixed in cool skim milk or water.

1/2 cup meat juice, defatted
1 cup cool water, skim milk or evaporated skim milk
2 tablespoons cornstarch or 1 tablespoon cornstarch and 1
   tablespoon flour, or 2 tablespoons flour
Pepper to taste

Heat the defatted meat liquid in a nonstick skillet. Mix the water
with the cornstarch and the seasoning, and add it to the drippings, whisking or stirring continually over low heat until the
mixture thickens. If you are using flour, sift it over the heated
drippings, whisking constantly until it thickens. If you are using
half cornstarch and half flour, mix together with the liquid before
adding it to the heated drippings, then whisk until thickened.
Serve immediately.

- **Per Tbsp:**      Saturated fat: Trace   Total fat: Trace   Cholesterol: Trace
                     Sodium: 37mg     Calories: 7     Calories from fat: 1%

## SKIM MILK GRAVY
Use 1 cup of skim milk instead of water.

- **Per Tbsp:**      Saturated fat: Trace   Total fat: Trace   Cholesterol: Trace
                     Sodium: 44mg     Calories: 13     Calories from fat: 2%

## THICKER SKIM MILK GRAVY
Use one packet of instant nonfat dry skim milk stirred into 1 cup
of skim milk instead of water.

- **Per Tbsp:**      Saturated fat: Trace   Total fat: Trace   Cholesterol: 1mg
                     Sodium: 75mg     Calories: 33     Calories from fat: 2%

## THICKEST GRAVY
Use 1 cup of canned evaporated skim milk instead of water.

- **Per Tbsp:**      Saturated fat: Trace   Total fat: Trace   Cholesterol: 1mg
                     Sodium: 55mg     Calories: 20     Calories from fat: 2%

# CHICKEN OR TURKEY GRAVY

MAKES ABOUT 1-1/2 CUPS

Turkey gravy, like chicken and beef gravy, doesn't have to have any fat to be delicious. Using defatted chicken or turkey stock (fresh or canned) makes a more glistening, clearer gravy, and the evaporated skim milk makes a creamier, whiter version. On the rare occasion you don't have enough drippings to degrease, add a small amount of water, and place it in a metal bowl in the freezer for 10 minutes, or until all the fat has risen to the top, making it easier to remove. (You'll have plenty of turkey drippings if you cook the skinned breast in an oven bag, either in the microwave or regular oven.) You may not be able to reheat this gravy as the cornstarch breaks down (for reheating, mix 1 to 2 additional tea-spoons of cornstarch in 1/4 cup of cool skim milk, water or the thin gravy). A one-step way to mix the ingredients is to take all of them (if they are cool), put them in a jar with a lid, and shake it up to mix.

**Drippings from the pan to make at least 1/2 cup of liquid, defatted by chilling or with a defatting cup**
**1 cup defatted chicken or turkey stock**
**2 heaping tablespoons cornstarch**
**2 tablespoons flour**
**1/2 cup of cool defatted chicken stock**

Pour 1 cup of defatted poultry stock in a nonstick pan and heat over medium heat. In a small bowl, blend the flour and corn-starch and mix them, whisking well, with the half cup of cool stock. Add the cornstarch mixture to the pan, and stir or whisk continually as it cooks, until the mixture thickens. Serve immedi-ately.

◆ Per Tbsp:      Saturated fat: Trace   Total fat: Trace   Cholesterol: 1mg
                 Sodium: 49mg     Calories: 3     Calories from fat: 5%

## WITH HALF EVAPORATED SKIM MILK
Substitute 1/2 cup of evaporated skim milk for half of the defatted chicken or turkey stock.

◆ **Per Tbsp:**      Saturated fat: Trace    Total fat: Trace    Cholesterol: Trace
                         Sodium: 39mg      Calories: 7      Calories from fat: 3%

## WITH ALL SKIM MILK
Substitute 1 cup of skim milk for the cup of defatted chicken or turkey stock and soften the cornstarch in 1/2 cup of skim milk.

◆ **Per Tbsp:**      Saturated fat: Trace    Total fat: Trace    Cholesterol: Trace
                         Sodium: 8mg      Calories: 8      Calories from fat: 3%

## WITH WHOLE MILK AND FLOUR
Substitute whole milk for the cup of skim milk or chicken or turkey stock and 1/4 cup flour for the cornstarch. Don't premix the flour in liquid but add it directly to the pan before the milk is added, cooking the flour and defatted drippings very slightly. When adding the milk, whisk constantly.

◆ **Per Tbsp:**      Saturated fat: Trace    Total fat: 1gr    Cholesterol: 2mg
                         Sodium: 8mg      Calories: 14      Calories from fat: 33%

## WITH SKIM MILK AND GIBLETS
In the all skim milk version, add any cooked meat you can get from the neck, plus the heart and gizzard, diced into 1/2-inch pieces.

◆ **Per Tbsp:**      Saturated fat: Trace    Total fat: Trace    Cholesterol: 2mg
                         Sodium: 21mg      Calories: 11      Calories from fat: 29%

# CLEAR WHITE SAUCE

This is a smooth simple white sauce, good as a macaroni base to which you add cheese, or use over vegetables, fish and poultry. It can be seasoned with herbs, spices or wine, but do so sparingly.

1-1/2 cups defatted chicken stock
1/2 cup defatted cool chicken stock
2 tablespoons cornstarch
1 tablespoon flour
Several shakes white pepper
Low-sodium salt (optional)

In a saucepan, begin heating 1-1/2 cups chicken stock. In a covered jar or open bowl, shake or whisk the 1/2 cup cool stock, cornstarch and flour, blending them completely. When the cooking stock is nearly boiling, lower the heat and slowly, stirring with a whisk, add the stock and cornstarch mixture, whisking until the sauce is thickened and cooking, for about 2 minutes. Pepper and salt to taste.

♦ **Per Tbsp:**  Saturated fat: Trace   Total fat: Trace   Cholesterol: 0
Sodium: 67mg    Calories: 3    Calories from fat: 7%

## WITH MARGARINE AND FLOUR

This is closer to the traditional white sauce. In a saucepan add 1 tablespoon of margarine, 2 tablespoons of flour and 1-1/2 cups of stock and seasonings. Heat while whisking, until thickened.

♦ **Per Tbsp:**  Saturated fat: Trace   Total fat: 1gr   Cholesterol: Trace
Sodium: 36mg    Calories: 12    Calories from fat: 38%

# THICK WHITE SAUCE

MAKES ABOUT 2 CUPS

This is a lovely, thick white sauce that is good on fish, chicken and as a base for macaroni sauce.

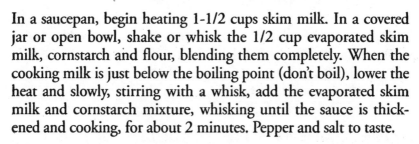

**1-1/2 cups skim milk**
**1/2 cup evaporated skim milk**
**2 tablespoons cornstarch**
**2 tablespoons flour**
**Several shakes white pepper**
**Low-sodium salt (optional)**

In a saucepan, begin heating 1-1/2 cups skim milk. In a covered jar or open bowl, shake or whisk the 1/2 cup evaporated skim milk, cornstarch and flour, blending them completely. When the cooking milk is just below the boiling point (don't boil), lower the heat and slowly, stirring with a whisk, add the evaporated skim milk and cornstarch mixture, whisking until the sauce is thickened and cooking, for about 2 minutes. Pepper and salt to taste.

♦ **Per Tbsp:**     Saturated fat: Trace   Total fat: Trace   Cholesterol: Trace
                    Sodium: 11mg     Calories: 11     Calories from fat: 3%


WITH MARGARINE AND FLOUR
This is closer to the traditional white sauce. In a saucepan add 1 tablespoon of margarine, 2 tablespoons of flour and 1-1/4 cups of skim milk and seasonings. Heat while whisking, until thickened (more skim milk can be used).

♦ **Per Tbsp:**     Saturated fat: Trace   Total fat: 1gr   Cholesterol: Trace
                    Sodium: 18mg     Calories: 16     Calories from fat: 41%

# CURRY SAUCE

MAKES ABOUT 1 CUP

Curry sauce is excellent over hot shrimp, cooked vegetables, rice, baked potatoes, fish, chicken, and scrambled egg substitutes.

1/4 cup minced onion
1/4 teaspoon sugar
2 teaspoons curry powder
1/8 teaspoon ground ginger
1 tablespoon flour
1 tablespoon cornstarch
1/2 teaspoon low-sodium salt (optional)
1 cup defatted chicken stock

In a large nonstick skillet, cook the onion in several tablespoons of water, stirring and letting the water nearly evaporate. In a bowl, mix the sugar, curry powder, ginger, flour, cornstarch and salt. Add the chicken stock and mix well. Add the liquid to the skillet, stirring or whisking until the mixture thickens. Serve hot.

◆ **Per Tbsp:**   Saturated fat: Trace   Total fat: Trace   Cholesterol: 0
Sodium: 67mg   Calories: 6   Calories from fat: 9%

CREAMED CURRY SAUCE
Substitute 1 cup of evaporated skim milk for the chicken stock.

◆ **Per Tbsp:**   Saturated fat: Trace   Total fat: Trace   Cholesterol: 1mg
Sodium: 36mg   Calories: 18   Calories from fat: 4%

# HAM SAUCE

MAKES ABOUT 1-1/2 CUPS

This is from my friend Lillian Pulitzer Smith of New Orleans. I've had it several times and it is delicious over lean ham or pork tenderloin.

1 cup cranberry sauce with whole berries
1/2 cup grape jelly (with grapes if possible)
2 tablespoons cornstarch
1 cup orange juice

In a saucepan, mix the cranberry sauce with grape jelly, the cornstarch in the orange juice and heat over low heat for several minutes until thickened. Serve hot or cold.

◆ Per Tbsp:    Saturated fat: Trace   Total fat: Trace   Cholesterol: 0
               Sodium: 3mg     Calories: 24   Calories from fat: 1%

# CRANBERRY SAUCE

MAKES ABOUT 2-1/2 CUPS

If you've never had fresh, homemade cranberry sauce, you're in for a delicious treat. Cranberry sauce is simple and takes only the effort of putting the berries in a saucepan, adding some sugar, juice, zest and cinnamon, and turning up the heat for a few minutes, and since I'm cooking other foods anyway, I don't count the 5 to 10 minutes of cooking time. Homemade cranberry sauce is foolproof, tart, thick and very good. It doesn't need any special effort to jell, as it gets thick all by itself. Homemade cranberry sauce needs no sour cream, nuts, marshmallows or anything else. If you'd rather have a smooth sauce, process or blend it for a few minutes. You can do it right in the pan with an immersion blender.

**2 cups cranberries**
**1/2 to 1 cup sugar**
**1/2 teaspoon orange or lemon zest (grated rind)**
**1/2 cup orange juice**
**1/8 teaspoon cinnamon**

In a large, nonstick saucepan, heat all the ingredients over medium heat, uncovered, until the berries have all burst, then (optional) cook about 5 more minutes (or longer) over very low heat. Serve cold.

◆ **Per Tbsp:**     Saturated fat: Trace   Total fat: Trace   Cholesterol: 0
                          Sodium: Trace     Calories: 23    Calories from fat: 1%

## COCKTAIL SAUCE

MAKES 1 CUP

For shrimp, crab, lobster or other seafood. This is fresher and spicier than the commercially prepared.

**1 cup ketchup**
**1 tablespoon prepared horseradish**
**1 teaspoon Tabasco or hot sauce**
**1 tablespoon lemon juice**

In a small bowl, mix all the ingredients.

◆ **Per Tbsp:**     Saturated fat: Trace   Total fat: Trace   Cholesterol: 0
                          Sodium: 162mg   Calories: 15    Calories from fat: 4%

# BARBECUE SAUCE

MAKES ABOUT 1-1/2 CUPS

The addition of a tablespoon of bourbon takes this sauce south, grated orange peel takes it west. Oil is never necessary.

1 cup V-8 Low Sodium Cocktail Vegetable Juice
2 tablespoons light brown sugar
3 tablespoons vinegar
2 tablespoons minced onion
1 clove garlic, minced
1 teaspoon dry mustard

In a small saucepan, mix together the V-8 juice, light brown sugar, vinegar, onion, garlic and dry mustard. Bring to a boil and simmer 5 minutes. Use to barbecue or bake chicken, beef and pork.

◆ **Per Tbsp:**  Saturated fat: Trace  Total fat: Trace  Cholesterol: 0
   Sodium: 45mg  Calories: 8  Calories from fat: 1%

# CHICKEN OR FISH SAUCE

MAKES 2 CUPS

1 cup V-8 Low Sodium Clamato juice
1/2 cup dry white wine
1 clove garlic, minced
1/2 teaspoon crushed tarragon leaves
2 tablespoons cornstarch
1/8 teaspoon pepper

In a small nonstick saucepan, whisk all the ingredients together and heat, whisking until thickened.

◆ **Per Tbsp:**  Saturated fat: Trace  Total fat: Trace  Cholesterol: 0
   Sodium: 42mg  Calories: 6  Calories from fat: 2%

## ASIAN ZESTY STIR-FRY FLAVORING AND THICKENING SAUCE

MAKES 3/4 CUP

Perfect for a stir-fry where you want some heat, but only add it when the vegetables and meat are all cooked, as this takes 30 seconds to heat and thicken.

1/2 cup defatted chicken stock
2 tablespoons cornstarch
2 teaspoons brown sugar
1/4 teaspoon hot oil sauce or several shakes hot sauce
1/4 cup chopped scallions
1/4 cup low-sodium soy sauce

Mix the stock and cornstarch together, whisking out any lumps. Add the brown sugar, hot oil, scallions and soy sauce, mix and add to any cooking stir-fry vegetable, chicken or beef dish.

◆ Per Tbsp:    Saturated fat: Trace   Total fat: Trace   Cholesterol: 0
                Sodium: 361     Calories: 12   Calories from fat: 3%

## GARLIC SALSA

MAKES ABOUT 1 CUP

This can be salsa itself or it can be added to commercial salsa to freshen and make it stretch. To make it very hot, instead of using hot sauce, use habanera peppers; to make it more mild, use pepperoncinis.

3 very ripe tomatoes or canned tomato wedges
1 onion, cut in chunks
2 cloves garlic, minced
Half a green pepper

1 tablespoon cider vinegar
2 tablespoons lemon juice
1 stem cilantro
1 stem parsley
Several shakes hot sauce
1/2 teaspoon sugar

Garnish:
Lemon or lime slices

In a food processor, add all the ingredients and process coarsely. Serve hot or cold.

◆ **Per Tbsp:**   Saturated fat: Trace   Total fat: Trace   Cholesterol: 0
Sodium: 2mg   Calories: 7   Calories from fat: 8%

## SALSA

MAKES 2 CUPS

Salsa now outsells ketchup, and with good reason. If it is vegetable based (it can be fruit salsa too) it is an absolutely delicious, versatile, quick, nonfat topping that can be used as a side for fish, beef or pork, as a dip for chips and celery, in tacos, over baked potatoes or as a spicy side for plain beans, in the center of guacamole, as a base for setting a piece of chicken that is wrapped in foil and grilled or barbecued, as a topping on hamburgers, as a spread in pita, over substitute scrambled eggs, and it can be used as a base for soup or as a dollop in soup. You can add half a cucumber to this mixture.

3 red ripe tomatoes
1 onion
1/4 cup cilantro (optional)
1 stalk celery
Half a yellow pepper, seeds reserved

1/2 teaspoon cider vinegar
2 tablespoons lemon or lime juice
1/2 teaspoon sugar
1/2 teaspoon low-sodium salt (optional)

Garnish:
Diced avocado

In a food processor, add all the ingredients and process. Do not puree.

◆ **Per Tbsp:** Saturated fat: Trace  Total fat: Trace  Cholesterol: 0
Sodium: 2mg  Calories: 7  Calories from fat: 8%

## YOGURT CHEESE TARTAR SAUCE

MAKES ABOUT 2 CUPS

Tartar sauce is a traditional favorite with fish. It's also good as a sandwich spread.

1 cup nonfat yogurt cheese
Skim milk to thin
1/4 cup finely chopped onions
1/2 cup finely chopped scallions
1/4 cup finely chopped dill pickles
1/2 teaspoon sugar
1/4 cup finely chopped pimento or red pepper
1/4 cup chopped parsley or watercress
1/2 teaspoon dry mustard

Mix all the ingredients together and serve.

◆ **Per Tbsp:** Saturated fat: Trace  Total fat: Trace  Cholesterol: Trace
Sodium: 21mg  Calories: 10  Calories from fat: 3%

# MAYONNAISE TARTAR SAUCE

MAKES ABOUT 2 CUPS

If you like your tartar sauce sweet, look at the
recipe for sweet tartar sauce below.

1 cup nonfat mayonnaise
1 tablespoon skim milk
1 tablespoon lemon juice
1/4 cup finely chopped onions or scallions
1/4 cup finely chopped dill pickles
1/4 cup finely chopped pimento or red pepper
1/4 cup chopped parsley
1/2 teaspoon dry mustard

Mix all the ingredients together and serve.

◆ **Per Tbsp:**    Saturated fat: Trace   Total fat: Trace   Cholesterol: Trace
Sodium: 75mg    Calories: 12    Calories from fat: 3%

# SWEET TARTAR SAUCE

MAKES ABOUT 2 CUPS

1/2 cup nonfat mayonnaise
1/2 cup nonfat cottage cheese
1 onion or 3 scallions
4 sweet pickles or 1/3 cup sweet pickle relish
1 red pepper, stem removed, seeds reserved
1/2 teaspoon dry mustard
Skim milk to thin

In a food processor, puree the mayonnaise and cottage cheese, add
the remaining ingredients and lightly process. Serve cold.

◆ **Per Tbsp:**    Saturated fat: Trace   Total fat: Trace   Cholesterol: Trace
Sodium: 102mg   Calories: 7    Calories from fat: 1%

# HOT AND SPICY BARBECUE SAUCE

MAKES ABOUT 2 CUPS

For shrimp, beef, hamburgers and pork, or use as a dip.

1 cup chili sauce
1/4 cup onion, minced
1/4 cup maple syrup or brown sugar
1/4 cup chopped green olives
2 cloves garlic, minced
1/3 cup chopped pepperoncini peppers, drained
1 teaspoon low-sodium soy sauce
1 to 2 tablespoons chili powder
Several shakes hot sauce

Combine all ingredients.

♦ Per Tbsp:     Saturated fat: Trace   Total fat: Trace   Cholesterol: 0
                Sodium: 154mg   Calories: 20   Calories from fat: 14%


# HONEY MUSTARD SAUCE

MAKES ABOUT 1/2 CUP

Good with fish, chicken and even fruit, this is a very easy sauce to make. You can use a hot Chinese-style mustard for a more spicy version. Heating it thins it, but it tastes just as good.

6 tablespoons lemon juice or good dry white wine
2 tablespoons coarse grain mustard
2 tablespoons honey

Mix all the ingredients together. Serve hot or cold.

♦ Per Tbsp:     Saturated fat: Trace   Total fat: Trace   Cholesterol: 0
                Sodium: 39mg   Calories: 17   Calories from fat: 7%

# APPLESAUCE

MAKES ABOUT 4 CUPS

Homemade applesauce is better than any canned, frozen, or sauce-in-a-jar variety and takes little time or effort. A high-sided loaf pan is suggested for cooking in the microwave because the sauce can be pureed right in the pan with an immersion blender if desired.

6 tart apples such as Granny Smith's or Gravenstein, unpeeled,
    cored, and coarsely chopped
1/3 to 1/2 cup brown sugar or maple syrup or sugar substitute
1 to 2 tablespoon lemon juice
Small pinch of nutmeg
Larger pinch or a few shakes of cinnamon
1/4 cup raisins or currants (optional)

In a glass loaf pan, mix all the ingredients except the raisins, tossing them well. Cover with a perforated plastic wrap and microwave for 12 minutes, stirring once. Remove and semi-puree with an immersion blender. Stir in the raisins. Serve hot or cold.

◆ **Per Tbsp:**      Saturated fat: Trace   Total fat: Trace   Cholesterol: 0
                     Sodium: 1mg      Calories: 14    Calories from fat: 3%

# DESSERTS

Rum Bananas • Fresh Fruit Cup
Fruit and Ice Cream • Frozen Fruit Frappé
Strawberry Shortcake • Peach Melba
Sugared Dates • Banana Split
Ricotta Pears • Frozen Banana-Berry Parfaits
Microwave Extra Thick Berry Sauce
Raspberry Sauce • Orange Sauce • Sour Cherry Sauce
Honey Lemon Sauce • Chocolate Sauce
Free-Whip Skim Milk

# Desserts

**B**irthday parties, weddings, holidays—ice cream, cakes thick with frosting, pies laden with syrupy fruit—the sweet endings dreams are made of, and the oohs and ahs of these sweet indulgences still remain after a few easy low-fat changes.

How lucky that markets abound all year with fresh fruits from around the world. And you can highlight them with the wide array of nonfat cookies, cakes, ice cream and frozen yogurts now available.

Add some delicious topping—a sauce or whipped skim milk—and your dessert is as beautiful and unique as a snowflake.

# RUM BANANAS

Your very ripe bananas are perfect for this rich, nonfat dessert. Serve hot for a soothing end to a winter's meal. Serve cold with a whipped topping to refresh a summer's eve. Try topping with whipped skim milk, a vanilla nonfat yogurt or nonfat ice cream and a colorful garnish. Whether in silk or jeans, your company will love this sweet ending.

4 large, ripe, peeled bananas
1/2 cup brown sugar
1/2 cup maple syrup
1/4 cup dark rum, cognac or pear brandy
1/4 teaspoon vanilla extract

Garnish:
Maraschino cherries
Blueberries

Cut the bananas in half and then diagonally into 4-inch lengths. In a nonstick skillet add all the ingredients, cover and simmer over low heat for 15 minutes or until the bananas are translucent. Add the blueberries and cherries during the last minute of cooking. Serve hot.

◆ Per Serving:    Saturated fat: Trace  Total fat: 1gr    Cholesterol: 0
                    Sodium: 17mg    Calories: 339  Calories from fat: 2%

# FRESH FRUIT CUP

SERVES 8

Fresh fruit is always a perfect close to a meal. This mixture can have different kinds of fruit. However, use fresh fruit, mixing red, yellow, orange and green colors for eye appeal.

1/2 cup pineapple juice
1/2 cup orange juice
1/4 cup dessert sherry or champagne
2 cups fresh pineapple chunks
2 cups fresh strawberries, sliced
1 cup green grapes, sliced lengthwise and seeded
2 kiwi fruit, peeled, sliced lengthwise, then crosswise into
    1/4-inch-wide slices
2 medium pears, cored and diced

Garnish:
Mint leaves

Mix together the juices and sherry. Reserve. Prepare the fruit and toss gently with the juice mixture. Serve in stemmed dessert glasses, garnished with mint leaves.

◆ Per Serving:  Saturated fat: Trace  Total fat: 1gr  Cholesterol: 0
Sodium: 3mg   Calories: 107  Calories from fat: 6%

# FRUIT AND ICE CREAM

SERVES 4

Fruit such as pineapple or pureed berries drizzled over nonfat ice cream or frozen yogurt is a delicious treat. Almost anything you can do with high fat ice cream, you can do with the nonfat substitutes, most are so good.

4 sweet and ripe pineapple quarters, or 1 pint raspberries, blueberries or strawberries
Juice of 1 lemon (if using berries)
Few shakes ground cinnamon (if using berries)
Rind from one lemon, cut into several strips (if using berries)
1/4 cup sugar (if using berries)
1 pint nonfat vanilla ice cream or frozen yogurt

Garnish:
Fresh berries
Mint sprigs or holly leaves
Chocolate shavings

If using pineapple, slice under the rind and crossways into bite-size pieces (the lemon, cinnamon, lemon strips and sugar won't be used with the pineapple). Divide the pineapple onto 4 plates. Add a scoop of nonfat ice cream or yogurt next to the pineapple, tuck a spring of mint into the ice cream, top with some berries and serve.

   If using berries, save a few, 15 or so, and puree with the lemon juice, cinnamon, rind and sugar. Place a scoop of nonfat ice cream or yogurt on a plate, pour 1/4 of the puree over the each scoop, or on the plate with the scoop, top with berries, a sprig of mint or a couple of chocolate shavings and serve.

◆ **Per Serving:**    Saturated fat: Trace   Total fat: Trace   Cholesterol: 0
                      Sodium: Trace       Calories: 151   Calories from fat: 2%

## WITH CHOCOLATE SHAVINGS
Top the dessert with several chocolate shavings, crumbles from a candy bar such as Heath Bars, enough to make 1/2 ounce.

◆ **Per Serving:**    Saturated fat: Trace   Total fat: 1gr   Cholesterol: 0
                      Sodium: 1mg        Calories: 169   Calories from fat: 8%

# FROZEN FRUIT FRAPPÉ

SERVES 4

Made of ice and fruit, this couldn't be more delicious. I use raspberries, but many other fruits such as blackberries can be used.

1 16-ounce bag frozen, sweetened raspberries
Juice of 1/2 lemon
Pinch cinnamon
20 to 30 fresh raspberries

In a blender or food processor, process the raspberries, lemon
juice and cinnamon until mushy but still frozen, much like the
consistency of a typical frozen drink. Spoon into individual dishes
and garnish with fresh fruit. Serve cold.

◆ Per Tbsp:     Saturated fat: Trace   Total fat: Trace   Cholesterol: 0
                Sodium: 7mg        Calories: 125   Calories from fat: 2%

# STRAWBERRY SHORTCAKE

SERVES 6

Strawberry shortcake can be made very
quickly using prepackaged biscuits as a base or,
for a more elegant look use angel food cake.

1 pint strawberries, hulled and cut
2 tablespoons sugar
6 baked, prebaked, or packaged refrigerator biscuits
   (reshape the 8 biscuits into 6)
2 tablespoons sugar
2 cups free-whip skim milk (page 275)

Garnish:
**6 large strawberries with stems attached**

After hulling and cutting the strawberries, sprinkle with sugar, cover with plastic wrap and place them in the refrigerator for several hours so they exude their juice. On each plate, place the two halves of a split biscuit, spoon on the strawberries and some of the juice, top with the whipped milk and garnish each with a whole strawberry.

◆ Per Serving:    Saturated fat: 1gr    Total fat: 3gr    Cholesterol: 3mg
                  Sodium: 416mg    Calories: 174   Calories from fat: 18%

## PEACH MELBA

SERVES 4

This variation of the traditional dessert, named for a singer, is probably one of the prettiest dishes you can serve.

**1 cup raspberry sauce (page 272)**
**2 fresh peaches, peeled and halved**
**2 cups nonfat vanilla ice cream**

Garnish:
**Almond slices**
**Fresh mint leaves**
**Fresh raspberries**

Place peach halves in dessert dishes. Top each with 1 scoop of ice cream. Spoon about 1/4 cup warm raspberry sauce over each serving. Garnish and serve immediately.

◆ Per Serving:    Saturated fat: Trace   Total fat: Trace   Cholesterol: 0
                  Sodium: 46mg     Calories: 275   Calories from fat: 1%

# SUGARED DATES

MAKES 30 DATES

This is a simple and lovely fruit. Garnish with fresh grapes for a buffet or for dessert. Another way to sugar the dates is to cut them lengthwise down the center, not completely in half, but enough to remove the pit and to turn them wrong side out so the sticky part is on the outside. Roll them tightly so a sticky edge keeps them closed. Then roll the outside sticky part in the sugar.

**White granulated sugar**
**1/2 cup honey or corn syrup**
**30 dates**

Put the sugar in a flat plate and spread it out. Place the honey or syrup in another dish. Moisten each of the dates with the honey or syrup, roll in the sugar, pressing down hard and coating well, then set aside on waxed paper to thoroughly dry.

- **Per Serving:** Saturated fat: Trace  Total fat: Trace  Cholesterol: 0
  Sodium: 1mg  Calories: 53  Calories from fat: 1%

WITH WALNUTS
Stuff each date before rolling with a walnut half.

- **Per Serving:** Saturated fat: Trace  Total fat: 1gr  Cholesterol: 0
  Sodium: 1mg  Calories: 63  Calories from fat: 14%

# BANANA SPLIT

SERVES 4

This indulgent dessert contains almost no fat. It looks like and tastes like the old soda fountain favorite—absolutely scrumptious.

4 bananas, peeled and cut in half lengthwise
1 pint nonfat vanilla ice cream
1 pint nonfat chocolate ice cream
1 pint nonfat strawberry ice cream
1/2 cup chocolate sauce (page 275)
1 pint whipped skim milk
1/4 cup chopped pecans
4 maraschino cherries

In 4 glass banana boats, arrange 2 banana halves side by side. Place one scoop each of nonfat vanilla, chocolate and strawberry ice cream on the bananas. Drizzle a small amount of chocolate sauce over the ice cream, add the whipped milk, sprinkle with nuts and top with a cherry. Serve cold.

◆ Per Serving:   Saturated fat: Trace   Total fat: 7gr   Cholesterol: 2mg
                   Sodium: 240mg   Calories: 551   Calories from fat: 11%

# RICOTTA PEARS

MAKES 4 SERVINGS

This soft dessert is just the right finish to a spicy meal.

1 cup part skim ricotta cheese
2 tablespoons orange juice
1 tablespoon honey
1/4 teaspoon almond extract

2 tablespoons slivered almonds
2 tablespoons carob chips or chocolate chips
2 tablespoons currants or chopped raisins
1 teaspoon grated orange rind
2 fresh ripe pears

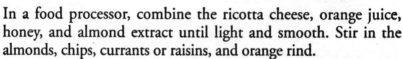

Garnish:
Strawberries or raspberries
Sprinkle of carob or cocoa powder

In a food processor, combine the ricotta cheese, orange juice, honey, and almond extract until light and smooth. Stir in the almonds, chips, currants or raisins, and orange rind.

Place one pear half in each of 4 individual bowls. For each serving, top the fruit with about 1/4 cup of the ricotta mixture and garnish.

♦ Per Serving:     Saturated fat: 4gr     Total fat: 10gr     Cholesterol: 19mg
                    Sodium: 79mg     Calories: 210   Calories from fat: 35%

## FROZEN BANANA-BERRY PARFAITS

MAKES 4 SERVINGS

When bananas begin to ripen, freeze them and use them in this parfait. Peel the bananas before freezing, then wrap in plastic bags. Make this just before you are ready to serve it.

3 medium-size bananas
1/2 cup nonfat yogurt
2 tablespoons honey
1 cup sliced strawberries
1 cup blueberries

Garnish:
Whole strawberries and blueberries

Cut bananas into 1-inch slices while still frozen. Place yogurt and honey in food processor fitted with a metal blade, gradually mix in the banana slices and puree.

Spoon into parfait glasses, alternating with a layer of sliced strawberries and a layer of blueberries. Garnish and serve immediately.

◆ **Per Serving:** Saturated fat: Trace   Total fat: 1gr   Cholesterol: Trace
Sodium: 26mg   Calories: 159   Calories from fat: 4%

VARIATIONS
Add a dash of vanilla extract to the banana-yogurt mixture. For a different flavor and a nice pink color, add strawberries (about 1 cup) as you are blending the mixture.

## MICROWAVE EXTRA THICK BERRY SAUCE

MAKES ABOUT 2 CUPS

This sauce only takes 2 to 4 minutes in the microwave and is delicious over cake or ice cream, nonfat of course.

1/2 cup fresh or frozen berries, partially thawed and drained
1 teaspoon lemon zest
2/3 cup sugar (if the berries are unsweetened)
2 tablespoons cornstarch
2 tablespoons lemon juice
1 cup berry, apple or grape juice

In a small microwavable bowl, add the berries, zest and sugar and toss. In a small bowl, mix the cornstarch, lemon juice and berry juice. Add to the berries, place a paper towel over the dish and microwave for 1 minute. Check and stir. Microwave for 1 minute and repeat until you have the thickness you desire.

◆ **Per Tbsp:** Saturated fat: Trace   Total fat: Trace   Cholesterol: 0
Sodium: Trace   Calories: 23   Calories from fat: 1%

# RASPBERRY SAUCE

MAKES ABOUT 1 CUP

Serve this sauce right after mixing or, if you want a thicker sauce, heat for a few minutes.

1 cup fresh or frozen raspberries, partially thawed
2/3 cup sugar (if the berries are unsweetened)
2 tablespoons cornstarch
2 tablespoons apple juice or water
1 tablespoon lemon juice

In a small saucepan, add the berries and sugar. Tip the pan and on one side add the water and lemon juice and mix in the cornstarch. Turn on the heat and stir until thickened, about 3 minutes.

♦ Per Tbsp:     Saturated fat: Trace   Total fat: Trace   Cholesterol: 0
                Sodium: 1mg      Calories: 39    Calories from fat: 1%


# ORANGE SAUCE

MAKES 2–3 CUPS

This is a tart sauce for crepes, over pancakes, under angel food cake and even on poultry. It can be made thicker by substituting instant tapioca for the cornstarch. The oranges, if fresh, can be cut in pieces. Mandarin oranges, because they are more uniform in size, give a tidier appearance to the sauce.

1 pint orange sections, seeds and membrane removed, or
    mandarin oranges, drained
1/2 cup sugar (depending upon the bitterness of the berries)
1/4 cup orange juice
1/4 teaspoon cinnamon

1 teaspoon orange or lemon zest
1/2 teaspoon 1-inch slivers of lemon peel
1/2 teaspoon 1-inch slivers of orange peel
4 tablespoons fresh lemon juice
2 tablespoons cornstarch

In a nonstick saucepan, heat over low heat one third of the fruit with the sugar, orange juice, cinnamon, zest and peel, until the fruit is hot. Mix the lemon juice with the cornstarch and stir in with the fruit until the mixture thickens. Serve hot or cold.

◆ **Per Tbsp:** Saturated fat: Trace  Total fat: Trace  Cholesterol: 0
Sodium: Trace  Calories: 6  Calories from fat: 2%

## SOUR CHERRY SAUCE

MAKES ABOUT 2-1/2 CUPS

Fresh or canned sour cherries have become scarce, but dried cherries from Michigan work beautifully in this sauce. Dried sour cherries are in gourmet shops and are beginning to appear in supermarkets. The sauce is not too sweet, so it is good with duck or pork, too.

3/4 cup dried sour cherries
1-1/2 cups cold water
1/2 cup sugar, or to taste
1 tablespoon cornstarch mixed to a paste with 3 tablespoons
   water

In small saucepan combine cherries, water and sugar. Stir over moderate heat until sugar is dissolved. Bring to a boil and simmer 15 minutes. Stir in cornstarch paste and bring to a boil. Stir constantly. Cook until translucent, 2 to 3 minutes.

◆ **Per Tbsp:** Saturated fat: Trace  Total fat: Trace  Cholesterol: 0
Sodium: Trace  Calories: 15  Calories from fat: 1%

# HONEY LEMON SAUCE

MAKES 1-1/2 CUPS OR 8 SERVINGS

This sauce is excellent on a variety of desserts. Refrigerate it for a day or two. Serve with bread pudding or crepes filled with bananas or oranges for a spectacular dessert.

1 tablespoon finely granulated sugar
1 tablespoon cornstarch
1/3 cup honey
3/4 cup boiling water
Dash nutmeg
1 tablespoon canola oil
2 tablespoons lemon juice

In a nonstick saucepan, blend the sugar and cornstarch. Stir in the honey and boiling water. Stir over low heat until thickened and clear and remove from the heat. Add the nutmeg and oil and stir until blended. Stir in lemon juice.

♦ Per Tbsp:     Saturated fat: Trace   Total fat: 1gr    Cholesterol: 0
                         Sodium: Trace    Calories: 22   Calories from fat: 22%

# CHOCOLATE SAUCE

MAKES ABOUT 1 CUP

This is an easy chocolate sauce, delicious and sweet over an angel food cake or ice cream.

2 tablespoons canola oil
1 or 2 tablespoons unsweetened cocoa powder
1 to 1-1/2 cups granulated sugar
1 teaspoon vanilla extract

In a small, nonstick saucepan over medium to medium high heat, whisk the oil with the cocoa powder, and whisk in the sugar until dissolved. Add the vanilla and use hot or cold.

◆ Per Tbsp:     Saturated fat: Trace   Total fat: 2gr     Cholesterol: 0
                Sodium: Trace    Calories: 76    Calories from fat: 20%

# FREE-WHIP SKIM MILK

MAKES ABOUT 2 CUPS

A delicious, nonfat whipped topping can be made by whipping skim milk with an immersion blender or a very strong electric beater. Put the beaters and bowl into the freezer for 1/2 hour before using. Some milk has stabilizers which prohibit it from whipping. A whipping stabilizer called Whip It from Oetker (1-800-8-FLAVOR) helps greatly. It may be found in a fancy food market of ordered from a catalog.

2 cups very cold skim milk
1 package Whip It (optional)
1/2 cup sugar
1 teaspoon vanilla extract

If using an immersion blender, use a large aluminum or stainless steel bowl and add ice cubes and water. Add the milk to the vertical container that comes with the immersion blender, sink the container into the larger bowl with the ice cubes, insert the blender with the proper blade in the milk, and with a rapid up-and-down motion, beat on high until it forms soft peaks. Add the stabilizer, if using, and add the sugar. Beat until well mixed and fold in the vanilla extract. Serve cold.

◆ **Per Tbsp:**  Saturated fat: Trace  Total fat: Trace  Cholesterol: Trace
Sodium: 8mg    Calories: 17    Calories from fat: 1%

## USING 2 PERCENT MILK
Substitute 2 percent milk for the skim milk.

◆ **Per Tbsp:**  Saturated fat: Trace  Total fat: Trace  Cholesterol: 1mg
Sodium: 8mg    Calories: 21    Calories from fat: 13%

# MENUS

Middle Eastern Asian Dinner • Gourmet Dinner
Puerto Rican Fall Luncheon • Formal Elegance
Asian Summer Supper • Quickie Lunch
Manga, Manga Italian Style • Winter Comfort Food of
Chicken & Noodles • Elegant Brunch • Middle Eastern Lunch
Light and Fresh Feast • Simple Middle Eastern Dinner
Family Dinner • No Cooking Cocktail Party
Festive Tex/Mex Gathering • Italian Delight
Tex/Mex South of the Border • Winter Soup Meal
Fish Dinner • Bella Italiano • Do-Ahead Party Buffet
Morning Glory Brunch • Elegant Stir-Fry Special
Pasta Picnic • Hearty Pasta Dinner • Country Cuisine
Soup and Salad • Kids Galore • Quickie Company Dinner

# Menus

**P**lanning your menu really helps you to formulate not only your shopping list but what you will be eating. This way you don't end up eating too many fruits and not enough vegetables or letting the leftover chicken dry out when you could have used it the next night in a stir-fry or salad.

When choosing food for meals, you may want to select a theme, even if it isn't a special occasion. A Middle Eastern theme would include some couscous, hummus or a Persian salad. An Italian dinner might have an appetizer of caponata, a seafood pasta or a Caesar salad. For a Tex/Mex night, you might go for black bean soup with rice and onions, a guacamole salad, some corn chips and rum bananas and nonfat ice cream for dessert.

The more organized you are, the easier and quicker a meal is to prepare and the more time you have to enjoy it and those dining with you.

Here are some suggestions for keeping the spice in your dining life.

1   Save energy on the everyday drain of thinking what to serve by creating a few weeks' worth of menus. Stock your cupboard and freezer with ingredients so you'll need to run to the market only for the fresh foods.

2   Avoid repeating ingredients in the dishes you serve in a meal. If there are tomatoes in the sauce, try and use something else in the salad.

3   Keep texture in mind—something smooth and soft in a salad like tomatoes and avocados is more interesting when you add crisp celery, radishes, carrots or onions.

4   For variety in a food such as pasta sauce or chili, vary the length of cooking time for some of the same vegetables such as onions and peppers, putting some in at different times. Well-cooked onions taste different and have a different texture than do the half cooked or raw.

5   Plan for variety in color. Dress up a pale rice dish with some slices of red pepper, a few steamed green beans on the top, or some ripe olives on the plate.

6   Dress up platters with interesting garden leaves, maybe a flower or two, or some extra color from pickled kumquats.

7   Include proteins in meals, such as large amounts of beans, lots of vegetables, rice and pasta, but small amounts (3-1/2 ounces) of animal products such as meat, fish, poultry, dairy and eggs.

8   Use a variety of vegetables. Those with rich nutrients and more vitamins exist in the more brightly colored vegetables. But serve all kinds.

9   Look for a balance of rich and light, dark and pale foods. A cream sauce vegetable meal might need a dessert of sliced pineapple or sorbet. And a good soup always benefits from a rich, crusty bread and a salad.

10  In season, freeze some foods you can't always get, such as concord grapes, ripe garden tomatoes (if small to medium, freeze whole to add to pasta sauce), berries to add to a sauce later in the year, or freeze Temple orange juice to save for a dessert several months away. Keep frozen pear and banana slices on hand for quick sorbets.

11  Any meal becomes an occasion when you use a theme in your food and table decor. For a Tex/Mex look try arranging brightly colored flowers for your centerpiece, or buy a piñata, and use different colored napkins and plates at each setting. You might even want to label some of your dishes or serving pieces with their Spanish names. If you prefer a Middle Eastern effect, set your table in hues of mysterious purple and black. Use brass candlesticks and paisley napkins and perhaps burn some incense. For a dramatic Asian look, place a single lily in the center of the table. Use chopsticks and then if you are adventurous, serve dinner on your coffee table with diners sitting on cushions around it.

12  For entertaining, select mostly cold foods, or dishes you prepare ahead of time so your party can be fun for you too.

13  Remember light that is higher than the head is more flattering for everyone, so use very tall candles on tall candlesticks, or if all you have are the tiny, low votive candles, make sure there aren't too many and that they aren't as bright as a lit overhead fixture so your guests don't look macabre when lit from below.

14  Lighting adds to the enjoyment of a meal. Too much can make you feel like you're on stage and too little may keep you from finding your plate. If there are candles on the table, always have them lighted. Lit candles always seem to make a table warm, while unlit candles appear unfriendly—like you're saving them for another, better event.

15  If you've given up alcohol, don't give up your beautiful wine glasses. Serve white concord grape juice, sparkling cider, nonalcoholic champagne or wine in them or even a frothy dessert.

## MIDDLE EASTERN ASIAN DINNER
*Baba Ghanoush with Pita Crisps
*Persian Cucumber Salad
*Saffron Rice with *Curry Sauce
*Rum Bananas with Orange-Raisin Sauce

❧

## GOURMET DINNER
*Monkfish with Mustard
*Fennel
Avocado Slices with *Seafood Dressing on Lettuce
*Frozen Fruit Frappé

❧

## PUERTO RICAN FALL LUNCHEON
*Black Bean Soup
*Corn Salad
Sliced Apples and Commercially Baked
Nonfat Gingerbread or Cake

❧

## FORMAL ELEGANCE
*Prosciutto and Melon
*Scallops on Spinach
*Creamed Onions
*Asparagus with *Hollandaise Sauce
*Raspberry Sauce on Commercially Baked
Nonfat Angel Food Cake

❧

## ASIAN SUMMER SUPPER
*Dan Dan Noodles
*Eggplant, Asian Style
Cucumber and Tomato Slices on Lettuce with
*Viniagrette Classic Dressing, Sprinkled with Sesame Seeds
*Honey Lemon Sauce over Commercial Nonfat Ice Cream

*Recipe in book

## QUICKIE LUNCH
*Hamburgers with Stretchers*
*Pineapple and Cottage Cheese Salad*
Fat-free Commercially Baked Chocolate Chip Cookies

❧

## MANGA, MANGA ITALIAN STYLE
*Caesar Salad*
*Stuffed Manicotti*
*Asparagus and Parmesan Cheese*
*Peach Melba*

❧

## WINTER COMFORT FOOD OF CHICKEN & NOODLES
Tossed Salad
*Orzo and Chicken*
*Peas, Carrots and Mushrooms in Cream Sauce*
*Banana Split*

❧

## ELEGANT BRUNCH
Champagne with 3 Strawberries or Raspberries in the Glass
*Chicken Salad*
*Frozen Banana-Berry Parfait*

❧

## MIDDLE EASTERN LUNCH
*Hummus and Pita Crisps*
*Couscous and Tomatoes*
*Sugared Dates*

❧

## LIGHT AND FRESH FEAST
*Chicken, Duck or Pork Stir-Fry*
*Cellophane Noodles*
Fresh Sliced Tomatoes with
Sweet Basil, Mozzarella and Balsamic Vinegar
Commercially Baked Nonfat Chocolate Brownies

## SIMPLE MIDDLE EASTERN DINNER
*Mock Caviar (Eggplant) and Pita*
*Couscous with *Curry Sauce*
*Persian Cucumber Salad*
Commercially Baked Nonfat Pound Cake with *Orange Sauce*

❧

## FAMILY DINNER
*Spaghetti Marinara*
*Steamed Carrots*
*Strawberry Shortcake*

❧

## NO COOKING COCKTAIL PARTY
*Clam Dip with Commercially Bought Lavosh*
*Ranch House Dip with Crudités*
*Black Bean Dip with Corn Chips*
*Baba Ghanoush with Pita Bread*
*Sweet Cherries*

❧

## FESTIVE TEX/MEX GATHERING
*Gazpacho*
*Guacamole on Lettuce*
*Beans and Rice*
*Rum Bananas with Whipped Cream*

❧

## ITALIAN DELIGHT
*Antipasto*
*Gnocchi*
*Caesar Salad*
*Frozen Fruit Frappé*

❧

## TEX/MEX
*Tacos*
*Cheese and Bean Burritos*
Commercially Baked Nonfat Swirl Cake
with *Chocolate Sauce*

### SOUTH OF THE BORDER
*Meatless Meaty Chili
Green Salad Tossed with Mild Jalapeños and
Nonfat Corn Chips
*Fresh Fruit Cup

❧

### WINTER SOUP MEAL
*Easiest Chicken Soup
Crusty Bread
*Cobb Salad
Fruit and Nonfat Ice Cream

❧

### FISH DINNER
*Carrot, Pineapple and Raisin Salad
*Filet of Sole with *Tartar Sauce
*Braised Leeks
*Steamed Green Beans
*Frozen Banana-Berry Parfait

❧

### BELLA ITALIANO
* Easy Stuffed Mushrooms Sprinkled with Sweet Basil
*Fettuccine Alfredo
*Fennel
Dinner Salad with Italian Dressing
*Ricotta Pears

❧

### DO-AHEAD PARTY BUFFET
Vegetables and Ranch House Dip
*Crunchy Rice Salad
Pickles and Hot *Stuffed Mushrooms
Meatballs in Chafing Dish
Fresh Fruit Plate with Whole Kiwi Fruits
(served with fancy soup spoon to scoop, poached egg style)

## MORNING GLORY BRUNCH
*Tomato-Ricotta Omelet
Fresh Fruit and Nonfat Yogurt
Commercially Baked Nonfat Pecan Coffee Cake

❧

## ELEGANT STIR-FRY SPECIAL
*Chicken, Duck or Pork Stir-Fry with Ginger Sauce
Brown Rice
*Peach Melba

❧

## PASTA PICNIC
* Quick Pasta Salad
Cold *Steamed Green Beans with *Greek Dressing
Sliced Summer Tomatoes with Blue Cheese
*Sugared Dates, Fresh Grapes, Apples, Peaches and Cherries

❧

## HEARTY PASTA DINNER
*Fettuccine Alfredo
Salad with Italian Dressing
*Broccoli and Garlic
Commercially Baked Nonfat Vanilla Cupcakes

❧

## COUNTRY CUISINE
*Glazed Ham Slices with Pineapple
*Country Green Beans
*Mashed Potatoes
Nonfat Ice Cream with *Berry Sauce

❧

## SOUP AND SALAD
*Minestrone
*Fennel, Beet and Carrot Salad
Farm Bread
Commercially Baked Nonfat Oatmeal Cookies

### KIDS GALORE
*Turkey Breast on Bread with *Turkey Gravy*
*Natural Corn*
*Nonfat Chocolate, Vanilla and Strawberry Ice Cream with Sprinkles*

ॐ

### QUICKIE COMPANY DINNER
*\*Juicy Roasted Chicken*
*Green Grapes*
*Commercially Baked Italian Bread Sticks*
*\*English Green Peas*
*\*Coleslaw*
*\*Frozen Fruit Frappé*

# *Glossary of Foods, Chemicals, Additives and Ingredients*

There are many food terms used or associated with lowered fat in commercial food and home-cooked food. You need to know what they mean so you know which ones to avoid and which ones, though they look ominous, are really okay. Anything with *hydrogenation* should be avoided, but *agar-agar* and *carrageenan* are just seaweed and are good for you. So, don't let manufacturers who are giving you high fat products scare you into thinking these stabilizers and gelatins are not healthy for you.

The following glossary will help take the mystery out of the food you eat.

## Agar-Agar
This is a clear flavorless sea vegetable. It acts like gelatin.

## Animal Protein
Any product from animals including fish, poultry, meat fat and muscle, blood, butter, roe, eggs, cheese, milk and all other dairy products. Check for words like *suet* and *tallow,* which are fats, and *rennet,* which is made from the lining of the stomach, and *gelatin* if you want to eliminate all animal proteins from your diet.

## Arrowroot Powder
A starch flour used for thickening—similar to cornstarch.

## Carrageenan

This product from seaweed is a stabilizing and thickening agent thought to be harmless.

## Cholesterol

There are two kinds of cholesterol. One kind is in the food you eat. The other is your own cholesterol number, which probably ought to be under current recommendations.

Cholesterol only comes from animals. It is a white waxy substance that does not dissolve in water. We humans, unlike some animals, need no extra cholesterol as we make enough of our own. It is suggested by the American Heart Association that we keep a blood total cholesterol count of under 200 milligrams and that we ingest no more than 300 milligrams of dietary cholesterol a day. Foods with high cholesterol are brains, liver, sweetbreads, kidneys, eggs, and lower on the scale but still moderately high is shellfish. Except for eggs, none of the above food contains much saturated fat. Shellfish contains omega-3 fatty acids, thought to help lower blood cholesterol.

## Cornstarch

Cornstarch is a corn flour that is used for thickening soups, stews, sauces and gravies among other foods, and it can be successfully mixed with flour. However, the mixing liquid always has to be cool. Add the cool liquid and blend to remove lumps. Then stir the mixture into hot, already cooking food. Heat causes it to thicken the other liquids, which takes about 30 seconds. It may not stay thick when reheated.

## Fats
All oil, grease, tallow, lard and animal fat from vegetables or animals is a combination of fat.

### Monounsaturated Fat
A clear oily substance made up of monounsaturated fatty acids that are liquid at room temperature. Some sources are olive, canola, and peanut oil, and it is the major fat in avocados. Most oils processed for human consumption have some amount of monounsaturated fat.

### Omega-3 Fatty Acids
A group of polyunsaturated fatty acids that are contained in some fish and like omega-6 fatty acids, are thought by some to help prevent heart disease.

### Polyunsaturated Fat
A clear oily substance made up of polyunsaturated fatty acids that are liquid at room temperature. Some sources are safflower, sunflower and corn oil, although some amount of polyunsaturated fat is in most eating oils.

### Saturated Fat
Saturated fat is a white oily substance and is the fat that most experts think causes cholesterol to form in the blood and plaque to build in the arteries. There are saturated fats in both vegetable and animal products, with palm kernel and coconut oil and hooved animal fats having the greatest amounts. There is some in fish and very little in shellfish. Saturated fat is the main component in the marbling and fatty edges in meat, and the fat in poultry and is the most harmful of the fats in terms of raising blood cholesterol.

Foods such as cheese, cream, and butter and ice cream are high in saturated fat. As far as we know there is no biological reason to ingest saturated fat. The more the saturated fat in an oil, the harder or more opaque it is at room temperature.

## Flour

Flour can be used as a thickening agent. It can be mixed with cornstarch and will hold up under reheating. Unlike cornstarch, flour must be cooked for at least 2 minutes so it doesn't taste pasty.

## Gluten Flour

Wheat flour from which the starch has been removed. It can be used to make seitan (see below) or bread that has a high rise and dense volume.

## Guar Gum

A natural water soluble fiber found in bean seeds and used as a stabilizer in foods from commercial ice creams to sauces.

## Harvest Burger

A soy product of the Archer Daniels Midland Company, the Harvest Burger® is an all-vegetable, cholesterol-free, low-fat alternative to ground meat. Harvest Burger comes in seven flavors—original, herbs and spices, taco, Italian, chili, sloppy Joe and curry. You can purchase it in grocery stores in the Midwest and Texas or by calling 1-800-8-FLAVOR.

## Hydrogenated

A chemical process where a small amount of nickel is used as a catalyst to artificially harden fats. Hydrogenation causes fat, even largely unsaturated fat such as canola, to become saturated.

## Low Sodium

Sodium free, low sodium and reduced sodium all have different meanings. Obviously salt free or sodium free means little salt, less than 5 milligrams per serving, but check the serving size and the possible addition of other sodiums such as benzoate, phosphate or other sodium additives.

## Margarine

Usually, margarine is made of vegetable products. If it is listed as an ingredient on the label of a commercial cookie or cake, margarine may mean it has hidden ingredients such as palm oil, animal fat or other more saturated fats. The item listed first means it contains more of that item than any other.

Margarine, if it is pourable, may have less saturated fat. If it is tub or whipped, it may have up to 30 percent water, which is fine for heating foods, mixing in some foods where the fat content won't significantly change the recipe, or putting on vegetables, but it makes hot toast or popcorn soggy.

Read the labels on margarine for the amount of saturated fats and select the lowest brand. Know that the word *hydrogenation*, which is a hardening process, makes all fats saturated.

## MSG

Monosodium glutamate is an additive used to enhance flavor. Some people have an allergic reaction to it. MSG has become purposely hidden in food labeling under such words as *hydrolyzed vegetable protein, hydrolyzed plant protein, HVP, vegetable flavorings, malt flavorings, yeast extract,* and *vegetable flavors.*

## Nutritional Yeast

A dietary supplement and condiment that has a distinct aroma and is thought to have some nutritional value. It can be taken as a supplement.

## Oat Bran

A water soluble fiber that apparently can both lower cholesterol and add fiber to the diet.

## Oils

Oil, in the cooking context, is the liquid version of fat. All oils have the same calorie content and the same number of fat grams, but they differ in saturates, monounsaturates and polyunsaturates. All heated oils should be used only once, and oils do better refrigerated (even olive oil) so they don't become rancid. Both high heat and rancidity change the chemical structure of oil. The best oils with the least saturated fats are canola, safflower, walnut, sunflower, grapeseed, soybean and sesame.

### Fish Oil

Most experts conclude that the limited information available at present does not justify specific recommendations for fish oil. Others believe that, until there is more information, no fish oil supplements should be taken.

### Hearts of Palm

Although all palm kernel oil is extremely high in saturated fat, the hearts of the palm have little fat and can be enjoyed on a low-fat eating plan. Most vegetables are low in saturated fat, although their oil content may be high.

### Palm Oil

The oils, particularly those from the kernel of the palm, have extremely high levels of palmetic acids or saturated fats. Thought to cause cholesterol plaque.

### Vegetable Oil

A product labeled *all vegetable oil* is usually made from corn, canola, soybean, safflower and so on, but it can also contain palm, palm kernel, coconut and other oils with high saturated fatty acid contents.

## Organic Foods

Although few states or corporations yet have agreed upon uniform national standards for organic farming or the organic raising of animals or poultry, organic generally means grown or raised without pesticides, synthetic fertilizers, hormones or growth enhancers, or as close to natural conditions as possible. There is a growing movement within the food industry to standardize as more and more consumers wish to eat organically grown and raised foods. Beware, some foods labeled *organic* are not. Nationally certifiable standards are currently being developed and some states already have certification.

## Pectin

A water soluble fiber that apparently can lower cholesterol if taken in large amounts. It is used for canning fruits and is found in the white part of citrus fruit.

## Psyllium

A water soluble fiber from a weed grown in India that has been shown to lower blood cholesterol. One cereal manufacturer now adds it to one product.

## Salmonella

Salmonella is a bacteria often present in poultry and eggs. It is destroyed during cooking and washing. Washing hands, cutting boards, dishes and utensils used when working with raw poultry and eggs is important. Also be careful not to cross contaminate foods such as basting or marinating sauces from the raw to the cooked version. Raw eggs should be changed to substitute eggs in Caesar salads, egg nogs and hollandaise sauce which traditionally doesn't use thoroughly cooked eggs.

## Sea Salt

Although trendy, there is no healthy reason to eat salt from the sea over salt from any other area. Most commercial salt is highly processed and cleansed for human consumption, and any qualities inherent from the sea are lost in the processing, making sea salt identical to all other salt. The other salts come from dried salt lakes and salt mines which were most likely part of the sea once anyway.

Table salt usually has an additive of iodine, not necessary if you live on either coast where there is ample iodine, but helpful in the elimination of goiter for those who live in the central part of the country. Iodine adversely affects about 8 percent of Americans who suffer from a type of Germanic/Irish/English adult skin acne called rosacia (causes a red nose and red dots on the skin) which iodine exacerbates. To eliminate the iodine, look for noniodized salt.

Rock salt probably has the most minerals because it is the least refined.

Kosher salt is blessed by a rabbi, and is used primarily by religious Jews as well as many other cooks.

Pickling salt is used for brines and pickling, but any salt can be used.

Lite or low-sodium salt is a mixture of potassium chloride and has sodium chloride, and is used by people who want to lower their salt intake.

Kosher salt and sea salt don't contain starch stabilizers so these salts may clump together.

## Seitan
A mock meat mixture made of wheat flour, often used in vegan or vegetarian diets.

## Sulfites
Sulfites are chemicals that keep fruits, vegetables, processed foods, dried foods, frozen potatoes and especially the lettuce and fresh foods in salad bars, and most wines, looking fresh. Some people may have allergies to sulfites. You can't see or taste them. The government has eliminated sulfites from many products but read labels to be sure.

## TVP
Textured Vegetable Protein (TVP®) is a meat alternative made of soy. It's distributed by the Archer Daniels Midland Company. It is highly prized by vegetarians as a substitute to meat in chili, stew

and other meat dishes. If you can't find it in your health food store, call 1-800-8-FLAVOR. TVP is usually sold in bulk, often without directions but it is easily reconstituted with any liquid. TVP Harvest Burgers, also sold by ADM, have ample directions.

## Vegan

A vegan is one who eats no animal products and often no added fat. This would exclude gelatin, custard, eggs, fish, poultry, chicken or meat stock based soups, or milk or cream products. A vegan eats lots of grains, vegetables, fruit, pasta, rice, bread, potatoes, salads and may have better health than most of us.

## Vegetarian

Many people call themselves vegetarians which probably loosely translates to (and some studies have concluded) eating a diet composed largely of a wide variety of vegetables, pastas, rice and other grains, lots of potatoes, fruits, juices, teas, nuts, seeds, skim milk, and occasionally small amounts of chicken, fish, cheese and eggs and with added fats such as margarine, corn, canola and olive oil.

## Wheat Bran

A water soluble fiber that does not lower cholesterol but does add fiber to the diet.

## A Word About Labels . . .

Read labels. Look for the words (in order of importance) *saturated;* then glance at the *total fat* number, then *cholesterol* and finally, *percent of calories from fat.* Sometimes *polyunsaturated* and *monounsaturated fat* numbers are given. They are far less significant than *saturated fat,* but add up the total fat number. Look at the *sodium* number, and you may also be interested in how much sugar a product contains. Sucrose, honey, fruit concentrate, molasses, glucose, fructose, maple syrup, and corn syrup are all forms of sugar. NOTE: The Nutrition Labeling and Education Act goes into effect in May 1994 and requires the disclosure of nutrient values and standardized serving sizes.

If actual numbers aren't given on the label, ingredients have to be noted somewhere, and they are in order here, with the greatest amount listed first. You may see many unfamiliar items such as carrageenan (seaweed) or locust bean, and most are fine to eat or are in such minute amounts as to be unimportant compared to the saturated fat or total fat.

Ideally, you would keep the saturated fat number 0, but under 2 grams per serving with the total fat number under 10 is considered okay. Often the saturated fat number is the only one I look at. If that is low, ninety-nine times out of a hundred, the total fat number will also be low.

Generally, you want the percent of calories from fat to be under 20 percent. But that is general. With oil, that number will be 100 percent no matter what the brand or type of animal or vegetable oil you use, and there is no reason to eliminate all oil from the diet. What you are looking for is a low daily, even low weekly percent of calories from fat. It doesn't mean that the majority should be low.

Be alert to the words *no cholesterol* found on peanut butter, some cookies, corn oil, coconut oil and many other items. No vegetable product such as corn oil ever has cholesterol. It is only in animal products. However, the saturated fat in peanut butter, some cookies, corn oil and especially coconut, or palm kernel oil or palm oil can be enormously high. Pay close attention to the serving size because in items such as part skim milk ricotta cheese, cheese, salad dressing, sour cream and nondairy creamers, etc., the serving size can vary by 100 percent, since some use ounces, others tablespoons. Understandably, the manufacturer wants to paint the best picture possible, and most products are nutritious, but to be accurate, one must be a little diligent.

With all that in mind, first and foremost, enjoy your food. Food isn't medicine. Some of it just contains some items you'd rather not put in your body. Use food as a good fuel to compliment your healthy body and active mind so you can do the things that are important to you in your life.

# Index